BLESS AND TELL

BLESS AND TELL

Written by
Richard Sullivan

First published in the United Kingdom in 2004
by MuseumWare Publishing

ISBN 1–905097–00–X

Edited by Lynda Watson
Illustrations by Amélia Rashley
Rear cover photograph by Photography Department,
Open University, Peterborough
Printed by AST Print Group Limited, Cardiff

MuseumWare Publishing
Westway Farm
Bishop Sutton
Bristol BS39 5XP
United Kingdom

Telephone + 44 (0) 1275 33 1177

To all those who believed in me

Contents

Acknowledgements

I wish to acknowledge the contribution made by all those who feature in this book, named and anonymous. By inviting me into your lives you taught me much about myself.

Especially I am indebted to Rt Rev. Arthur Roche, Bishop of Leeds, for taking the time to write the Foreword, to Helen Whitty my mentor and guide over the years, to Nicola Haigh who painstakingly proof-read numerous drafts without a word of complaint and to Caroline Day for her watchful eye as the book matured.

To Peter Wells for his enthusiastic encouragement and to Lynda Watson who edited the book I am deeply grateful.

I would like to acknowledge individually all those who have had a direct influence in my life as I have stumbled from one crisis to the next. Suffice to say that without the NHS. I wouldn't be alive today. And without my Family, the Salvatorians, the Loreto Sisters and the British Army, my life would have been much less colourful.

In the words of the poet Francis Thompson:

'To you O dear givers, I give your own giving.'

Dedication of Poems (1893), To Wilfred and
Alice Meynell in *The poems of Francis Thompson*

Foreword

The shock of reading one's own obituary is rare. It happened to Alfred Nobel who was a powerful and wealthy manufacturer of weapons. When his brother died the national printer printed Alfred's obituary by mistake! In it he discovered that the world would remember him as a purveyor of mass destruction. He was so shocked by this opinion of him that he was determined to be remembered by something else entirely.

This book also recalls such a shocking and life-altering moment in the life of a little boy who learnt from a teacher he respected that *nothing good would ever come of him!* Such a dispiriting indictment ultimately conspired to be the springboard for something very different. Richard Sullivan distinguished himself in the army and became a priest and a scholar. He did not allow the sun to go down on his childhood disappointments. With courage and great faith, he turned them into an opening for something much more noble.

I was one of the boys he taught at Christleton Hall and I well remember his industrious application to work and study and his encouraging patience and fine example to us students. His strength of character, his deference in dealing with others, that self-deprecatory sense of humour are as present in these pages as they were back in the sixties.

It is not given to all of us to read our obituaries nor to know what others will say of us when we are gone, but what is clear is that there is nothing that comes our way that does not also bring with it a moment of great grace. This record of a life has much to say not only about a man born in 1926, but lessons to impart to those of us who face the same challenges even in today's enlightened world. There is something here for everyone.

+ *[signature]*

Rt Rev. Arthur Roche

Introduction

Recently I was asked to conduct a service for children leaving the local prep school prior to their going on to secondary education. This was a major step for them and I tried to think of something to say that would inspire them.

I thought back to the days of my own childhood and remembered people always going on at me, 'What are you going to do when you grow up?' I knew very well at the age of seven what I was going to do with my life but I wasn't going to tell them. But it occurred to me that even now at the age of seventy-seven, I am still asking myself that question, 'What am I going to do when I grow up?' I suppose I am really asking myself what am I going to do next. For my life is full of dreams and no sooner have I realised one than another comes as a new challenge. Somebody once said that the day a person stops dreaming is the day that person dies.

I wondered how to get this across to the children so I began with a story I came across sometime ago. It's called 'A Vision for the Future':

> The leader of a certain Indian tribe encamped at the base of a mountain was dying. The chief summoned his three sons and said, 'I'm dying and one of you must succeed me as head of our tribe. I want each of you to climb our holy mountain and bring back something beautiful. The one whose gift is the most outstanding will succeed me.'
>
> After several days the sons returned. The first brought his father a flower which grew near the summit and was extremely rare and beautiful. The second son brought his father a stone which was colourful, smooth and round having been polished by rain and sandy winds. The third son's hand was empty.

He said, 'Father, I have brought nothing back to show you. As I stood on top of the holy mountain, I saw on the other side a beautiful land filled with green pastures and a crystal lake. And I have a vision of where our tribe could go for a better life. I was so overwhelmed by what I saw and by what I was thinking that I could not bring anything back.'

The father replied, 'You shall be the tribe's new leader, for you have brought back the most precious thing of all – the gift of a vision for a better future.'

I told the children that when somebody asks you what you are going to do when you grow up they are really asking you, 'What is your dream? What is your vision for the future?'

And I told them of a vision I had long, long ago. I was seven years of age when I first asked myself, 'What shall I do when I grow up?' And without thinking any further I knew that one day I would be a priest. Many years passed and lots happened to prevent my realising my dream but I never wavered. I was determined that one day it would come true. It was twenty-eight years later at the age of thirty-five when Bishop Murphy of Shrewsbury put his hands on my head and made me a priest. And do you know what my first thoughts were? They were not very holy I'm afraid. I thought, 'At long last, I've made it and no one can ever take it from me.'

I told the children that whatever their vision is now, no one can prevent them fulfilling it if they have the determination and will to succeed.

These pages tell the story of my vision and how, against all the odds, it came to pass. They tell of the wonderful life I have had as a priest as one dream gave way to another. And all because:

> Somebody said that it couldn't be done,
> But he with a chuckle replied
> That 'maybe it couldn't,' but he would be one

Who wouldn't say so till he'd tried.
So he buckled right in with a bit of a grin
On his face. If he worried he hid it.
He started to sing as he tackled the thing
That couldn't be done, and he did it.

'It Couldn't Be Done' by Edgar A. Guest

Hundreds and hundreds of people have welcomed me into their lives over the years. Welcome into mine.

Richard.

PART ONE

The Beginning 1926–1939

A student went to a Jesuit chaplain for counselling after she failed her finals. His response was, 'I am sorry I can't help you. I have never failed anything in my life.'

I think almost everybody has failed, especially in their early years, and consequently in the majority of cases see themselves failures.

Some go through life being failures, one failure reinforcing another. Others are fortunate enough to be picked up by circumstances or caring people and translate failure into success. I was one of the fortunate.

1

One Step Forward

It was 6.30 in the morning and pitch black as we queued to get into the chapel. It was only a small chapel and as I walked in and made my way to one of the seats I nearly bumped into a white marble statue in the middle of the aisle. I was just about to lay my hand on the shoulder of this statue to steady myself when I heard it groan. I looked again and it was Pope John Paul II kneeling at his pre-dieu saying his private prayers before Mass. A few of us, in Rome for an International Conference, had been invited to say Mass with the Pope in his private chapel and to meet him afterwards in the papal apartments. Having recovered from the shock of nearly molesting the Pope I made my way to my seat a few chairs away. We had about twenty minutes before Mass was to begin and I thought, 'What on earth am I doing here in the Pope's private chapel where Popes like Pius XII, John XXIII, Paul VI and John Paul I had knelt at that same pre-dieu a few feet away from me?' I think, that in those few moments I came as near to ecstasy as I am ever likely to encounter in my entire life, and I have lived a long and wonderful life.

The Pope's secretary had rung us up the night before to ask what language we would like the Pope to use for the Mass. We were a mixed bunch so we asked for various parts of the Mass to be said in different languages. Hymns were sung in English, Spanish and German. The prayers were said in Polish and the rest of the Mass in Latin. I wonder if you could possibly capture the awe of that moment when the Pope got up from his pre-dieu, approached the altar and began the Mass and I was saying it with him.

"Sorry your Holiness...... I thought you were part of the furniture!"

From the time I can remember all things papal had a fascination for me. When other boys were playing with their trains I was playing at saying Mass. When other boys said they were going to be train drivers or firemen when they grew up I always said I would be the Pope. I never quite made it but that morning in the papal apartments made up for all the disappointments of my life.

How can I describe that moment when the Pope actually shook my hand, smiled at me and gave me a present, actually gave me, the lad from Everton, in Liverpool, a present. May God forgive me but as the Pope moved on I thought, if only that old so-and-so Mr Hignet could see me now. He was the teacher who told my mother nothing good would ever come of me – and I believed it. In fact, in the early years of my life I seemed to go out of my way to prove it. But let's leave Rome for a while and go back to the beginning.

THE BEGINNING

I was born in Everton, Liverpool, on 2 June 1926 but my life really began one morning in March in 1945 in the city of Rotterdam in Holland. I had arrived the day before on a troopship carrying reinforcements for Montgomery's Second Army and as we disembarked we were issued with live ammunition. I'll never forget that moment. Previously when we had been training for this moment it had seemed as though we were playing war games. Now, issued with live ammunition, the war suddenly became real. True we had experienced air raids back in Liverpool and, in fact, we had been bombed out of our home, but sitting in an air-raid shelter listening to dog-fights going on in the skies above us seemed somehow rather remote from the present situation. But now with live ammunition in our webbed pouches we became very aware that the enemy was very close. Soon we would meet them and we were expected to kill them or be killed.

We were sent to a reinforcement holding unit and on the way, from the back of the lorry, we could see a train drawing into the railway station as we passed. We were held up in traffic and as we waited we saw army personnel being disembarked from the train; arms, legs, heads bandaged, with the blood still seeping through the cloths.

That night there was a film, *When Irish Eyes are Smiling* in the NAAFI cinema and a few of us went to see it. We found ourselves sitting behind some of the soldiers we had seen on the train. They told us that they had been shipped from the front line for treatment and rest and recuperation. They were still bandaged but more cleanly now and during the interval they began to tell us of their exploits finishing with, 'it's your turn tomorrow'.

The front line had reached the Rhine at Bonn and we were destined to go and assist in the crossing of the Rhine, a major step towards the ultimate surrender of Germany.

We didn't sleep much that night and the next morning we were all on parade waiting to be taken by lorry to the station and thence to the front line. As we stood there a sergeant major came on parade and made an announcement. He was looking for volunteers to go on a special operation.

He couldn't tell us what it was but I thought anything would be better than going to the front line as an Infantryman. So when he commanded all volunteers to take one pace forward, I took that step. Future events proved that it was akin to being born again, leaving a womb of failure caused by circumstances, some of my own making, some caused by others and some due to the environment in which I lived. That step was when I truly began my life.

I was eighteen at the time and prior to this my life had been a case of one failure after another. The sad thing was that I had never realised I was a failure. This was just me and though I had ambitions it didn't occur to me that, one day, they might be fulfilled. Failure just seemed to be a way of life which I had come to expect as the norm for me. I had failed the scholarship, the equivalent to the eleven-plus. As an evacuee I was the last out of about 300 to be chosen for a billet. I was asked to leave school because it seemed obvious that I wouldn't pass the School Certificate, today's GCSEs. From then until I was called up I worked in a chemist's shop, filling shelves, cleaning the cabinet windows and keeping the cellar tidy, among other things.

And now, here was somebody really important taking notice of me. A panel of officers interviewed those of us who had stepped forward. We were asked our background and I realised that the senior officer seemed rather impressed after I had spoken. I had always been taught to speak well and my Liverpool accent had virtually disappeared. It seemed to register with the panel that I had been to a Jesuit College and that I had a 'posh' accent, well, posh for a lad from Liverpool, anyway.

Looking back, he must have made some notes on my records in view of what happened to me when the war ended, but more about that later. For the first time in my life I felt somebody was impressed with me and it was almost as though an earthquake had erupted within me. I was being singled out and I was accepted for this particular operation. I can still see that Officer's look when I spoke to him. He turned to the rest of the panel, nodded to them in the form of a question and they all seemed to agree with him. My form was stamped and signed and I walked out with my head held high. I had been appointed bodyguard-cum-batman to the Officer leading the team I was to join. I shall come back to this but I can honestly say that my subsequent success in life goes back to that moment when I saw an Officer of the British Army look impressed with me. Perhaps I was beginning to realise subconsciously that failing doesn't make a Failure.

2

Born in Liverpool Down by the Docks

Born into a large family in Liverpool in the days of the Depression when survival depended on the largesse of the pawnbroker, poverty was the name of the game. With parents unable to communicate with each other, thoughts of failing didn't exist as we were all in the same boat. Failure was a way of life which we presumed was normal. We were protected by the innocence of childhood. Rousseau once said that if we left children to their own devices and did not force our values upon them, they would grow up perfectly normal. It was only when we mixed with people who were not poor that we realised our particular state of poverty.

As I said, I was born naturally in Liverpool in 1926, the year of the General Strike. In those days children were born at home and I was born in 11 Margaret Street, Liverpool 6. I don't remember too much about it but I expect my three sisters were quite thrilled to find they had a brother. Whether I was thrilled to find myself with three sisters is another matter. Like all those in Everton at that time we were truly poor, not relatively so but in true fact. Helen Forrestor has written at length about Liverpool in those days and I won't bore you with details that don't concern this story in the immediate sense. But poor as we were I remember my parents had standards and even among the Everton population there was a class system. There were the shawlies, those who wore shawls, and then the posh poor who wore hats. My mother never went anywhere without a hat so you could say that we were among the posh poor. Certainly I was brought up by my mother to feel different than others. As I said earlier even my accent was different from my own sisters and brother. I should have mentioned that my brother came along four-and-a-half years after me. I remember him being born also in Margaret Street.

My father was the seventh son of a seventh son and the year of my birth was just eight years after the Great War during which my father and six uncles served the King. One by one, five of them were killed so I grew up with one uncle and an aunt. My mother had been an only child and so there were no relatives on that side of the family. Not all that long before my mother's death in 1994 we, the children, learnt that my mother's father was a German and had left his wife when my mother was aged two. Her mother, an Irish lady named Burke married again and we had a Welsh step-grandfather named Davies though I remember very little about him. As through a haze I can see him sitting by the fireside smoking a pipe. My father's parents were both Irish and, though he never set foot in Ireland, he worshipped the Irish to his dying breath. For some reason my mother was very anti-Irish. My last grandparent died when I was two years of age so I never knew grandparents in spite of having five and to this day I don't really appreciate their role in the family set-up. I am constantly surprised when a divorced mother will tell me she has to take the children to see her ex-husband's parents, 'After all,' they say, 'they are her grandparents.' — such luxury!

Being three-quarters Irish and one-quarter German and with a Welsh step-grandfather came in very handy in terms of personal relationships in the student world. I was able to empathise with the English, the Irish, the Welsh and the Germans at a rather personal level.

But getting back to my parents, sadly, my mother and father never really got on and I remember one night listening to them fighting from the top of the stairs. I remember vaguely hearing the word divorce and later realised they had been talking about splitting up but wouldn't because of the children. Divorce hardly existed in those days and was unheard of among Catholics. My course to the priesthood lasted nine years. From time to time during those years I very nearly left the seminary wondering why on earth I had given up a good job and prospects of marriage. But whenever I was tempted to desert my vows, my parents' example gave me the strength and inspiration to continue. It still does. They lived in very difficult times when survival was the name of the game. Kisses and cuddles never played a part in my upbringing and it was a question of where the next penny was coming from to buy the tea.

I hardly remember having any conversation with my father. As a child, I remember 'playing boats' with him. We had one of those galvanised baths, an oval-shaped bucket really, and Saturday nights were bath nights—in front of the fire. After being washed, my dad would get the toy boat out and we would sail it on the water, sinking it with great relish, recovering it, racing it with imaginary other boats. Sometimes we would go to the park and sail it on the lake. But there our boat always sank in the wake of the boats owned by the 'posh kids'. They had luxury yachts of course. It was the same when we would take our home-made kites to the park. Having made them from bits of wood and coloured paper and string we would take them out proudly only to be scorned by those who had actually bought theirs from the shops. But ours went as high as theirs if not higher.

Talking of baths reminds me that as we got older our galvanised bath gave way to something much more sophisticated. To have a real bath we had to go down to the public baths on a Saturday morning and wait in the queue with a lot of other scruffy, dirty Everton children for a slipper bath to become available. To this day I don't know why they were called slipper baths. They were like little bathrooms of today with just a bath in them. We, my sister Flo and myself, would sit on a long bench clutching our towels and soap with the other kids and wait for a bath to become available. A man would go around cleaning the bath after each person and then, when your turn came you paid six old pence for the privilege of getting rid of your dirt. To give you an idea of the value of six pence in those days, you could get fish and chips and peas at the local chip shop for two pence. It was called a two-penny (pronounced tuppenny) special and was a real if rare treat. Today six old pence is worth two-and-a-half pence (decimal currency).

On Saturdays my dad would make the supper and I remember the menu was always a large Spanish onion each. They would be oozing with butter, well marge really. We used to love it when dad cooked because it was always something tasty—a bit like the fast food of today. Corned beef grilled on toast was always a favourite. But my mum always kept us well fed even if she did have to learn how to serve up mince in a variety of ways to make us think it was different each time.

Back to conversation with my father, another time my dad and I used to talk was when we went to bed. I didn't tell you, did I, that we lived in a three up and two down—but that was only the bed. It was a double bed and my three sisters used to sleep heads to the wall and Bernie and myself would sleep with our heads towards the end of the bed, five pairs of feet entwined happily. Can you imagine? Somewhere among the legs and arms was the hot-water bottle. This took the form of a hot flat-iron or a hot brick warmed in the oven and wrapped up in newspaper. Woe betide us if we forgot to put the brick in the oven or the iron on the stove in time for bed.

Well, as we grew up we were separated and Winnie and Lily had their own room. I think Bernie slept with my mum and dad. Flo and myself had one bed between us and every night our pre-sleep entertainment was searching the seams of our clothes for nits. Nit-picking in the real sense.

When we found one we would crush it with great glee between our thumbnails and wait to hear the 'click' as the nit was exterminated. I won't say what we did with the bugs. This great adventure would always end with my dad coming in to tell us our bedtime story. Each night it was another episode of his adventures in the army in Mesopotamia during the Great War and how they had to sleep with their rifles at the side of them and how one time he was gassed.

A lovely story emerged later in life when we discovered that being gassed had caused him to lose his sense of smell. He used to love flowers and when we went for walks in the park he would pick them and ask us if they smelt nice. As time went on he developed a great devotion to 'The Little Flower'. This was the title given to St Therese of Lisieux. She was a Carmelite nun who entered the enclosed order of Carmelites at the age of fifteen and died nine years later from TB. During the years in the convent she would describe herself as an ordinary person who could do only ordinary things. But she was determined that she would do those ordinary things in an extraordinary way. She was canonised by Pope Pius X1 in 1925 and was appointed patron of the Missions and the Armed Forces. When my father died we asked the stonemason to carve the image of the little flower on his tombstone. It was some time before we revisited my father's grave but when we did we found that the mason had carved an image of a bunch of little flowers on the stone. Of course we should have made it clear to the mason what we wanted. But we never did anything because my father loved flowers as much as he had loved the 'Little One'. I'm sure they both had a little chuckle in heaven.

Whether it was because we were nearest in age, Flo was two years older than I was, or because we shared such exciting pre-sleep exploits, I shall never know but the two of us became great friends and to this day we give each other great support. Perhaps the greatest support she ever gave me was when I used to go to the toilet at night-time. We called it the 'lav', loo hadn't been heard of then. The lav had a latch, no lock and because our feet couldn't reach the door to stop people coming in we would sing to let people know it was occupied. I think that's why Liverpool became so famous for its singers. Also there was a big gap between the bottom of the door and the floor—a Mecca for cats. I was scared of cats in those days and so whenever I went to the toilet at night Flo would stand at the back door and talk to me. I remember I would say to her, 'Say Hail Mary the cats won't come, Flo.' How holier than that can you get? And, you know, the cats never came. Flo must have been as holy as me for God certainly listened to her those nights

I remember one year when I was stationed in London; I wanted to give her a special birthday present. We have never been a demonstrable family, I think we were too busy trying to survive to give cuddles and hugs and so on. But I wanted to show her how much I appreciated her. Why couldn't I have said I loved her?

I must have been in my cups when I was wondering what to give her. Something different and special I thought. Then I got this brilliant idea of 'lunch in Paris'. I thought this would be fantastic and so I suited the action to my thoughts and got on to Eurostar. They had a special offer. One day return for £90 and I could take a friend free. So Flo came down the night before and at 8a.m. on her birthday we set off for Paris. It was a wonderful day. We had our lunch, avoiding French food, of course, and then set off for a walk along the Champs Elysees. There we sat drinking cognac and coffee. Can you imagine it? From nit-picking to the most famous boulevard in the world! You can be sure we took a lot of pictures to show the neighbours back in Liverpool. And before anybody asks, I paid for it out of gifts given me for Christmas—with the permission of the Superior of course (I think)!

But back to my parents. I don't ever remember what my mum did of an evening. My dad seemed to be always at work and the only time we saw him was when he came in for his supper and then went out to the pub. He must have worked twelve hours a day. She probably spent the time looking after the five of us kids. We never had books in the house of any sort and reading materials consisted of the Liverpool Echo. This doubled up as a tablecloth and later, cut into neat squares, as toilet paper. If there was an evening service at church we would go to that. There was no telly of course so perhaps we listened to the wireless.

I remember her taking us to the beach at Seacombe. Helen Forrestor called one of her books, *Two Pence to Cross the Mersey*. In our day it was three pence to go to Egrement and a shilling to go to New Brighton. We would go to Egrement for three pence and pitch our camp at Seacombe. The posh kids of course went directly to New Brighton. Sometimes we would walk to New Brighton along the Prom almost a mile away. There were all sorts of entertainment there such as donkeys, fairgrounds and so on. We would paddle and make sand castles with our buckets and spades. We were never allowed to do anything dangerous, consequently from that day to this I have never learnt to swim or take part in any sport that might have been seen as dangerous.

I shall tell you more about my mother later when I come on to my church activities. You might have noticed that though I have talked about what we did with my dad and with my mum, I haven't said anything about what we all did together. As I said earlier, sadly, they never got on. I don't ever remember them going out together. This could well have something to do with having five children. Every night my dad would go down to the local 'just for a pint' and my mother would go to the whist drive run by the church. This in time, of course, gave way to bingo which became a great money raiser for the churches. In fact, for a while, bingo became associated with the Catholic Church until the abandoned cinemas found a use for their buildings and commercial bingo was born.

Years later, soon after I was ordained, I used to see families out in their cars having picnics on the side of the road. I thought back to the days when we had nothing. Why not give mum and dad a real treat, I thought. I couldn't drive and certainly did not have a car. But, and it is a big but, I was in the Territorial Army (TA) by this time and they were encouraging members to learn to drive. I enrolled for this and was given a one-week crash course, a rather unfortunate expression perhaps! The sergeant instructor was very strict and carried a stick with him. Whenever my hands slipped from the 'ten to two' position he would wrap my knuckles. But worse was to come. To teach starting on a hill he asked me for my wristwatch. He put it behind the back wheel and then said, 'Now start.' I passed my test on the Saturday with flying colours. I was thirty-seven at the time and must have been in one of my success phases. All I needed to do now was to get a car. I hired a Ford Anglia and drove it back to Christleton Hall with great pride. I turned into the drive and, of course, drove it straight into the bushes. It was scratched! My fellow priests knew the answer to that one. 'Get some brass polish', they said, 'and smear it over the scratch.' It worked in those days and the surrounding paint merged over the scratch and there wasn't a flaw to be seen. I was ready to take my mum and dad on a picnic just like those posh people I had seen. I collected them and they seemed so proud to be driving along with me. We stopped at a suitable place and I set up the table and chairs and got out the food hamper I had prepared. My dad sat with his hat on and seemed to be enjoying the cup of tea I had given him. Likewise my mum until she started: 'Take your hat off', she said to my dad. He didn't budge. He hadn't heard her or was pretending not to. It must have been the latter for after three or four calls to him to take his hat off, he took it off. Then he flung it into the middle of the nearby road and said, 'Take the bl... hat.' That was the end of the picnic. I never tried again.

But I am quite convinced my parents loved each other in their own way. My father would do anything for my mother, even to going without his pint to keep her company if there was no one at home. My mother couldn't bear to be left on her own and often I would stay in so that he could have his pint. In later years Bernie took over that role and stayed in almost every evening to keep my mother company.

Whenever I think of those dreadful rows they used to have I think particularly of Christmas. My father worked twelve hours a day all the year round apart from one day in the year—Christmas Day. He was a sorter in the post office and the only full day he had at home was Christmas Day. And what Christmas Days we had. Virtually the whole day was spent rowing, before, during and after the Christmas dinner. My father would be out at the pub while my mother would be getting the dinner ready. We used to have goose, as it was the cheapest bird in those days. Ironically it is now reserved for the 'posh people'. Turkey and chicken was out of reach of the poor whereas today it is the cheapest meat available. People condemn the practice of battery hens but it did bring 'luxury meals' to all and sundry. When I eat chicken these day I still think I am living it up. The first happy Christmas I had during that time was when I was in the army in 1944. I had been in the army six months and I remember I was one of the lucky ones who drew the ticket for home leave that Christmas. I remember swapping it with someone so that I would have a good reason not to go home.

But before the days when we were not aware of the trouble or perhaps before it began, Christmas was a happy time. We believed in Father Christmas and we would always hang up our stockings on the end of the bed before we went to sleep on Christmas Eve. They were real stockings— socks really, none of your Christmas sacks that they have these days which would almost hold a grand piano. We would always find an orange and an apple and some chocolate gold coins in a little string bag in the stocking. Sometimes there would be a little toy. I can't remember what our big present was except for one Christmas when Flo and myself woke up to find that I had a real desk, just like a school desk and she had a big doll. I remember another year when I got a chemistry set. I can still experience the joy I felt then when I think about it. My eyes nearly fell out of their sockets. Looking back I wonder if my parents were psychic. Thirty years later as a priest I lived in academia for thirty years and some of that time was spent teaching chemistry and physics. I loved it.

In fact, my mother often said that my dad was psychic. I mentioned he was the seventh son of a seventh son and sometimes he would tell the fortunes of family and friends. He forecast the life of my Auntie Louie and it came true to the very day and manner of her death. He wanted to tell me mine before I left for the army but my mother wouldn't let him.

Once my mother was going to see a medium/psychic for a bit of fun and she was going to ask her about my father. This was supposed to be a joke as the church strictly forbids such behaviour. She was told to take some article of my dad's clothing with her and so she took a tie. Now at that time, my father had a terrible cold and was coughing and spluttering a lot. As soon as the medium took hold of the tie she started coughing and spluttering. I shall return to this subject when I tell you of my being an ordained exorcist which in the old days was one stage on the way to the priesthood (see Chapter 20).

When people ask me what sort of a childhood I had I normally say dreadful, but looking back, particularly to the years before the war broke out and writing this up, I suppose it was a happy time within the context of those days. We had fun playing in the streets, chasing the girls and the old 'stop me and buy one' ice cream carts. I actually remember chasing a girl when I was five years of age. She got away of course—the story of my life but more about that, also, later.

Perhaps our greatest fun came from going round during the week collecting empty jam jars. Every Saturday morning the rag-and-bone man would come around and give us halfpenny for them. This gave us the entrance money for the Lytton, the local fleapit (cinema). It was a halfpenny in the front and a penny at the back. Of course we always got the front seats and we would have money left over for ice cream at the interval. I think that cost a farthing. We would sit enthralled watching Laurel and Hardy or Tarzan hurtling his way through the jungle leaping from branch to branch with his family of animals. Always the film would end with him in great danger and just about to be killed. Off we would go determined to get enough jam jars to get in next week to see what happened.

What cast a shadow on those days was my parents' relationship. It was always there, the rows eventually giving way to silence. I received a letter from my sister just recently reminding me that there were never rows, only silence. There was the inevitable poverty, the unemployment of the thirties, the Depression and so on. Survival was the name of the game. My father worked all the hours he could to get sufficient money to pay the rent and buy the food. My mother and I would meet him outside work on a Friday night to collect his wages. We would go straight to the pawnshop to redeem our good clothes to wear at Mass on Sunday. Monday saw us back in the pawnshop with them. I had to laugh recently. Just a few months ago I was having a meeting with the parish youth and their leaders. I began to reminisce and started telling them about my days in the pawnshops. Out of the corner of my eye I saw the young people looking at each other and muttering. It suddenly dawned on me that they thought I was talking about 'Porn Shops'! They had never heard of the other sort. My goodness, I thought, how the world has changed.

Our parents took good care, as far as they could, to shelter us from the hardships of those days. I don't remember ever being hungry, for example, though how they managed to feed and clothe five of us in the days of the Depression in addition to their own problems is incomprehensible. They took care to see that these things didn't touch us specifically but with hindsight I can see now that those days contained the seeds which were to shape us and form our personalities as we grew into adolescence and adulthood. It was only in later years that I realised the effect it was having on my character and the development of such character traits as insecurity, stubbornness, and attitudes to authority, and in my teenage years my relationships with the opposite sex.

But all this will come out as my story unfolds. Suffice it to say that negative character traits were being built into my system, which made me ripe to believe I was a failure even before I began my formal education.

3

The Black Sheep in a Family of White Ones

During my counselling course a question came up: if a person has a problem and is not aware of it should that person be told he/she has a problem? The same can be asked about a person who fails. If he/she is not aware they have failed, should they be told? Awareness of failure for me began with competition in school. Competition rears its head and breeds a failure/success class system. At school this concerned two areas of life, namely academic and sport. I was no good at either and so was ripe to be considered a permanent failure. At home, as I said previously, there was no competition. We simply struggled to survive. Perhaps these were co-related.

My formal education and what one might call indoctrination of failure began the day my mother took me to the parish infant school. I remember vaguely the hustle and bustle of the first day and that suddenly I was on my own. I didn't know anybody. Nobody knew me except my mother and she had just gone. I have wondered since if that was when my being a loner began. From that day to this I have never felt that I belonged in any particular group to which I have physically belonged. It was as though that first day set the pattern of my life in terms of relationships.

Throughout my school career which began that day I only ever related seriously to two boys who became friends for life, Tony Walsh and Pat Mackrell. Tony served my First Mass almost thirty years later and we still see each other from time to time. Pat sadly died some years ago. In fact it was Pat who introduced me to the mystery of women and it was from him I received my first lessons in sex education. Most of it took place one day walking up Brunswick Road on the way home from school. Now I come to think of it he also taught me how to shave. God grant him peace.

Another boy from those days emerged much later. We had been to school together but whereas I was normally in the C stream he was in the A stream so we didn't see a lot of each other at school. It was years later when I did a supply for a priest at Moels that I discovered him in the congregation. After the Mass we re-introduced ourselves. John Styles was now a successful accountant and married with three children. Moels is a small village in between Rock Ferry and West Kirkby in The Wirral on the other side of the Mersey about twenty-five miles from Chester. I went over to Moels on supply every weekend for three years and became a regular visitor to John's family who lived in the parish. Sadly, he too died long before he reached his threescore years and ten.

But back to Day One of the worst years of my life! It didn't take me long to realise I was not the wonder boy my mother had tried to make me believe I was. The Head Teacher of those days was a Mrs McQuirk, and I remember her telling me that I was the black sheep in a family of white ones. I was made to stand in the corner with my back to the class more often than I care to remember. This was the first line of defence for teachers in those days to be followed by the cane or strap if the misdeeds continued. The day began and ended with prayer and it was a common expression at the beginning of the day to be told, 'Join your

WHO SAID BLONDES HAVE MORE FUN?

hands, close your eyes and look at the statue.'

Yes, it was 'Quackers', as Mrs McQuirk was called, that first drew my attention to my being a failure both as an academic and a person. But she only sowed the seed. The person who really went to town in germinating that seed was Mr Hignet in the elementary school. He told my mother, while I was standing there, that 'nothing good will ever come of him'. I can see him now standing in front of a row of desks talking to my mother. His remarks stayed with me and governed my life until that day when the Officer nodded to his companions on the panel in Rotterdam. And even to this day whenever I do anything right I think of him. I believe I am still trying to prove him wrong.

Looking back this must have been a terrible experience for my mother who believed I was absolutely wonderful. Even worse was to follow years later when she was asked to take me away from the college because I would never be likely to pass the school certificate, the GCSEs of those days. Thank God other events later in life made up to her for it.

You know, I thought of that experience the day I saw her lying in her coffin. She lay in peace and around her hands was bound a small towel. This was the towel that bound my hands during the ordination ceremony when I was made a priest. In the days before the Second Vatican Council, during the ordination ceremony the priests hands were bound after they had been anointed by the Bishop. It was later in the ceremony when the newly ordained priest was given the power to say Mass that the hands were unbound. The towel, called a purificator, was tucked into the newly ordained priest's girdle (cingulum) and later handed to the mother to be kept for her burial. I like to think that the wonderful moments of my priesthood in which my mother took part made up for the abysmal failure she was made to believe I was.

Talking about the cingulum reminds me of the time when Adrian, a fellow student, and myself went on holiday to Turin. We were looking around the Dominican church and we came across a glass case on one of the pillars. In the case was a cingulum. Cingulum is the Latin for girdle and is really a long rope that a monk wears around his waist in the manner of a belt. Under this girdle in the glass case was a small title, 'Cingulum Castitatem'. Translated this means 'The Girdle of Chastity'. As we gazed at it a young Dominican monk came up and explained it to us. Actually we knew what it was but we didn't want to undermine the obvious insecurity of the Dominican in the presence of the Salvatorians. When the great St Thomas Aquinas told his parents he wanted to enter the monastery they were horrified. They did everything to persuade him to change his mind. In desperation when they realised they were not succeeding, they locked him up in a tower. Then, to put his virtue to the test they sent in a 'loose woman' who did everything to tempt him from his decision. But Thomas was resolute and in fact picked up a poker from the fireplace and chased her from his room. Legend has it that an angel then appeared to him and girded him with this girdle of chastity which was now hanging in Turin. It is said that as a result of wearing this girdle, Thomas was never tempted again. The young monk told us all this and then burst into uncontrollable laughter. We wondered!

Thankfully or sadly, I am not sure which, I was never girded with the 'Cingulum Castitatem' but enough said about that for the time being.

Most of the boys in the parish began their education in the infant school and then went on to the elementary school. The latter is the equivalent to what was later called the Secondary Modern. But there was an alternative for boys who passed what was called the scholarship. This would be equivalent to the eleven-plus later on and determined your academic future. Boys who passed the scholarship were offered a place in the Jesuit-run College, which was very elite and considered far superior to the elementary school.

As you would expect I never passed the scholarship and was destined to remain in the elementary school with the so-called 'thickies'. There was great antipathy between the elementary school and the college boys as they were called. Many an evening the elementary lads would lie in wait for the college toffs and make them run the gauntlet on their way home Actually, the only happy memories of my school days come from my time at the elementary school. One was the great picnics we would have at Ainsdale, near Southport. We would go off by train in the morning with buckets and spades, sandwiches and fizzy drinks. As the train moved out we would all sing the school song with great gusto:

> SFX the school of our youth
> of honour and of fame so real.
> May the hopes that we cherish
> and memories come true
> keep us faithful to our ideal.
> Onwards and upwards rally one and all.
> Victories in class and field we can recall.
> And as youth goes by we shall live and die
> Sons of St Francis Xavier

I should have mentioned that SFX referred to the infant, elementary schools and the college. They all came under the umbrella of the parish of St Francis Xavier.

At some time or other I must have mentioned in my sleep that I wanted to be a priest because I know it became ingrained in me that this was my destiny. The Jesuits were really on the ball and when they discovered this desire of mine they offered me a place in their school, not the local college but Mount St Mary's, their Public School in Sheffield. I was actually offered a place in a Public School. This was due to no academic brilliance on my part for I had failed the scholarship and had already begun academic life in the local elementary school. However, I was to be disappointed for my mother couldn't afford to keep me there with the 'swells'. A free place was one thing but to provide books and suitable clothing was another. I remember now how disappointed I was (another failing) but I got over it. It gradually drifted into my subconscious and remained there for many years until one day when I was talking to some freshers at Keele University and I asked them what school they had attended. You can imagine the memories rushing back when they said 'Mount St Mary's'.
However, the Jesuits were not to be defeated, (were they ever?) and I was

36

offered a free place in St Francis Xavier's College which was situated in the parish. Fortunately, a boy whose mother was a friend of mine was leaving the day I began and she gave me his uniform. Maroon blazer with the crest of SFX and a cap with a badge of the same. We were expected to wear them with pride but sadly for me the cap became the cause of my lining up outside the ferula office many an evening after school to receive nine of the best – the automatic punishment for being seen not wearing the school cap.

So in 1938 I entered St Francis Xavier's Jesuit College and began what can only be described as the un-happiest years of my life. There were consolations during these years but they came from outside the college as I shall describe later.

A perfect fit

The Headmaster was Father Brinkworth. He was a Chinese priest and whenever I think of him it is with a picture of a benevolent, caring priest. He loved sport and the cabinets in his office were filled with school trotrophies. Sadly, very soon after I began my college career he was replaced by Father Neylon, whose first act was to empty the cabinets of their trophies and replace them with scholarly tomes of the classics. He was a disciplinarian of the first order. Pat Heery has written a history of the college recently and sums up this priest admirably. He recalls the story of when he was asked about fire regulations, Father Neylan replied, *'In the event of a fire make sure that the boys studying Greek get out of the building first.'*

Of course, 1938 was overshadowed by rumours of war. The world was waiting for the Second World War to break out and this was by no means the ideal time for starting formal education in terms of college life. Everything was prefixed with, 'of course if war breaks out!' Towards the end of that first academic year we spent a great deal of our time practising how to use our gas masks and what to do in an air raid. Special attention was given to how to do our homework in the air-raid shelter if the siren went after school hours and as the academic year came to an end priority was given to what to do if war broke out during the school holidays. War did break out of course and life was changed for everybody. I don't think anybody who was not alive during the war years could possibly imagine the difference the war made to everybody. There are as many stories of heroics and tragedies as there were people and I have attempted to describe some of these later in the book.

Our school was evacuated but, bit by bit, boys returned home when there were no signs of air raids and it was not long before the whole school returned. Normal school life resumed and it was very rare to experience daylight air raids. But the night air raids were a different matter and most of our homework had to be done by candlelight in the air-raid shelters. That might have been all right for the clever lads but for an ignoramus like myself it became a nightmare. I have to admit that I hadn't a clue about school work. It just went right over me and I knew that every piece of work I would hand in would be rubbished by the teacher. As this meant a steady stream of white bills, I took to deliberately pouring candle grease over my theme book to give the impression it was due to vibrations caused by the dropping bombs. But the Jesuits had no mercy and a much more personal war was going on at that time within the school. This was between the boys and the Jesuits and their cohorts, the lay staff.

The Jesuits are renowned for their strict system of discipline. Based on the spiritual exercises of St Ignatius it is fair to say they exercised the discipline upon themselves. This seemed to leave them devoid of emotion. In those days before the time of Vatican II, religious life emphasised discipline seemingly more or less for the sake of discipline and it was almost as though the object was to depersonalise the members of the particular Order. Thus, in the Constitution of the Order to which I belong there was a rule which said, 'no member must be singular' thus emphasising the need to detach oneself totally from material concerns and desires and cling solely to God by obeying the rule. Unfortunately, the Jesuits enforced this on the boys they taught forgetting they were not members of the Order but ordinary boys growing up with human failings, not to mention academic failings. Their great ally in this was the ferula.

The administration of the ferula was liturgy at its best. Whatever the offence was the form master would give you a slip of paper four inches by three inches called a white bill. At the top was printed 'Ad Majorem Dei Gloriam'. This was Latin for 'To the greater glory of God'. Then underneath was written the number you were to get and beneath that the offence, then it was signed by the form master. You then had to take it to the Prefect of Discipline, the Jesuit Deputy Head Teacher, who gave you a telling off and signed it. The worst was to come. The ferula is defined in the Oxford English Dictionary as a 'Jesuit form of torture'. It was allegedly a piece taken from the tongue of a whale, and cut into slipper-like forms There were three thicknesses: thin, medium and thick. The thin ferula was

the most painful and reserved for the worst crimes like not doing your homework or not wearing your school cap!

To become a Jesuit priest in those days a candidate had to undergo a fourteen-year course from entry to ordination (slow learners we believed) and three of those years were spent teaching in one of their schools. So in any given Jesuit school there were three students, called scholastics, among the ordained priests. It was the scholastics who administered the ferula. It would be given twice a day, after morning and after afternoon classes. So twice a day a queue could be seen outside the ferula office at twelve noon or 4 p.m.

Until I went to the Jesuit College I had associated with the Jesuit priests working on the parish. These were very saintly men, wonderful preachers and very caring pastors. Any skills I may have in the preaching area came largely from listening to those men preach on Sunday evenings at the service called Rosary, Sermon and Benediction. My first big mistake when I entered the college was expecting the 'school Jesuits' to be similar. And what a mistake. A few days after beginning my school career with them I was in an art class listening to the art master giving us some instructions. A couple of boys were talking and the master turned on them and shouted, 'the next boy to talk gets four' (the least they ever gave incidentally). I whispered to the boy next to me, 'He doesn't mean it' and there I was in the ferula queue for my first experience. I have to say I became very familiar with the ferula office. I still shiver and my hands smart to this day whenever I think of it.

But it was not all punishment. There was a reward system as well. If a boy did something very well such as excellent homework or was always punctual etc., he was given a red bill with a certain number on it. This was similar to the white bill except instead of your crime being written, your particular good work was noted on it. If you were given a white bill you could exchange your red bill for it and so escape the punishment. In the four years I spent at that school I only ever received one red bill and that for six. It was so precious to me that I never exchanged it and I have it with me to this day. It is dated 1942 and I have framed it and it hangs over my bed.

Actually, it came in handy when as Provincial I was asked to speak at the Achievement Ceremony in our Salvatorian College. I took it with me and showed it to the boys telling them it was the only thing I ever achieved in all my school days.

The college staff were not all Jesuits. There were a number of lay staff all equally imbued with the cruel streak of their masters, if not more so. One of the these was the P.E. master. These days he wouldn't get away with it but then he would walk around the boys in the gym, the hall used for physical education, and if they were not doing the exercises properly, he would give them a whack across the bottom with a little whip he carried. Remember, in the gym all we had on were thin sports pants and shirts. Many were the whacks I received which had me shinning up the ropes like nobody's business.

Years later I was reminded of those ropes when we had to master a rope bridge across a raging river in our intensive basic training in the army. As soon as the Sergeant Major bellowed out his command my mind went straight back to those school days. Fortunately the Sergeant Major didn't have a whip—only a gun!!

But talking of achievements, believe it or not, I did achieve something else in those days. I managed to get expelled from the same school as Jimmy Tarbuck though his distinction came some years later.

But my poor mother! She was summoned to the school and told that this wonder boy of hers was almost certainly unlikely to pass the school certificate and would she please take him away. I can still visualise the scene. We were not even in an office but the school entrance. I can see the teacher bringing me out of class and handing me to my mother as though I had the worst disease imaginable. My mother had done everything she could for me. With the pittance my father earned, she had put money aside for me to have private Latin lessons and even piano lessons. Remember it was the Jesuits who had asked me to go to that school in the first place. They are noted for their successes but it is fairly obvious why.

It was 1942. I had no qualifications to offer an employer and had no ambition except that I still wanted to be a priest. From the day I was asked to leave I never heard from the school until twenty years later. I was ordained at the age of thirty-five and the college wrote and asked if they could publish the event in the college magazine. And some years later when the college was moving from Everton to Woolton I was invited back to say the closing Mass, I replied, 'I would be delighted'. Talk about 'Success has many fathers, failure is an orphan!'

I mentioned earlier that I not only went to a Jesuit college but I also belonged to the adjoining Jesuit parish. And, fair dos, the parish Jesuits were a different kettle of fish altogether. These were the men who had worked among the people in the slums of Everton and had been able to adapt the spiritual exercises to people of all classes living in all conditions. I met many of them and I can honestly say that I never met one whom I could not describe as saintly.

It is to these Jesuits that I shall always be in debt. In desperation, after my expulsion, my mother turned to one of these parish Jesuits and asked for his help to get me a job. Father Joseph Ryland Whittaker had entered my life earlier soon after I started serving Mass. He had been a heart surgeon before becoming a Jesuit and one day when I was on the altar he noticed how pale I looked. He took me up to his room and examined me with his stethoscope and came to the conclusion that I had a weak heart or something the matter with it. He advised my mother to change my diet and he said that with care I would live to be forty at least. Of course we couldn't afford the diet he suggested. It was long after I was forty that I was rushed into hospital for emergency heart surgery but Father Whittaker saw something all those years before. I will tell you later about the village doctor in Norfolk diagnosing the killer Sub Acute Bacteria Endocarditis (SBE) in my aortic artery. I wonder if Father Whittaker could make out those bacteria beginning their evil work even then.

I owe so much to this priest that even now, sixty years later, I offer Mass for the repose of his soul to thank him for what he did for me then. He had a friend who owned a chemist's shop down in Great Homer Street near Scotland (Scotty) Road and he asked him to give me a job. He did, and so I became a chemist's assistant dispensing cough mixtures, making up powders but, above all, making up buckets of leg make-up every Friday for the girls. Clothing coupons were soon used up and leg make-up was all the rage. Lucky were the boyfriends who got to paint the seam! I also made haircream and lipstick. It didn't appear to be the ideal preparation for the priesthood but I have since discovered every experience is useful to the priest.

It was here in the chemist's shop that I first became aware of the opposite sex in the adult form! Across from the shop were I worked there was a bakery and when I looked across the road I could see this lovely girl serving from behind the counter. I fell in love with her and every morning I would spend my pocket money buying almond cake so that I could get close to her. It was during those days that I first experienced what moral theologians taught me years later were 'commotiones', (irregular movements of the flesh). I think this means, in today's language that 'I fancied her'.

My employer, Mr Murphy was a strong Catholic and belonged to the Catholic Pharmaceutical Guild. He used to take me along to their meetings and I was beginning to think of studying pharmacy when I came out of the army. In fact I began studying with Wolsey Hall to get the College of Preceptor's exam which was the entrance ticket to the College of Pharmacy. I discovered my results sheet recently. It seems I took the exam twice as was my wont and the September 1943 results read: Marks out of 100: English

I'm almond-caked out!

30, Geography 21, Algebra 11, Geometry 8, French 23, Chemistry 5.

The March 1944 results read: English 45, Arithmetic 35, Algebra 34, Geometry 13, French 19, Chemistry 28. Who knows where I would be today if I had taken the exams a third time? The pass mark for pharmaceutical students was 45. Without compunction the examiner would write 'F' next to the subject with less than 45. I remember the day I received those first results. My mother was up a stepladder in the parlour fixing curtains. I went into her with the results and told her that they were all 'F's. All she said to me was, 'You didn't expect anything else did you?' I swore that day that one day she would be proud of me. I might have been still failing but I no longer saw myself as a failure. And in the next exam I got one pass. I was over the moon.

At some of these meetings of the Pharmaceutical Guild they would have entertainment and members were encouraged to 'do their thing'. My boss fancied himself as a conjurer and, fair dos, he was good at it. On one occasion he was performing and he asked me to assist. Well! with great aplomb and pride, qualities for which I later became famous, I mounted the platform and helped him out. I think I held his cloak. When 'we' had finished our act there was a standing ovation. I thought it was for me and I went centre stage and took the applause. Talk about embarrassment when I realised they were applauding Mr Murphy! But that wasn't the most embarrassing moment I have experienced. That came a few years later when I was at a Reinforcement Holding Unit in Rotterdam waiting to be sent up to the front line.

I remember the first morning making my way to the latrines for the morning ablutions. This was simply a square compound shut off from the rest of the camp and formed by the erection of canvas sheets. We would take our mess tins filled with cold water and toilet equipment. There we washed and shaved. While this seemed primitive at first it turned out to be luxurious when we came to visit the loo. This was a huge square tent and on entering it the first thing noticeable was that three sides of the tent were lined with long benches with holes in at strategic points. These were the toilets, and if ever there was an example of community at its most intimate this was it. One advantage was that you had the choice of two early morning papers to read if you cared to look at your next door neighbours' papers. In fact some chose their seat according to who was reading what. Many soldiers took all this in their stride but I must confess that I began to pray for constipation before we moved out.

And that, strangely enough, brings me back to the Jesuits. Our school toilets were highly respectable. But not always used for the purpose intended. The more daring would use them for a quiet smoke while the more notorious of us would use the iron bars erected there to cool our hands after receiving the ferula. I am not sure of the purpose of the iron bars. They seemed to stretch down the length of the toilet building like grills dividing it in two, I suspect they were merely decorative. Our hands would be almost red raw and by pressing them on the cold bars we would get some relief. But before leaving my school days let me tell you how the Jesuits saw me, the academic Jesuits that is.

My school report of Lent 1941: Moderate ability and tries, more exercise in the open air would be beneficial. Report of Summer 1941: Very moderate intelligence. Willing and obliging. A little careless of his appearance. I wondered; is 'very moderate' more moderate or less moderate than 'moderate'?

Of course the boys could never win that war with the Jesuits but it did prepare us for a war of another kind which was much more personal and tragic, the war between the Orange and the Green.

4

The Orange and the Green

I begin to discover an area of life in which I appeared different to others and at which, without at first realising it, I was a success – the church. Among the altar staff I wore a 'uniform' and I was different to other children in the body of the church. Pride in ones own personal success rather than team effort was seen as a vice and consequently discouraged. Though I began to feel different I was still held back by the emphasis placed on the virtue of humility. To see oneself 'as a worm and no man' to quote Thomas à Kempis was drilled into us and thus I was brought up with a warped spiritual life.

I remember attending a retreat once when the Retreat Director asked us all to draw a tree with many roots and branches. We were asked to label each root with incidents, experiences, etc. that had happened to us in our earlier life and then to trace their influence to the present day. How this influence affected our present behaviour had to be written on the appropriate branch. The object of the exercise was to see how things that happened in our lives influenced us and still influence us and make us the person we are. It is possible that things in our roots have never yet been taken on board in our adult life and lie dormant waiting for the right moment.

Sadly my life has been greatly influenced by one particular series of events that happened in Liverpool in my early childhood. Although the infant and elementary schools made no impact upon me as regards my academic education I remember vividly the impact religious affairs had upon me at that time.

It was in the infant school on 12 July that I first became aware of the Orange and the Green', the Protestants and the Catholics. The Protestants were called 'The Orange' after King William of Orange who defeated the Irish Catholics at the Battle of the Boyne in 1694. Catholics were known as 'The Green' as most of them living in Liverpool were immigrants from the days of Irish famine.

These were the days when the Original IRA were active on the mainland, though in a much minor capacity than in recent years. The biggest atrocity in those days was exploding bombs in telephone boxes, an experience equally practised by Moseley's Black Shirts who were also active in those days. Every twelfth of July the Orange Lodge would celebrate the Battle of the Boyne and the Liverpool Lodges would celebrate by going off to Southport for the day. The trouble began in the evening on their way home. They would march through Liverpool with flags flying and pipe and drum bands blaring away all the antipapist songs they could think of. And of course they would march through the Catholic quarters of Everton and Bootle banging away on their big drums. On the previous Sunday they would also have been banging away outside our church during the 11a.m. Mass. When it came to the Consecration, somehow or other they would know and that was when they really went to town on the big drum. Of course Irish Catholics did not take this lying down and they would line the streets of the processional route armed with green sods and bottles which they would hurl at the procession. Looking back it was a really sad occasion. The children and grown-ups in the procession were dressed beautifully and two children would ride on horseback representing William and Mary of Orange carrying the Bible opened at the relevant page. These were particularly the objects of attack. I remember one year when it was especially bad outside our church. Father Dukes, our Jesuit parish priest was out in the street ranting and raving at the Catholics to go home. I can still see him there racing up and down Shaw Street with his hair all over the place and the wings of his habit, as the sleeves were called, billowing in the wind.

But of course the Green were equally 'bad'. Their turn came on 17 March, St Patrick's Day, when Liverpool would be awash with shamrock. Every Catholic Church would have a ceremony of the blessing of the shamrock on the eve of the feast. On the Feast itself the Liverpool 8th Battalion of the King's Regiment, the 8th Irish as they were known, would march through the streets to the swirl of the Irish Pipes and the twirl of the kilt. They would march along Lime Street and as they passed the St George's Hall the Lord Mayor of the day would take the salute. The truly great day came when the Lord Mayor happened to be The Revd Longbottom who also happened to be the Leader of the Orange Lodge. Can you imagine him having to stand there taking the salute of the Liverpool Irish, servants of the scarlet woman of Rome. I was there that day and if ever there was a two finger exercise that's where it began on that day.

In those days, sadly, Liverpool was divided between the Orange and the Green and it was as dangerous to stray into each other's territory then as it is today in Belfast. Those days are particularly precious to me for two events. One to my shame, the other to my credit. The shame results from one twelfth of July when I denied my faith, the other when I got up from my bed in a barrack room full of soldiers to go to Mass. I can still hear their jeers more than fifty years later. But let me explain. When I was in the infant school, as the twelfth approached and tensions were high we would often be met outside school by the members of the Orange Lodge and battered all the way home. Every twelfth the windows of our house would be smashed and we gradually learnt to stay in and avoid trouble – even to the extent of staying off school. All my childhood was coloured by the battle of the Orange and the Green and continued well into my adult years. Even in the army I remember one night in a barrack room of 200 men, Northern Irish Conscripts (Protestants of course) and Southern Irish volunteers (Catholics) taking their bayonets to each other.

I was about twelve or thirteen when I experienced what I consider to be the most shameful event of my life. I was walking home from school when this big fellow grabbed hold of me by the collar. He seemed a giant though he was probably only about three years older than I was and not much bigger. He flung me against the railings of Grant's Gardens which was within about 100 yards of our house and he said to me in a voice I can remember to this day, 'Are you a Catholic?' I think on my deathbed I shall remember my response, 'No', I said and I could almost hear the cock crow. I wonder now how my life would have changed had I said 'yes'. But the memory of that incident continues to have a profound effect on me. You might remember that earlier I said that I was still trying to prove Mr Hignet wrong when he said that no good would come of me. I wonder if my reason for joining the Catholic Evidence Guild years later was an attempt to cleanse myself of the betrayal I still feel when I think of that incident. For years later, I stood proudly on the platform of the Catholic Evidence Guild at Speakers Corners around the country teaching the Catholic Faith to all who would listen. The C.E.G. as it was called was a national society, the aim of which was not to evangelise but simply to teach. Our remit was to take a particular teaching of the Catholic Church, explain why the church taught it and why we believed it to be true. The speaker would then take questions. But we were forbidden by Guild rules to evangelise. If somebody expressed interest in joining the church the Guild member would refer the person to a priest for further instruction.

But long before the days of the C.E.G. I had the opportunity to recant on my apostasy. It was in the army and I was billeted with about 200 men in the one huge barrack room. Being a Catholic in the army was a mixed blessing. Those were the days of compulsory church parades on Sunday mornings but the army always recognised freedom of religion. Although we had to parade with everybody else, when it came to the point of marching off to the church there always came the command, 'RCs and Jews fall out'. The army didn't seem to recognise other religions or atheism because everybody else was marched into the Anglican Church. As you can imagine we used to get quite a few converts on Sundays but they didn't last beyond midnight.

I would try to find a Catholic church in the area wherever I was billeted. Hail, rain or shine I would get up and go to Mass. I had to go to an early Mass because we were not excused parades once the Anglican Church Parade was over. I remember once being stationed five miles from the nearest Catholic church. On the first Sunday I got up to go to the early Mass. Those who were awake in the barrack room jeered and cat-called at 'Holy Joe' going off to Mass in spite of a heavy snowstorm. The next week another soldier, a Catholic, got up and came with me. Before long five or six Catholics were coming to Mass regularly and those who had been doing the cat-calling would keep our breakfast warm for when we returned. I felt that I had made up for my apostasy.

Another sacrifice we had to make for our faith came as a result of Catholics not being allowed to eat meat on Fridays in those days. Some camps would serve alternative food on Fridays out of respect and would also be sensitive to the Jewish laws concerning food, but others would not. Because of these experiences I can fully understand the difficulty of vegetarians when they go visiting. With my own experiences behind me I always cook a special vegetarian dish when they visit me as a matter of respect for their holding to their principles. In my army days vegetarians didn't exist. We were glad to get whatever food we could and of course during the war years bully beef and biscuits was our staple diet. Vegetarianism really came to the fore in the 1980s.

I became conscious of the variety of people's needs in terms of food in a very striking way one evening in the days of Keele when I gave a dinner party for a few students. I used to do this about once a week and would try and mix the group of about eight in terms of sex, culture and religion. On this particular night I had prepared Bœuf Bourguignonne and was happily about to serve it when a Muslim present asked what it was. Even as I told him it dawned on me with a shudder that there was bacon in it. I had forgotten all about the Muslims not eating pork.

Those dinner nights were very productive in terms of getting to know the students. As I said, I would make sure that the group was very mixed. Being men and women of social grace they would invite me to a return meal and of course it would be into their own groups that each of my guests would welcome me. I called this the spider's web approach to the apostolate. That reminds me of the day the Bishop of Lichfield invited the three chaplains to tea at the cathedral. A new Anglican chaplain had been appointed and I think this was a gesture on behalf of the Bishop to integrate him into the team. Over the tea, served in the best china, remember this was the Potteries, the Bishop asked us, 'If I was to begin as a chaplain, what would you recommend I should do to get to know the students?' 'Well,' one of the chaplains said, 'I would arrange a Bible study.' Another said, 'I would arrange a prayer group.' 'And what about you?' the Bishop said, turning to me. Without hesitation and even without thinking I replied spontaneously, 'I would throw a party.' And that has been my policy since I began teaching and doing chaplain's work over a period of thirty years. I would have Freshers' Parties. But the best way of getting to know the students and for them to get to know each other was to share an experience. And from 1961 until I finished student work in 1993 I would take students away at the beginning of the academic year for a rough weekend into North Wales. There we would sleep in a bunkhouse or under canvas and climb Snowdon. Friendships formed during those weekends lasted forever. Sometimes we would go to the bunkhouse in Ystradgynlais and twice I even took thirty students, all female, to Zermatt where we attempted the Matterhorn. I shall be returning to Snowdon from time to time in these pages.

But back to the Orange and the Green! Liverpool has always been noted for its two obsessions, Religion and Football which is almost an extension of their religion. And the Orange and the Green played their part here also. Everton were Catholic and Liverpool were Protestant and many a fight took place on a Saturday after a derby match. For a happy weekend it wasn't sufficient to have your team win but the other team had to lose. There was no give or take in this area.

The international language

Thankfully things have changed out of all recognition. Economics have changed the membership of the football teams and Church leaders worked really hard to bring the Orange and the Green together. Archbishop Heenan began the process and how successful the efforts have been can be seen in the nicknames given to the Catholic Archbishop Worlock and the Anglican Bishop Shepherd – 'Fish and chips, always together and never out of the paper'.

The Orange Lodge can still be seen marching on 12 July and the St Patrick's Day parade takes place on 17 March. But now it is a case of live and let live.

I began this chapter by mentioning how things that happen in childhood can colour our whole lives. Such was the influence of the Orange and the Green on me. To this day I find ecumenism very difficult and I find I cannot go into an Anglican church without thinking of 'those days'. Ironically, I now say Mass every Sunday in an Anglican church. In my youth we were not even allowed to go into one.

You will have gathered from all this that I had a very strong Catholic upbringing. My family lived in the Jesuit parish of St Francis Xavier and I was born into a strong Catholic family where everything revolved around the church.

We all attended Mass every Sunday and I remember being taken to every other service that took place on the Sunday evening and during the week. I can't remember any of my sisters or my brother being taken now I come to think about it. Rosary, sermon and benediction? I was there. Stations of the Cross? I was there. Novenas to almost every saint in heaven? I was there. I lived and breathed church.

It was no problem for me when, on a Monday morning, we had to show our stamped Mass cards to the teacher to prove we had been to Sunday Mass. Actually, during the war, we had to show them every morning as well to prove that we had been to prayers in the church the night before. Would you believe it, a priest, normally Father Dukes, would go around the parish ringing a bell at 8p.m. every evening. On the sound of the bell we would have to go into church for night prayers and we would have a card which was stamped each evening. Woe betide anybody whose card was not stamped, the strap was given unmercifully. I think this was the only period in my school years when I scored above my fellow pupils, a success of a different colour. Never once was my card not stamped. My mother saw to that, God bless her.

You will gather from this that my mother was a very holy woman in her own way and certainly a woman of prayer. Her one ambition was to go to Lourdes before she died. Of course, she never had the money for this so when I was demobbed from the army I gave her my demob money as a gift and off she went to Lourdes. She was ecstatic. Before she died she had been to Lourdes five times. I am told it is addictive though I have never been myself.

As a little boy I would wear red velvet knickerbocker suits with lace collars and walk in the processions of the Blessed Sacrament. There would be ten of us. The one in the front and the one at the back would wear black velvet and then four pairs in between would wear the red. We would walk forwards and every few steps turn around, take petals out of the baskets each of us carried and strew them on the floor before the monstrance carried by the priest. I can still remember the prayer we said as we did this: 'O Sacrament we thee adore, O make us love thee more and more.' Years later after I was ordained a priest I was invited to preach on the occasion of the Annual Outdoor Procession.

In addition to church services there were all sorts of religious groups we were invited to join. My sisters were in the Guild of St Agnes for young girls. Then as they got older they joined the Children of Mary. These were really prayer groups of one sort or another. I joined the St Vincent de Paul Society (SVP). The SVP used to collect money and clothing and give them to the poor – yes there were people much poorer than we were. I remained in this group for quite a long time. At Christmas members would be given addresses of the poor and we would take them money collected from the parishioners. One year I was given the address of a very old person and given half a crown to take to him (twelve-and-a-half-pence now). It was a small fortune then.

He lived in the really poor area of the parish and when I knocked at the door he invited me in. It was smelly, dirty and the furniture consisted of a bed, a chair and a table. He was drinking tea from a cup on a saucer. The poor had standards! He asked me if I would like some tea and I told him I would. I dreaded the thought of it especially when he took the cup and poured half of his tea onto the saucer and handed it to me. I shuddered at the thought of drinking it but then I realised he was sharing exactly half of what he had. That thought certainly sweetened the drink and I don't think I have ever been offered such a valuable present, not to say lesson.

I sang soprano in the choir and a very handsome choir it was too. We sang all the great Masses and I couldn't wait each year to join in the great Alleluia Chorus on Holy Saturday. When my voice broke I joined the altar staff. Now that was when I first experienced real discipline.

The standard of altar service at SFX could only have been equalled in the Basilica of St Peter in Rome. A Master of Ceremonies (MC) every bit as thorough as the strictest Regimental Sergeant Major (RSM) ensured that every altar server and priest knew his role. Just as the RSM has authority over all ranks when it comes to parades and military discipline so the MC is in full control of all 'ranks' during religious ceremonies, be that rank of the lowliest altar boy or the Pope. He would conduct a religious service with an eye to every detail and can well be compared to a conductor of a large orchestra.

The MC was the most prized and envied person on the altar, so much so that years later, when I had the opportunity to succeed to this role I seriously thought of making it my life's vocation rather than becoming a priest. It was Brother Mulligan, the Sacristan, who convinced me otherwise. Space prevents my doing justice to this subject and there is material enough for a book on the subject alone. Suffice it to say that when the Thurifer with his boat bearer, eight torch bearers, two acolytes and the MC lead the celebrants to the altar it was with a dignity and reverence unequalled anywhere. I served at the altar until I left to become a priest. Nine years later, a few weeks before my ordination, two boys came from Liverpool and asked me what gift I would like from the altar staff to commemorate the occasion. I chose a lavabo spoon. This is a little spoon the priest uses to pour a drop of water into the chalice during the Mass. On my ordination day I was presented with such a spoon inscribed, 'From the SFX Altar staff 1961'. To this day forty-two years later, I use it at every Mass I say. One of those boys is now a Salvatorian priest and the other a Jesuit Brother.

Who will forget the great occasion at SFX when 'Dickie Downey', as the sainted Archbishop of Liverpool was affectionately called, ordained four men to the priesthood. Archbishop Richard was one of the old school and although he was only of small stature he was one of the last triumphalist bishops. To the choir singing the majestic, 'Ecce Sacerdos Magnus' (Behold the great High Priest) he would process into the church as solemn as any potentate. On this occasion he was ordaining one of the men as a Jesuit priest, one as Diocesan, one a Salvatorian and the other a Mill Hill priest. Mill Hill priests were missionaries and this one went straight to Borneo after his ordination. He would send us letters and photographs and spoke of the wonderful people of Sabah where he was serving. I swore that one day I would visit Borneo, another of my wild dreams. Many years passed and would you believe, I met some Sabahan students at Keele University. They belonged to the Kadazan tribe which was now ninety-nine per cent Catholic and they invited me to visit them. I went. The students met me and took me to their village of Penampang deep in the rainforest. On our journey from the airport they told me that there was a reception for me in the village hall that evening and that I was to have a speech ready. I nearly dropped dead at the thought. That evening they came to the presbytery where I was staying and took me to the hall. As I approached I could hear the sound of gongs being hit right, left and centre. I asked my friends about the noise and they told me it was their welcome – the sort of thing we do on church bells. They gave me a tape of this welcome afterwards.

As I walked into the hall I saw emblazoned across the wall behind the stage the words, 'Welcome Father Richard'. There in the jungle was this welcome to the lad who would never come to any good. Talk about being gob-smacked. The children had prepared a play for me and afterwards the Chief of the village made a speech welcoming me. He said that they get so few priests they like to ensure that those who visit get a great welcome. I forgot to mention that when I first met the parish priest earlier that day he had just come from a Mass centre (parish) deeper in the rainforest. He was covered in leeches. I asked him how many Mass centres he had and he replied nonchalantly, thirty. There were two priests in the whole diocese. Anyway, I got up to reply to the speech and I told him about the ordination I had attended over forty years before and that I had sworn I would visit Borneo before I died. I mentioned the name of the priest whose ordination I had attended, Fr McCarthy. The parish priest stood up after me and told me that as a boy, he had been taught by that very same priest.

Then a few of the old ladies came forward and said the same. I couldn't put a foot wrong after that and, please God, I will go back some day. I could tell you a lot of stories about that visit. Well, why don't I? After all this is a 'Bless and Tell' book. I will tell you about the engaged couple I blessed after the prospective groom had bartered for his potential wife. The going rate was two buffaloes but because he was American he got her for one buffalo and an English degree which she had gained at Keele. I think he is still paying for that buffalo.

And I will tell you about the minibus driver I blessed after he took me to the airport. In Sabah buses don't run according to a timetable, they run when the bus is full. I was sitting on one waiting for it to get me to the airport but, of course, the driver was waiting for it to be full before setting off. They had 'agents' touting for custom but the response was slow. I had visions of missing the plane and my host, Mary, could feel the vibes. She told the driver I was a Catholic priest and was worried about missing my plane. Without hesitation, he closed the door and immediately set off for the airport. Never mind about blessing him, I nearly kissed him. I am sure he lost a lot of custom because of his noble action.

I'm sorry I am getting carried away.

As you can imagine such an upbringing as I have described lead inevitably to my forming a value system based on a very strict conscience ruled by guilt and law. (Everything pleasurable was sinful.) Without the Sacrament of Confession as it was then called I would have gone crazy. I remember to this day the classroom. I can see the teacher in front of a blackboard telling us about it. I can distinctly remember thinking then, 'this is great. I can do what I want and then go to confession afterwards'. She must have been a dreadful teacher for she gave me exactly the wrong interpretation of the Sacrament. And it stayed with me for quite a while. My conscience developed so strictly as to border on the scrupulous and I would be seen in the queue for confession sometimes twice a week. Of course it was counterproductive and only reinforced feelings of guilt, feelings that stayed with me until I went to university at the age of thirty-nine. I shall tell you later how this influenced the members of the province when it came to their electing me as Provincial, or not electing me as the case may be.

I cannot remember a single incident where we were taught about Christ as a person. We must have been taught so in preparation for First Holy Communion but it obviously made no impression on me. I have told elsewhere the story of my First Holy Communion day. It wasn't until I was twenty-two after I came out of the army that I met Christ as a person. And that was due to a throwaway remark by a speaker on the CEG platform. I had always been interested in prayer but I had never cracked it until that day. It was always quite a complex process for me but quite suddenly it all seemed so simple. My prayer life has never given me any trouble since then.

During this period a priest arrived at SFX who was to have a profound influence on my life. Father Tom Conlan! He would stand in the pulpit and give the most inspiring sermons. He appeared to me as another St Francis Xavier and he even seemed to be a look-alike. He spoke with such passion about the man and his works that I was overcome with hero-worship which is still with me to this day. It was listening to his sermons that made me determined that one day I would go to the Island of San Scian in the South China Sea where SFX died. It took me more than sixty years to fulfil that ambition which I did in 2002 (see Chapter 25).

Fr Tom was a very apostolic man and introduced me into the world of the apostolate – prayer in action. He was a true apostle. At this time the Communists were very active in Liverpool operating in cell groups. Fr Tom formed Christian cell groups in the parish and I belonged to one whose task it was to get those shops selling 'dirty books' in the parish closed. Two of us would go to a suspect shop and ask for a particular book. There were certain titles that book shops were not allowed to sell by government law. These were always sold from underneath the counter and our object was for one person to buy one of these and the other to witness the sale. A number of so called 'sex shops' were closed through our apostolic zeal. I think it was because of Father Tom's influence that I decided to join such an active religious order when the time came for me to 'join up'.

I do believe that it was during those days that the seeds of my vocation planted years before began to germinate.

Often people ask me why I became a priest and when did I first decide to 'do it'. To understand my first response to the call I need to remind you of the lifestyle we lived in Everton in the 1930s. I wrote earlier how seven of us lived in a small rented house with one wage-earner. Sometimes he was out of work and it wasn't unusual for us to wonder where the money for the next meal would come from. To this day I find myself eating every scrap of food on the plate at meal times and I never throw anything out. This actually paid dividends when I became Chaplain at Keele University. Every Sunday there was an open house for lunch in my cottage. Forty or fifty students would turn up after Mass and, of course, there were always leftovers. These I would put through the blender and make the most delicious soup to be served the next Sunday. I became famous for my soups and people would ask for the recipes. What could I tell them? Every edible thing imaginable went into the soup from bits of the choicest meat to pieces of lettuce and even salad cream if there was some left in the bottle. During the nine years I served Sunday lunch at Keele not one student ever had stomachache.

Almost exactly like the Liverpool folk song, I was born in Liverpool down by the docks. My religion was Catholic, and under old overcoats each night we slept. I told you earlier that I lived in a three up and two down and that was only the bed. I don't remember if we wore nightshirts, pyjamas were unheard of or only for cissies like those who used underwear. It was unheard of for the boys from Everton to wear underpants. In fact, the first time I wore any was when I was issued with them when I joined the RAF. But looking back, perhaps it was only me and my brother that didn't. Who knows? Anyway, it was from this sort of background that I used to go down to the church and help one of the priests in the priests' house library. There were about twenty Jesuits or more there and it was an extensive library. I used to help a Father McDonald put the returned books back on the shelves and sometimes catalogue them. I think I was about seven at the time. After helping him he would invite me into his room to sit in front of a beautiful coal fire and give me orange juice and biscuits.

He had his own collection of books lining the walls. It was so quiet and peaceful. To get to his room from the library we had to go through the refectory, the first time I did this my eyes nearly popped out of my head. There were bowls of fruit on the table – real fresh fruit. It was around this time that I heard the call. I thought if this is the way priests live then this is for me.

This idea about a 'call' came back to me years later when I took a group of girls to climb Snowdon. We used to go from Mary Ward College annually and there was one girl who came every year but would never make the climb. We kept on at her, thinking she was nervous and reassuring her, but in vain. Eventually on one of these excursions she drew me aside and told me the reason. As true as I am typing these words she said to me: 'My mother always told me that when God calls a girl to be a nun he does it on a mountain. I don't want to be a nun, so, just in case, I don't climb.'

Others benefited from the Jesuits at this time. There was old Father Joe Hughes. He had been blown up in the First World War and buried for three days in a trench. Another bomb came over and he was blown out. Ever afterwards he suffered from shell shock. There is a professional name for it now, 'Post Traumatic Stress Syndrome', and victims of it have special therapy. His therapy took the form of helping himself to the fruit in the refectory and taking it to the poor of the parish – and there were plenty. Sometimes he would be seen furtively sneaking through the streets at night making his way to the hard-up with a jug under his habit. He had been to the pubs and begged beer for them. A wonderful man but a terror in the confessional! If you were last in the line, after he had given you absolution, he would just put the light out, walk out his side into the priests' house and leave you in the dark to find your own way out to the church. These were the days when confessionals were like cupboards divided by a wall with a screen in the middle. This little screen was covered with a purple cloth so you could be heard but not seen. I remember once a loud cry coming out of the box, 'Nellie where am I? I can't see anything.' A poor old lady had been plunged into darkness and couldn't find her way out. But he was great with the penances. You could tell him you had committed murder and he would simply say, "How many times? Say three Hail

Marys'. I used to serve his Mass and I would like to think some of his holiness came through to me.

So it was at the age of about seven I thought of becoming a priest and I can honestly say that the thought never left me as I grew up. And if old Fr Joe influenced my spiritual life, Fr Tom fired my enthusiasm for the apostolic life.

And so my teenage years were drawing on, always shadowed by the war. The question of what we would do when we grew up had to be put on hold. We didn't know if we would be fortunate enough to grow up.

But let's have a break.

First Interlude

The Silver Sixpence

In the midst of this a silver sixpence assumed value out of all proportion to its real value.

In today's decimal world an old sixpence is now worth two-and-a-half new pence.

Actually sixpences have played quite a large part in my life. There was that time when I made my First Holy Communion. I was walking down the aisle with hands joined, head down, contemplating transubstantiation (as if). I think I must have read somewhere about when saints made their First Holy Communion they had visions and doves flew over their heads. Well, I was expecting all this but imagine my shock when, as I passed the bench where my Auntie Louie was sitting, she suddenly reached out and pushed something into my hand. It was silvery and so I presumed it was a medal. As I approached the Lady Chapel where we were to receive Holy Communion for the first time I glanced into my hand and there I saw a silver sixpence. Almost immediately thoughts of transubstantiation left me. Do you know for the rest of the Mass and even during actually receiving my First Holy Communion all my thoughts were on how I could spend my new-found wealth.

I told you earlier how it cost us sixpence to have a slipper bath down at the Public Baths every Saturday didn't I? Many a time Flo and myself thought of spending the money on sweets and pretending we had had a bath. But as you can imagine we would have been found out very soon for obvious reasons, not the least eau de Everton or should that be eau d'Everton?

Then there was the time when, as a student at Christleton Hall, I went into Chester for confession. Christleton Hall was our major Seminary where British Salvatorians were trained for the priesthood. To go out we had to have the permission of the superior. If he gave it we would then have to go to the bursar and ask for whatever money we needed for wherever we were going. We were encouraged to have a personal confessor outside of the Salvatorian Community and I used to go into the Friary where the Franciscans had a church. You could always get permission to go to confession. Some of our number abused this privilege of course and said they were going to confession when, in fact, they had other intentions (not me of course). In fact, in those days I was very holy. Enlightenment came some time later. Anyway, I got the fare from the Bursar to get the bus into Chester and back. I was told to be back for supper at a particular time, I've forgotten what time now. Anyway I came out of confession and went to get the bus back home when I discovered to my horror that I had lost the fare—sixpence. I was absolutely 'gob-smacked' as they would say today. Not to be on time for meals was an unforgivable sin and I knew that if I walked the three miles, I would be late. I prayed fervently to find sixpence. Do you know, as I walked along, my eyes on the ground, there I saw a silver sixpence in the gutter. (Definitely grounds for a canonisation don't you think?) I was back in time and nobody knew of that miracle.

Then there were the sixpences of Ystradgynlais. Sounds like a good title for a book! Ystradgynlais is a large village in Powys with a population of native Welsh and immigrant English, Poles, etc. The Salvatorians founded a parish there back in the 1940s and many of our priests have served there as parish priests or as assistant priests. One of the parish priests founded a bunkhouse in the parish and I used to take students there to go hill-walking on the Black Mountain. One of the parishioners has a most interesting cabin at the bottom of his garden. It is a disused railway carriage and he had equipped it with all sorts of naval paraphernalia. In addition to this all sorts of artefacts had been installed over the years, one of which was a 'one-armed bandit'. This was a sort of fruit machine. You had to place your money in the slot and a variety of fruit spun around until the machine stopped. If, when it stopped you had three of the same fruit lined up you won the jackpot. Well, the money used was old sixpences and Frank used to keep a supply for when children called. They were not supposed to take the sixpences away with them if they won but gradually Frank's supply dwindled until it was almost non-existent. A great source of joy to children was in danger of being lost. Then one day, I was clearing

out one of our houses in Norfolk, a presbytery which we had to hand over to the diocese and so we were sorting out the contents. Imagine my joy when in the process I came across a hoard of old sixpences. That was in 1997 and Frank is still using them.

I mentioned earlier that I had been given sixpence on the day of my First Holy Communion in 1933. During my fortieth anniversary of priesthood celebration I told the guests this in my response to the Toast. I was opening my cards the next Christmas when out of one fell a 1933 sixpence. A friend who was at the ceremony sent it to me as a Christmas present.

But enough about sixpences!

PART TWO

The War and Post-war Years 1939–1952

A number of major events were happening at this time that must have had their effect on my personality and spiritual development.

Having lived with failure it came as no surprise that I would be left to the last in being given a billet when I was evacuated. We were losing the war and rationing was influencing family harmony, such as it was.

A glimmer of England, as a whole, being in the failure class system is seen in the reaction to Dunkirk. It was seen as an occasion of rejoicing when in fact it was one of the biggest defeats of the war—a complete rout.

5

It Will All Be Over By Christmas

When war broke out I was thirteen. In accordance with instructions given to us at school the previous term we were taken to school the very next day after Chamberlain had made his famous speech, ending with the words uttered in a very grave voice, 'we are now at war with Germany'.

The sirens had sounded for the first time but nothing had happened. 'It will all be over by Christmas' was the greeting people gave each other now when they met on the streets. And certainly, the phoney war was over by Christmas. But by then we had been evacuated and returned.

What evacuee will ever forget the memory of those early days of the war? On 4 September 1939 we paraded at school and then were taken by buses to the railway station and kitted out with a gas mask and food parcel. Our school was evacuated to a little village called Dyserth in North Wales not far from Rhyl. With our gas masks over our shoulder and a name tag on the lapel of our school blazer in case we got lost we mounted the train waving to our broken-hearted mothers who thought they would never see their children again. No one knew which way the war would go but there were enough veterans of the First World War who knew that war was not a picnic. We had been given a parcel of food. Imagine a big brown paper bag filled with sandwiches, fruit and, above all, a 1lb bar of chocolate. The chocolate was so precious that some of us kept it all through the journey and still had it when we arrived at Dyserth. On arrival we were shepherded into a large village hall, I can't remember who supervised us at that time, whether it was the teachers or the villagers. We were to be billeted with the local people who would sort of foster us during our stay there and we had to wait in this hall for the villagers to come and select who they were prepared to take. It might rank as child abuse today because our numbers gradually dwindled until there were just three left in the hall with no one to take them. Guess who was among the three? Absolutely right. After a bout of feverish activity on behalf of the organisers I remember a lady bustling in and saying she would take the three of us. She took us home and the first thing I remember was that she took our food parcels off us and gave the chocolate to her son. To this day I can remember that incident. We lost our chocolate.

Years went by and the war went on so long that we were in the army and in the front line before it ended. As I shall tell you later, part of my war period was spent in repatriating prisoners liberated from German prison camps. There was one occasion when I came across a French prisoner who happened to be a Catholic priest. He had been imprisoned for quite a while. I had only met one army padre since I enlisted and so I took the opportunity of going to confession to this French priest before he was repatriated. Confession was very much a part of our Catholic lives then. I can't remember what I told him but I do remember very clearly him sitting at a very long, canteen table with his head turned aside and resting his chin in his hands as this young English soldier poured out his sins. After my confession was over I stayed with him for a little chat. As prisoners were liberated and prior to their repatriation they were given a food parcel to boost their meagre rations. Well, I was about to say farewell to my new-found French friend when he reached into his parcel and took out a huge bar of chocolate. He divided it into two and gave me one half. My mind raced back to Dyserth.

That chocolate was even more precious to me because of Dyserth but also in another sense. Each afternoon after school we, the three 'leftovers' from the village hall, would wander up the hill and sit on a bench overlooking the sweet shop down in the valley. One of them became a Bevan Boy when we were called up and worked down the mines. He later became an artist of some distinction. I should mention that there were various occupations classed as 'reserved occupations'. Men working in these were exempt from call-up because their work was seen as necessary towards the war effort. Miners were among these. But there were not enough and so conscientious objectors who refused to fight or had some other good reason not to be enlisted in the Armed Forces, such as health, were 'sent down the mines'. There was another class of person who was released from the Forces to join a reserved occupation. These were called 'class B release' and among them were religious orders. I remember visiting my cousin who was a monk soon after I joined the army. He was a monk of the Ramsgate Community of Benedictines. Obviously impressed with what he saw, the Abbot said to me, 'if you would like to join us I could get you a class B release'. Such bribery! But I wasn't tempted. While I was still determined to become a priest and was uncertain as to what sort, I knew that it was not to be a Benedictine monk, God bless them.

The third evacuee billeted with us went into the RAF. He was killed over Germany. An evacuee at the beginning of the war and killed in action before the war ended. That says something about the times in which we spent our childhood.

Looking down at the sweet shop we would watch the posh kids going in and out, opening their Mars bars and Milky Ways. These were boys from the posh parts of Liverpool like Grassendale, Formby, and so on. How we envied them. I would wait until the end of the week when I would get a half-crown postal order from home and race to the post office to exchange it for cash. Then straight to that sweet shop. I cannot see a Mars bar to this day without the smell taking me right back to that hill and that bench. It also reminds me of the terrible sacrifice my mother must have made for me, to send that much out of my dad's miserable wage packet. God rest her soul. I don't think any of the five of us were really aware of how much she and my father were doing for us in spite of such sadness in their own lives. How selfish we can be without realising it and what a disappointment I must have been to them in those early years. One failure after another.

We were only evacuated for a few months as there were no signs of the war in Liverpool. I absolutely hated being away from home. I was talking to my sister Flo about this recently and she told me how my mother would pace up and down worrying about me and how she could get me home. Flo also mentioned the trouble my mother went to to find that half a crown each week. These sort of scenes must have been going on all over the country at that time. A lot has still to be written about the Second World War, what you might call the alternative version. There were more unsung heroes than bemedalled ones. Bit by bit parents would call their children home until eventually the whole school had returned within six months.

Pat Heery writing in his book, *The History of St Francis Xavier's College, Liverpool 1842–2001*, says:

> the boys evacuated had been scattered around the district from Prestatyn to Rhyl to Dyserth and St Asaph. Father Neylan, [the headmaster] was content to leave the administrative and pastoral work to other priests and lay staff as he took up residence in Mia Hall a large country house outside Rhyl. Here he taught classics students—with their needs attended to by the college cook and the college secretary.
>
> (Pat Heery, Liverpool: 2002)

So, though I can't remember it clearly, we must have been split up with some staff remaining in Liverpool for those who refused to be evacuated or returned early like myself.

My memories of evacuation are centred on letters and postal orders I received from home and being put out into the field every Sunday night— hail, rain or shine—while our landlady and her family went to Chapel. Sometimes we would stand at the side of the road and watch the kids billeted with the posh people ride by in cars—such luxury!

But evacuation was another turning point in my life and in spite of the theft of the chocolate I owe a great debt to that landlady. Perhaps as a result of our sad home life I was still wetting the bed at the age of thirteen when I went to Dyserth. The landlady used to put a rubber sheet on the bed but that didn't seem to make much difference. One evening my room-mates and myself were chatting in the sitting room when she burst in. She might have overheard us talking about her or something but she was livid. She burst in and flung a hot-water bottle at me with some choice words, which of course, being an innocent little boy, I didn't understand. Looking back I can't remember what those words were but I can still remember the look on her face. Do you know that from that day to this I have never wet the bed. Perhaps in the whole of my life I have never received a gift of such proportion and consequence.

So we settled down again in Everton and the war seemed miles away. However, somebody knew something we didn't because brick air-raid shelters began appearing in the back gardens of those who could afford them. They were like one-room houses with seating and bunk accommodation. One such shelter appeared in our friends' house across the road and, God bless them, when the bombs began to drop they shared their shelter with us. Can you imagine it? In the early days sirens would go in the middle of the night and we would jump out of bed, put some clothes on and dash across the road. I remember one night when I was getting dressed my dad grabbed me and carried me across. It was only when I got into the shelter I realised I had no trousers on.

Who could ever forget the air raids? Gradually, as things got worse and the war got hotter every household was issued with a shelter. But the 'Council Shelter' was made of corrugated iron and was sunk partly into the ground at the end of the back yard. Consequently, we would sit there for hours, night after night, with our feet in puddles of water. We would go into the shelter about 6p.m. every evening. We would hear the bombs dropping and the dogfights as the battles between our fighter planes and the German bombers were called. The Royal Artillery with their mobile guns would dash from street to street to get a better 'pad' from which to fire their shells. My dad would stand outside the shelter and give us a running commentary on what was happening above us. We became experts at distinguishing our planes from theirs by the sound of the engine, and, by the same token, we knew whether it was a landmine, an incendiary bomb or a simple explosive by the sound of the explosion when they went off. We even began to be able to tell where the bomb had landed. Inevitably someone would say, 'Looks as if so-and-so is copping it tonight.'

Immediately the all-clear sounded we would come out of the shelter and dive for the houses that had been hit. It had become a hobby to search for bits of the bombs and grab them even though some were still red hot. Later that day, at school, we would swap a piece of landmine for a piece of incendiary and so build up a good collection of bomb fragments. I sometimes wonder what has happened to all those bomb fragments. In aeons to come, no doubt some archaeologist will be excavating and come across them and make a fortune.

Later in the day we would go to the local council offices to read the list of those who had been killed or injured the previous night. Who did we know that was on the list? Was he killed? Was he maimed? During one raid our house was irreparably damaged, probably by blast more than a direct hit. A high explosive would fall and directly hit and destroy a building, the force of the explosion would destroy or damage nearby buildings. This force was called 'the blast' and I have a vague memory of moving into the house from the shelter and finding it covered in dust and lots of broken furniture. We all got under the table in case anything fell on us and we had to give up the house in which we were all born and move around the corner. Such were the days of my youth.

Ironically, having returned from Dyserth because nothing was happening we were again evacuated later in the war. This was much different. Whole families would leave the city centre housing areas and travel by bus to Huyton a few miles outside of the city. We would spend the nights there and return next day. I don't remember who put our family up but I do remember what a posh house it was. They had a most beautiful kitchen and a real garden. None of your back yards in Huyton in those days

People laugh today when I say I was evacuated from Everton to Huyton—a distance of a few miles. Today Huyton is very much a part of the City of Liverpool and has joined the ranks of the poor but in those days it was countryside.

Then there was the rationing. We all had our ration books and we were allowed so much of certain foods every day. For those of us without much money it didn't make much difference apart from things like sugar and butter, well, marge really. We only ever had butter on Sundays with high tea in the parlour—ham salad and tinned fruit with evaporated milk. It was always known as best butter, perhaps because we kidded ourselves that marge was butter though we called it maggie-anne. I was in a super-market recently and saw some tins of condensed milk and was amazed at how expensive they were. Shoppers near me wondered what I was laughing at. I looked at the tins and immediately thought of the 'connie onny' we used to put in our tea instead of real milk because it was so cheap. It was in those days I gave up sugar. My dad would go spare if he came in from work and there was no sugar. This would happen if we had used up the ration and so I gave it up so as to make the family ration go further. Wasn't I the good boy then? I was telling one of my parishioners this only last week and he told me he had done the same. Unsung heroes!

And so life went on and I reached the age of sixteen. There was no sign of the war ending. I don't remember being frightened at the prospect of being called up. It just seemed another stage in growing up. War had become part of our lives, indeed, a way of life. One day I heard that if you joined the Air Training Corps (ATC) at sixteen you were guaranteed a place in the RAF when you were called up. This seemed much more preferable than the army which was certainly the most dangerous arm of the Armed Forces. So a few of us joined the ATC and, sure enough, when the time came we were enlisted into His Majesty's Royal Air Force.

6

Germany Calling

A question asked of all young people has been for ever, 'What are you going to do when you grow up?'

This has never really been a relevant question, for few ever get the opportunity to follow their star. For us in the war years, it wasn't a question of, 'What are you going to do when you grow up?' but rather, 'What will you do until you are called up?'

For us, youth was simply a time of waiting and preparing to take our place at the front.

Almost imperceptibly the war went on and eventually the tide began to turn. We began to win battles. The second front was launched and as with the change in national fortunes so a major change was about to take place in my life.

I may not have been enamoured with my school uniform and I shall always remember that happy day when I took it off for the last time. But came the day when I donned another uniform.

With great pride I wore the Blues of the Royal Air Force and to fit completely into the role I gave up smoking cigarettes and bought a pipe. It seemed to suit the image much more. I did my basic training with the RAF Regiment at Arbroath in Scotland. I had never come across the RAF Regiment before. They were in khaki like the army but had bits of blue scattered around their uniforms and they wore blue forage caps. I was very impressed with them until they began our eight weeks basic training on the promenade. It was as though they had collected all the Regimental Sergeant Majors (RSMs) in the army and transferred them to the RAF Regiment. RSMs were responsible for discipline in the army and everybody, including the officers, went in fear and dread of them. What a proud day it was when we passed out as airmen at the end of the training! In fact, our pride was only exceeded by our relief at having finished the course in one piece.

It was in Arbroath that I first developed my taste for sausages. On Saturday evenings there was not much worthwhile happening in the camp and a few of us, all Catholics, would go down to the Salvation Army. They used to have a sort of hymn sing-a-long and we had heard that anybody that requested a hymn would get a free sausage bun. I am not sure if it was a sin for us to go but a few of us, all Catholics, would go and call out a hymn. I can still taste those sausage buns, fat oozing out of them and the most delicious sausages you can imagine. These were the days before awareness of cholesterol of course.

So we passed out as airmen during a most fantastic parade. I was destined to train as a Radar Operator and I was all ready to begin the course when the letter arrived. Hundreds of us got a letter from the Minister of Aviation, Sir Archibald Sinclair: 'You have been selected to be discharged from the Royal Air Force.' We had only been in it for eight weeks and already we were being kicked out. D-Day had occurred and the casualties were enormous. They were looking for Infantrymen and so the RAF and the navy had to surrender some of their finest men for transfer. On the day of transfer we had to line up in a queue before two separate tables. At one we were discharged from the RAF. About ten yards away at the second table we were called up into the army. The Royal Military Police were there in force between the two tables in case we did a bunk. I was posted to the Durham Light Infantry and we were sent to a Reinforcement Holding Unit (RHU) to await our turn for the intensive training needed before we joined the front line.

It was in the barrack room of that RHU that I received my best education for my future life as a priest. I think I must have experienced or seen at first hand all that human nature was capable of. There were 200 men aged between eighteen and thirty-five from the four countries of the UK and from Southern Ireland, the Free State as we used to call it in those days. They came from very different backgrounds and, as you can imagine, there were almost as many different value systems as there were men. Of course we didn't call them value systems in those days, it was more a matter of 'what people got up to'. I remember my first counselling experience took place here, apart from counselling my family of course. Again we didn't call it counselling then, more a matter of listening, you might say. A young lad woke me up one night and sat on the side of my bed and opened his heart to me. He broke his heart crying. Picture the scene. Lines and lines of beds all exposed to each other. At any one time you could see the Northern and the Southern Irish soldiers taking their bayonets to each other; a soldier on his knees saying the rosary out loud and effing and blinding the Royal Military Policeman (RMCP) in between his prayers as he was told to get into bed; the usual snoring and nocturnal noises of the human animal as they settled to sleep. 'My client' and I were both eighteen when he came to me that night. I can still see his face. He had had his FFI (free from infection) inspection that day and discovered he had venereal disease. Of course he had been out with the local girls and his tears were caused because he was engaged to a girl back home and he would have to tell her. I wondered, as I listened to him, if he would still be crying if he hadn't contacted the disease. So many times in my life I have come across this sort of thing and wondered if tears are for the offence or for being found out. A lot to think about there, don't you think?

Free from infection examinations were, perhaps, the most degrading experiences of army life. Before and after leave, before and after postings, soldiers would have to line up and a corporal of the Royal Army Medical Corps would come out with a torch. We would have to expose our private parts for him to examine to see if we had contracted any disease of a sexual nature. Fresh cases of venereal disease and related diseases had to be reported each day. This went on throughout my army days, especially when we were in Germany. When the war ended each soldier received a letter from Field Marshall Montgomery forbidding him to fraternise with the Germans, male or female. Venereal disease had become a secret weapon and infected persons were deliberately infecting soldiers.

This might be the place to mention the mobile baths. At the front line we had no way of bathing other than out of a wash bowl on a stand in the latrines. From time to time, ideally weekly, mobile baths would come out. We would strip off and hand in our clothes to the attendants, get deloused and then go into a caravan-style shower chamber. On exiting we would be handed a set of clean clothes. Only God knew who had been wearing them before us.

But back to the RHU and the Durham Light Infantry (DLI). It seems the eight weeks basic training in the RAF didn't count and we embarked upon a period of intensive training prior to going to the front line. It made the RAF's training seem like an eight-week picnic with a few exercises thrown in for entertainment.

Eventually our turn came for battle inoculation. I was sent with hundreds of others to a battle inoculation camp in Omagh which, like Eniskillen, was a Garrison Town. The principle behind battle inoculation was to prepare us for the real thing before it happened. In the event the inoculation was worse than the real thing. A simulated battlefield was set up. With our rifles cradled horizontally in our arms and full kit on our backs we would have to crawl over open fields as the 'enemy' fired live tracer bullets over our heads. We had been told beforehand that the 'enemy' was allowed ten per cent casualties so they meant business. We would crawl digging our hands and knees into the field to move forwards keeping our heads down. All around us, antipersonnel mines were going off and then the occasional smoke screen would set us all off coughing and spluttering. Imagine this at night-time with the only light coming from the tracer bullets. But worse was to come for those who survived this.

The only time I ever really panicked in my life was the result of the next exercise we were put through: the gas chamber. Having survived the journey across the battlefield, we were told to put on our gas masks. Then we were marched up to what looked like an elongated prefabricated hut. We all sat around on benches lining the walls. After a short while we were told to take off our gas masks, then the fun began. It was a gas chamber and we were being given the experience of gasses the enemy might unleash upon us in the front line. We were coughing and gasping. It was impossible to breathe but the sergeant in charge would not open the door until we had had a good dose of it. It was then I really panicked and made a run for the door. I have never experienced an emotion like it before or since. Fortunately, the sergeant opened the door just in time and I was violently sick just outside. We were then made to run round in circles outside to get the gas out of our lungs. But more was to come. No sooner had we recovered than the medic came and applied mustard gas to our skins so that we would recognise it if we were exposed to it. Thank God we never had to put our new and very hard-earned knowledge to the test in battle conditions. Never once did I have to crawl over fields under battle conditions and, thank God, we never had to experience a real gas attack.

But I think the worst and most demoralising exercise we had to undergo was instruction in bayonet fighting. Being Infantrymen we were trained for hand-to-hand fighting, one form of which was 'going in with the bayonet'. In training we would be lined up about 100 yards from a line of dummy enemy and each soldier would have one of these sawdust filled dummies to himself. Before we were given the order to charge, we were worked up into a frenzy by the sergeant making us scream and shout and put on ugly faces. Then on the command 'charge' we would race towards our dummy screaming and shouting at the top of our voices and then plunge the bayonet into the dummy. The magic words of the instructor still echo in my ears, 'in, out, on guard'. The idea was that you plunged the bayonet in, twisted it to do maximum damage and then pulled it out. On guard meant having your rifle and bayonet in the correct position ready to meet the next person who might be coming at you. There was a variation on this theme. A more merciful way of killing your enemy with the bayonet was to hit him across the head with the butt of your rifle. Hopefully this would knock him unconscious and when he fell to the ground you went into the drill: in, out, on guard. We were encouraged to put our boot onto the victim to make it easier to pull the bayonet out. I wonder if this is where the expression, 'putting the boot in' came from? Before an actual bayonet charge in action the soldiers were encouraged to drink and drink. This was not so much to get them worked up as to anaesthetise them to what they were actually doing.

After eight weeks of intensive training we sere sent to another RHU up in West Hartlepool, there to wait being sent into action. It was 1945 and, thankfully, the war was nearly over. Each week a draft of reinforcements would be sent alternately to Europe and to the Far East. One morning we were marched to the railway station and railroaded to Tilbury docks where we boarded ships which would take us to the fighting zone. We had no idea where we were going but we knew that it was for real when we were issued with live ammunition.

For some reason, when I was posted to Germany I was transferred from the Durham Light Infantry to the 7th Battalion, Duke of Wellington's Regiment. This remained my 'outfit' until the war ended. I was not in it for very long but long enough to be included in the Roll of Honour published by the Battalion Commander once we were all back home, and I quote:

In these pages you will find recorded our roll of honour — those who were decorated, those who gave their lives and those who marched with the Battalion along the road from Yarmouth to the Ruhr in the great years of 1944 and 1945. Every name in this book is that of a man who was a member of a gallant Company of heroes.

Excuse me while I blush! But back to that line-up in Rotterdam when the sergeant major called out, 'Volunteers wanted'.

Those of us who had taken that momentous step forward not knowing what awaited us were marched into the office and lined up. An officer interviewed each of us. I can't remember the details of the interview but as I said earlier I do remember him being surprised by my well-spoken voice and my demeanour (Jesuits please note). Anyway, I was accepted for the operation and eventually we were informed that we were to join a particular operation, one just begun with the objective of travelling immediately behind the front line, going into the German prison camps and taking the surrender from the German commandants. We were divided into groups of three, an officer, an OR (Other Rank) driver and an OR batman/bodyguard. The officer was a major and I was his bodyguard/batman. My job was to guard the officer as he went forward into the camps, do his washing and cook for the three of us. The officer had the customary officer's revolver and the two of us had the old Lee Enfield 303 rifle. We had to hand these in complete with the live ammunition we had been issued and in return received small Sten machine guns with the appropriate live magazines. These were not the most stable of guns. Some months later I was escorting a German sergeant on the run from Belsen to the English Prison Cage as it was called. We were in the back of our truck with my Sten gun trained on him. I don't know who was the most scared. Every time we went over a bump, and there were many of them, there was the danger of the gun going off automatically. After seeing the treatment he got when he arrived at the cage, it might have been more merciful to have let the gun go off.

Our truck was a 15cwt motor and had been issued to us along with our Sten guns. It was to be home for the three of us for many months to come

We remained at Rotterdam for about three days and then because of the operation we were involved in we moved through Germany just behind the front line. We would go into the liberated prison camps and arrange for the repatriation of the prisoners. It was the most interesting period of my army years. It was on one of these occasions I met the French priest I talked about earlier. The camp was an Offlag (officers' prison camp) at Fallingbostel and there were prisoners there from every country at war with Germany. I was a humble private, of course but as part of the team I had to get the particulars of the different national groups prior to repatriating them. I remember going to a corner of the camp where the Russian officers were billeted. As I entered they stood up to a man and saluted — yes saluted me, a private from Everton. Was the tide of my life really turning I wondered.

One really good thing came out of serving in that camp apart from seeing the joy of the prisoners as they began their journey to their homes and loved ones. Montgomery would tour the liberated camps and give a pep talk encouraging the prisoners. He would always leave behind a carton of 200 cigarettes for each prisoner. We would include ourselves among the number of prisoners and so benefit from free cigarettes. This was all the more welcome in that tobacco was to become the currency in the immediate post-war Germany.

Alas, there was a lot of tragedy still to come for some of those prisoners. Lying in bed at night listening to shells going over we would also hear the occasional pistol shots from the woods. A nation group divided into Royalists and Nationalists imprisoned together had set about preparing for home by eliminating each other. And Belsen was within 'smelling distance'. Eventually, all the prisoners were repatriated who wanted to be and we continued on our way.

We continued north and it was at Schwerin that we reached the border with the Russian troops. As they had advanced the German civilians had fled so as to be in the British Zone when the war ended. It was there that I met Germans who would urge us to carry on and fight the Russians. As young men indoctrinated into believing that the Russians were our allies and, indeed, victims of the Germans, we had no time for such talk—little did we know.

Not only did we come face to face with the Russians, it was at Schwerin that I first met the Americans in action. I have to admit they were a pleasant bunch and we did a lot of swaps with our booty. I was very naive and thought I was doing a great deal swapping office material I had 'picked up' for a Luger revolver one particular American had 'found'. I thought I was quids in until when, returning to Blighty on board ship, we were ordered to throw overboard any weapons other than those that had been issued to us. All manner of threats were showered upon us if we failed to comply. The problem was that some men coming home from the front were finding their women had been unfaithful. Trained to kill, some soldiers were unable to control themselves and so the number of violent deaths had increased. With tears in my eyes I threw overboard my Luger and a Samurai sword I had found somewhere.

I was in Hamburg when the war came to an end. We didn't know it had ended until we saw soldiers across the River Elbe from us celebrating and we guessed. I had joined the front line at the crossing of the Rhine.

I saw action of various sorts from hand-to-hand fighting to waiting for a bomb to explode that had just landed ten yards away. Now the war was over but pockets of resistance occurred of course, and I remember one day I was cooking a meal over a primus stove in the billet. There was no such thing as a kitchen and it was a general-purpose room, anybody who has lived in a bedsit will know the feeling. As I was cooking I heard a noise behind me and when I turned my head, there, standing behind me with rifles trained on me, were three German Infantrymen. We were trained never to go anywhere without our weapons and mine was on the bed a few yards away. Swiftly I turned and reached for my Sten gun but it would not have done me any good. Had they wanted I could have been dead on the spot. But, would you believe it, they had come in to surrender. Their rifles were not trained on me. They were offering them to me.

What memories of those days! Some wonderful and, sadly, some quite shameful. We were a conquering army and whatever we found we believed to be ours. It is called looting. I remember we would find motor cars on the side of the road abandoned by fleeing Germans. We would drive them until they ran out of petrol and then pick up another one.

But thinking back to that Sten gun reminded me of sometime later when we had become the Army of Occupation, to be changed later into the British Army of the Rhine (BAOR) and ultimately the British Army on the Rhine. This is rather a subtle distinction but it emphasised the army of occupation as opposed to the army as guests of the German government.

As I said previously we had to take our guns everywhere with us. By this time I had surrendered my Sten gun for a 303 Lee Enfield rifle once again. There was no chaplain with us at that time and to attend Mass on Sunday we had to go to the local German Catholic church—with our rifles. I remember the first Sunday after the war ended. We were attending Mass in St Michael's Church in Hamburg. The time came for Holy Communion and with rifle over my shoulder I knelt next to Germans we had been fighting only days before. There is a message for our peacemakers somewhere there I think.

Gradually as hostilities ceased we settled down as the Army of Occupation. Infantry units were disbanded and the Infantrymen were transferred
to other Corps. I was transferred to the Royal Army Service Corps where I
was put to being trained as a clerk. I was sent on a course where I learnt to
touch-type and qualified as clerk Grade 3. Again this was an important
step for me for not long afterwards I was appointed senior clerk with the
rank of sergeant. I had been an LAC (Local Acting unpaid Lance Corporal) before this. Being promoted to sergeant was truly another step up the
ladder for this lad from Everton. I was a flop on the parade ground but
was completely at home in administration.

As the Army of Occupation we had great privileges—free theatre tickets
with the top stars coming from home to entertain us, free booze, free fags.
I remember seeing Ralph Richardson, Sybil Thorndyke and Laurence
Olivier on stage at the one time.

But the booze was wasted on me for I don't ever remember wanting a
drink even though it was free, or virtually so. We would get our ration of
duty-free booze when we were serving abroad and we would use the gin
to wash the car windows it was so cheap. Another privilege we got in
those days was a weekly ration of fifty free cigarettes, two bars of chocolate and three condoms or French letters as they were called in those days.
I worked in a bakery in some sort of management position. I remember I
had eight German girls working for me, two of whom I worked very
closely with. One had come from Posen as the Russian army advanced,
she had been raped and her family killed. I smoked cigarettes in those
days but I used to give the chocolate to the girls. They couldn't understand why I didn't want anything for them. It was dreadful to believe but
some girls were very cheap and a soldier could have a good night for two
cigarettes. Cigarettes and coffee were the currency immediately after the
war in Germany. Little boys would plunder the cinema queues waiting for
soldiers to drop cigarette ends. They would take them home and make
cigarettes out of them and thus buy coffee. They were sad days for everybody. We would have to watch out and search the workers as they left the
bakery at night. Some of them would be wearing vests made of dough so
short of food were they. Soup kitchens were the only source of food for

many.

But what about the free booze? Would you believe it, I never touched a drop of alcohol in my life until I entered religious life. We would celebrate the major feast days by having a special service and then a feast of sorts. There would be the aperitif, gin and tonic, and wine with the meal. These were the occasions when I first drank. And of course I have continued this ever since without waiting for feast days. Thank God I was never dependent on it in the sense of being an alcoholic. Soon after I was ordained, I asked my superiors if I could go back into the army as a full-time chaplain (padre). However, I was required to teach but I received permission to go into the Territorial Army. This meant one night a week in the local barrack room, one weekend camp a month and then a fifteen days summer camp. It was on one of the fifteen-day camps that I nearly met my match for drinking. A padre was allowed to mix with all ranks and thus was able to socialise in the NAAFI, the Sergeants' Mess or the Officers' Mess. One night I walked into the Sergeants' Mess in time to see the Regimental Sergeant Major (RSM) proudly boasting of the quantity he could drink. When he saw me, in a loud voice he invited me to have a drink with him. He was one of those men who thought that padres spent their whole time on their knees praying for the likes of him. In those days I drank rum so I called his bluff and asked for a large rum. He was quite surprised as we drank together and after the first drink he asked me to have another, quite sure I would decline. Well it became a drinking match to see who could drink whom under the table. It must have been like that when, in the old days, boxers would fight bare-fisted to the delight of the crowd baying for blood.

"Fancy another old chap?"

RSMs are probably the most unpopular men in the army by definition and so the men roared with delight when the RSM finally succumbed and sunk very ungraciously to the floor. On my wall near where I am writing this there is a picture of a railway engine. The unit I was with on this occasion was an engineers' unit and we had taken over the single-track railway at Blaenau Ffestiniog for the fortnight's camp. On the back of this picture of a railway engine is a message 'from the lads of the Sergeants' mess', it reads, 'to the best Padre in the British Army'. Obviously sanctity is measured in the army by the quantity of alcohol a man can drink. For my part I felt I had a duty that night to let the men know a padre is ready for any emergency. I saw it as a form of apostolate very much in keeping with the religious order I belonged to. Father Francis Jordan who founded the order used to say that we should evangelise by all ways and means!

But I digress. A lot happened very quickly when the war ended and I was in Luneburg when the German army came in to officially surrender. I remember the bedraggled men in their battered war-torn vehicles—the epitome of depression. It was good to see German women coming out of their houses giving them food and drink. Meanwhile in a tent on Luneburg Heath, General Eisenhower was accepting the formal surrender. Shortly after this I witnessed a scene that many a civilian at home would have given his right arm to see. When the air raids were at their height and it looked at times as though we would never see the morning we were plagued by a voice on the wireless coming from Germany, 'This is Gaarmany calling. This is Gaarmany calling', in what he thought was an Oxford accent. And then the voice would go on to tell us which city would be bombed that night and how Germany was the master race. It was the voice of the traitor William Joyce otherwise known as Lord Haw Haw because of the way he spoke. It was most peculiar. People hated him, were even afraid of him but felt compelled to tune in to the wireless and listen to him. He was one of Hitler's best secret weapons—though it was only his whereabouts that were secret. After the war he was captured. He escaped but not for long and that night in Luneburg I saw him being carried on a stretcher into a hospital I happened to be passing at the time. In the course of his capture he had been shot. He recovered and went on to earn the dubious distinction of being the last man to be shot for treason. As I saw him carried into that hospital I could almost hear the cheers of the folk back home.

Around this time the RASC posted me to an administrative unit where I was responsible for issuing Demobilisation (Demob) Books and other documents for soldiers being discharged. Soldiers who had been conscripted had signed up for the duration of hostilities and now it was a question of first in first out. We were issued with a demob number and were discharged when our number came up. I was Number 61. My job as chief clerk was to collect the necessary documents, references, etc., to make a soldier's passage into Civy Street that much easier. I was given another soldier to assist me and we became great friends. In fact, I can honestly say Bob Howe was the greatest friend I ever had in the army. Like myself he wanted to be a priest after the army but unlike myself he was an Anglican. We shared the same bedroom and many a night we would lie awake discussing theology and our future vocations well into the early hours. We were truly very close and kept in touch after the war for a long time. Unfortunately he was not accepted by the Anglican Church. Somewhere along the line we lost touch with each other but I would love to meet him again one day before I die. Many a day I wonder what has happened to him. The last I heard he was living in Rochdale. He had been a film projectionist before he joined up. Perhaps he returned to that.

And so 'my war' was coming to an end. It was time for me to return home. I remember one evening looking over a field in Buren shortly before I went home thinking, 'what's it all been for?' From the age of eighteen to twenty-two, the age of formation, of youth, joy and relationships, I had served my country. What was waiting for me back home? What had I got out of it all?

7

What Did You Get Out Of the War, Father?

A simple answer to that question is, 'I got a life'. While others were giving their lives for king and country the war gave me my life—a new life.

Living with others of different cultures, religions and other value systems I began to question my own values and philosophy of life.

I now belonged to a success class. I was on the winning side and had my name in the roll of honour of a distinguished Army Regiment.

I had worn my uniform with pride.

What did I get out of my time in the RAF and the army? At first it would appear not much.

I got a taste for bacon. Until those years I would never eat bacon. But in one particular camp going to Sunday Mass meant that I would have to miss breakfast because of a conflict of timing. But the cook would always keep food back for me, and of course, being Sunday, it tended to be bacon and egg. Rather than offend him I would eat it and gradually I got a taste for it. What better meal can there be than the full English breakfast of bacon, egg, sausage and tomato? I feel hungry now at the very thought of it.

During those days I learn the art of writing letters for I would write home every day—just a short letter but none-the-less daily. And I learnt to part with money in that out of my twenty-one shillings a week pay, fourteen shillings would automatically go home. An extra six pence a week was added to the weekly wage if we passed our efficiency test. This involved running five miles in full kit and then firing five rounds of ammunition being expected to hit the bull each time. We had a limited time to do this. I can't remember how much time but it was very little compared to the task.

I learnt to touch-type and the art of administration when I was trained as a clerk, and as chief clerk was introduced into the world of man management and leadership.

All of these skills stood me in good stead later in life. But I think what I got out of it especially was the opportunity to meet people of different values and the opportunity and desire to read. Talking of people of different values you have to remember that I had been brought up solely among Catholics. I was reminded of this many years later when as a chaplain at Keele University a student from Latin America came to see me. He was Catholic of course. He had started going out with an English girl and discovered she was not a Catholic. It came as a great shock to him that there were such beings in the world as non-Catholics. He hadn't a clue how to relate to her. He had never met a non-Catholic in his life until he came to England.

Similarly with myself, I now met men of every denomination and of none. I met Protestants of different sorts, Trappist monks who had left their monasteries to fight, Agnostics, Atheists, ordinary Catholic and fanatical Catholics like myself. Thank God, they caused me to question my faith and confirmed it.

I mentioned Bob Howe a bit earlier. There was another man whose name I can't remember now who was also a friend. He was a lot older than my-self and he was a very sound Catholic. We would talk a lot about relig-ion and my vocation. I don't know what happened to him after the war but somewhere along the line we were posted to different units and lost touch. He was a great sounding-board for me and helped me to ques-tion my vocation very earnestly. I remembered him for one particular incident. We were in the NAAFI one day having our tea and wad, as the cakes were called, when two soldiers came in and sat at our table. We got talking and as soldiers did, we asked each other what Unit we were with. They told us that they were with the Grave Diggers Unit. Their job was to go out to the battlefields and bring back the bodies of soldiers killed in action. In fact, they told us that they had just parked their truck outside the NAAFI and in it were about twenty bodies. They told us that when they recovered a body it was wrapped in a blanket and one shil-ling was deducted from their back pay, the pay that their relatives would inherit. 'Why not come and have a look at them', they said. So we did and stood in that lorry surrounded by the bodies of men who had given everything. We went back to my friend's digs and, in silence, lis-tened to a recording of 'Death and Transfiguration'. It was one of those moments that have a profound effect on a person but which cannot be put into words.

And reading. I hardly read a book at home but in the army there was always a lot of waiting around and books were available. I took up read-ing in a big way. We must have had access to libraries for most of my reading was in the subject of theology. By the time I entered the semi-nary I had studied practically the whole syllabus ahead of me and with great interest. This was just as well as all our formal studies were in Latin and, had I not already studied them, I would really have been in a mess.

But the most important consequence of my Service days and for which I shall always be in debt to the army was the opportunity to change. I re-member standing on the stairs coming up from the basement the day I left home. My mother took hold of me and almost vehemently said to me, 'Never change. Never change.'

While given with the best of intentions it is perhaps the worst advice a person could give to another. Had I not gone into the Forces I might not have changed and I dread to think how I would have turned out. Till the day I die I shall thank the army for changing me. I had no option. I was changed, almost imperceptibly. It wasn't until a long time later that I realised just how much.

I was still failing but only in the area of physical behaviour such as team sports, swimming, football and suchlike. In other areas of my life failure was beginning to give way to success. I had survived in the Armed Forces and had medals to prove it. I had accomplished all that had been asked of me with efficiency if not distinction. I was a sergeant and chief clerk. And to crown it all when my demob number came round I was offered the rank of sergeant major as an inducement to sign on for further service.

'One step forward march' the sergeant had said in Rotterdam. And I marched into a new life.

Failure was beginning to turn into success but I still had some way to go.

8

Anything to Declare?

Something for the weekend perhaps?

Alas it was to be another four years before I could follow my dream. I was demobilised and sent back to my own failure social class but with a new determination. I had questioned my values and the answer had been a resounding yes.

Though I continued failing I now knew that there was another world outside of my family and the failure mentality. I began to balk at the possessiveness I had previously taken for granted.

I was developing a self-confidence I had discovered in the army. This was reinforced by the emergence of moderate successes such as being accepted for HM Customs and Excise.

I had declined the invitation to stay in the army. It is interesting that since that invitation to stay on I have always been asked to stay longer wherever I have been. Surely the tide of my life was turning had I known it then but I was yet to become aware of it.

It was not heartbreaking but I was certainly reluctant to leave the army. As a sergeant I was 'something' and life in the Sergeants' Mess was enviable. I remember going down to breakfast each morning to find lovely freshly baked crusty bread rolls on the table and servants waiting to take our order for breakfast. I loved those rolls spread with real butter. I can still taste them.

I wasn't looking forward to returning to a chemist's shop as an assistant after an exciting four years with the Forces. But I was almost twenty-two and could put it off no longer.

You could always recognise soldiers travelling home on their demob leave even though they were now out of uniform. In fact they had exchanged one uniform for another—striped suit, trilby hat, shirt and tie and carrying a cardboard box containing other civilian clothes they had been issued with. But travelling home to what? I knew Mr Murphy would have to give me my job back and I think in this respect we of the lower ranks were fortunate. Men who had shown leadership skills had been promoted far beyond their civilian status so what could they return to? Had I reached officer status which, in principle, could have been quite possible, would I have wanted to return as chemist's assistant?

Skills for war were of no use in a land looking for peace. So unemployment and dissatisfaction began to mount. It became quite common in London to see some of the commissioned officers wearing the uniform of hotel commissioners. It was the only job some of them could get.

It was during February 1948 that my demob leave ended and I was once more a civvy. I was a fish out of water at home. I didn't know what to do with myself and I sank into depression. It was a fierce winter with one of the highest levels of snow-fall recorded. I sank deeper into depression and caught a dreadful cold. The doctor was sent for. Thank God, I have never given in to illness or sickness and I had hardly ever visited a doctor in my life. As my cold got better I gave up using the doctor's services. The next time I was to visit a doctor was in 1991, forty-three years later when I was almost manhandled and frog-marched to a surgery in a Norfolk village.

Thank God for Millicent Spence, she quite literally saved my life. She noticed that I was looking ill and insisted I visit the doctor who diagnosed endocarditis. I went into hospital and had emergency surgery which resulted in an implanted aortic valve. The NHS were superb and I cannot sing the praises of their staff highly enough. There is a full account of this in the third interlude entitled, 'The Operation'.

Well, I couldn't lounge about the house for ever and so one day I reluctantly dragged myself to Mr Murphy and asked for my old job back. He admitted that he had to give it to me but he put it to me that a lady had been working there in my absence. He couldn't refuse me my job but he hadn't the heart to tell this lady to go. He knew of a similar chemist's shop down the road where there was a vacancy and he asked me if I would consider going there. I wasn't really bothered so I said yes, and, without realising it, set in motion a chain of circumstances that eventually led me to applying to the Salvatorians to become a priest. I am constantly being forced to believe that there is no such thing as coincidence.

Mr Green, for such was the chemist's name, was not a Catholic and so, naturally, he was one of the 'something for the weekend' brigade. He sold contraceptives and, of course, expected me to do so. As I have said I was almost fanatical about my faith in those days and firmly believed in the church's teaching on contraception. Every Friday they would come in, the customers looking for 'French letters' as they were then called. I would hold them by the tips of my fingers and give them with a disgusting look—and I can be disgusting when I want to be!

I did this for three or four months and then decided I could no longer do so. I told the chemist that I was not prepared to sell these things and that I was prepared to resign. He asked me if I had another job to go to and I said, 'of course!' I was out of work for the next five weeks. It was the first time in my life that I resigned on principle.

As you will see, this resignation pushed me into an entirely different direction. Had I stayed with Mr Murphy or Mr Green I might well have gone on to be a pharmacist and spent the rest of my days in a chemist's shop. Who knows?

After five weeks I managed to get a job in a cold storage warehouse doing manual work and then after a while, I got a job in a warehouse office. Thanks to the RASC, I was able to put my secretarial skills to good use. They were happy days and not a lot of pressure was put upon me at work. Home was another matter. My mother kept assuring me that I was capable of better things and kept on at me to do the Civil Service Entrance Examination. I have to say that she always wanted the best for me and perhaps she was a bigger positive influence in my life than I have given her credit for.

I'm not sure how I prepared for the exam, Wolsey Hall was involved I remember, and I got down to it and studied hard. The subjects being examined were English, Handwriting, Arithmetic, General papers and General Intelligence. I took the exam and of course failed. Here we go again, I thought.

But I took it again in the October of 1949. Out of a possible mark of 650 I got 409. The pass mark was 355. Out of 224 successful candidates I was 67th. Because I was high on the list of successful candidates I was invited to join His Majesty's Customs and Excise Department of the Civil Service. The only Department higher than this was the Foreign Office. From the day I received those results I knew that I could pass whatever any Seminary Professor could throw at me. I was on my way—again.

Joining the Customs and Excise was another momentous step for me. I had proved myself in the real world and had obtained a prestigious job. I had arrived.

I won't bore you with the work we did in the Customs. So much happened between 1949 and 1952 as a result of my getting that job. We were sent to London to Adelaide House on London Bridge for training. I had digs at Plumstead and I used to go to Mass there at St Patrick's Church. I would go daily sometimes if my work allowed. There was a lovely girl about my age who used to go there and I lost my heart completely to her. I should say I have lost my heart a few times in my life but she was special. It's no wonder that the surgeon who operated on me years later told my sister that my heart was crumbling when he had taken it out to look at it in 1991. The number of times it has been broken is nobody's business. I never spoke one word to that girl but I loved her. I used to spend half my time at Mass just looking over at her and occasionally we would catch each other in mid-glance. I always waited for her to leave so I could see her walking out. I never asked her out. I didn't know how to for goodness sake and I had just come out of the army after four years.

It was now 1950 and the Pope, Pius XII, had declared a Marian Festival year. It was a Jubilee year dedicated to devotion to the Blessed Virgin Mary. Jubilee years began in the reign of Boniface VIII when he declared 1300 a Holy Year. A Holy Year was a time when, to celebrate the Redemption of the Human Race, the Pope proclaimed a Jubilee, as a special occasion when the faithful might obtain remission of sin by gaining the Jubilee Indulgence on visiting the tombs of the Apostles at Rome. It was meant to be held every hundred years but gradually it was reduced to every fifty years and eventually to every twenty-five years. The Jubilee Year of 1950 was held in honour of Our Lady and it was during that year that Pius XII made the infallible declaration that Our Lady was assumed body and soul into heaven after her death.

A great demonstration of faith was planned to be held at Wembley Stadium. Cardinals and bishops from all over the world converged on London and the stadium was packed on the day. Before that I had become aware of a Catholic Group called the Catholic Evidence Guild (CEG). I will be explaining the CEG at great length in the next chapter but suffice it to say at present that it was a group of Catholic men and women who would mount platforms at Speakers' corners throughout the country and explain the teachings of the church.

I joined it as a non-speaking member and it was with a group of likeminded people that I joined the crowds at Wembley. Among the group was a girl of great grace and beauty and I lost my heart again. This time, 'because we had properly been introduced' I did ask her out and we became very close.

Anyway our relationship developed and we saw a lot of each other while I worked in London. After my training I was posted to the London Royal docks until such times as there would be a vacancy in the Liverpool Collection. After about six months I returned to Liverpool and settled down to life in the Customs and Excise, a respectable citizen. Eileen, for such was the lady's name, wrote regularly to me in green ink and I kept all her letters with my army souvenirs.

By this time I had a battered old iron trunk at home and it contained my life: all my DWR newsletters, souvenirs from Germany, all the letters I had written home and so on. Sometime after I entered religious life my mother was having a great clear out and not realising the value of its contents, she asked the bin men to take it away. I still feel anger when I think of all I lost then.

In the Liverpool Custom House each officer had a desk. Mine was somewhere in the middle of a huge hall. I was still very apostolically minded and I had a small statue of Our Lady on my desk. I did this probably to give witness to my fellow Customs officers that there was more to life than the dirty stories they used to tell or the dirty postcards they would pass around during the coffee break. It must have worked because they would always pass me by as they handed the cards around. I can't think of another reason as I never really had a great devotion to Our Lady. I suppose it could have been there simply to demonstrate that I was a Catholic, but it did serve a very useful function as well. If anybody came to reception looking for me the receptionist would direct them to my desk saying, 'You can't miss him. He's the one with the Virgin on his desk'. Holy? Perhaps, but not that holy.

However, after a while when the staff saw I was no threat to them they accepted me and we became good friends, Catholics and Protestants, with their occasional teasing of me and my occasional preaching to them.

I was still writing to Eileen when another event occurred which took me one step further along the way to the priesthood. I joined the Liverpool branch of the CEG. Perhaps they were not as fussy as the Westminster branch or their standards were not as high but they quickly invited me to become a speaker.

Although I wasn't aware of it at the time, this was the last step, before finally leaving all things.

9

Any Questions?

My self-confidence increased through the medium of public speaking.

It was through the nature and the subject matter of my public speaking that that question came back to haunt me: 'What are you going to be when you grow up?' And throughout that haunting came the determination to govern my own life and make my own decisions.

What I didn't realise then was that my mind-set was too limited to things spiritual and religious. I was growing up lopsided. All my social life centred around the church with no social intercourse with the opposite sex or secular matters. This was to play havoc much later in my life.

This was the question the crowd were always waiting for and the question that the speaker feared the most.

Picture the scene. The Pierhead in Liverpool with six or seven platforms scattered along the promenade beside the river. Picture all sorts of speakers, mostly male, screaming their heads off plying their philosophies to anyone who would stop and listen. Agnostics, Atheists, Christians, Communists and a host of others including the Catholic Evidence Guild, were there teaching their particular beliefs to whomsoever would stop and listen

Quite often some platforms would be manned by one-man bands. I remember one such would-be prophet who used to read out the sexy and violent bits from the Bible. A member of the public reported him to the police. They came to arrest him on charges of corrupting the public but they couldn't touch him because, as he said, he was simply reading the Bible.

The Catholic Evidence Guild was highly structured and no one was allowed to mount the platform before they were fully trained in the particular subject on which they were about to speak. The speaker would mount the platform, give their talk and then ask for questions, but only on the talk they had just given. At each meeting there was a chairperson who had what was called a general licence. That meant they could talk on any teaching of the church and take questions on any subject. We were all strictly limited to teaching what the church taught and what the church condemned. As I said in a previous chapter we were not in the business of evangelisation, simply teaching. Converts occasionally emerged as a result of our teaching but these were always directed to their local parish priest for further instruction.

I remember once a few of us decided to take a platform and try a street corner in a more residential area. Every Saturday night for eight weeks we would man the platform and teach the church to a crowd composed of the Guild members only. Not a member of the public turned up. So on the last Saturday we announced to nobody that we were closing and wouldn't be there the following week. A lady came out of her flat and said she had listened every week and would like to learn more, she eventually became a Catholic. We never knew what good we were doing and often thought none.

When I first joined the Guild in Liverpool our platform was at the centre of the City opposite Central station. I shall never forget my first appearance. For hours before I had stood in front of the mirror practising my spontaneous gestures as Winston Churchill used to do. I would go through every possible question that could be asked on the subject which was the Infallibility of the Pope. I can remember vividly saying for the first time those awesome words, 'Any Questions?' In the event it wasn't really a baptism of fire. There were only a few in the crowd and I got one or two questions that I managed to bat fairly well. But being my first experience, I was filled with terror.

I gradually became qualified in a number of subjects and eventually received my general licence. Now that was an experience—standing on the platform saying 'Any Questions?' knowing that I was expected to be able to answer any that were asked on any subject. The climax of my CEG career came one lunchtime at the Pierhead when I mounted the platform towards the end of the lunchtime meeting. I got up at 1.30 intending to finish at 2p.m. I was still there at 5.30p.m. The questions came thick and fast and, thank God, I was able to bat every one. The crowd grew and office workers stayed beyond their lunch hour to listen to the debate. As I write this, my mind goes forward to the days when I was Chaplain at Aston University. I would say Mass in the Students' Union in a hired room

once a week. We would then go into my office for coffee. We would begin to talk about religion and a member of staff would be the heckler to my teaching. It was supposed to finish at 2p.m. for lectures but often students would miss their lecture to continue to listen. Absolutely fascinating. I can honestly say that some of my happiest moments have been publicly defending the faith. It happened again at Manchester

University, but more about that later.

I have often said that the Catholic Evidence Guild was the finest training ground for preaching. There was no captive audience, members of the crowd could just walk away if they were bored or if they couldn't hear you. People in the crowd would interrupt you, disagree with you and even vilify you if they had a mind to and you couldn't do anything about it other than through your natural wit. There is a story told about Fr McNabb, a great Dominican speaker. He had been speaking on celibacy of the clergy and a female heckler shouted up at him, 'If I was your wife I would feed you poison.' And he quickly retorted, 'And if I was your husband, madam, I would take it.' Hecklers would criticise you and even throw bottles at you. And there is nothing worse than to get on the platform after a good speaker and watch the crowd just dwindle away as you talk. Speaking in public like this also meant that you had to project your voice to make it heard to the background of six or seven other speakers, not to mention public transport passing by and the hooting of ships on the river Mersey. If the crowd couldn't hear you or you were not interesting they just walked away.

Of course there were techniques for increasing your crowd like having hecklers planted in the audience who would ask crowd-pulling questions such as on sex, the Pope, Our Lady and so on. Once the crowd was established we would then go into serious teaching mode. There were also techniques for dispersing the crowds of your neighbouring speakers but we won't go into that just now.

I could write a full book on my Guild experiences but you might be wondering why I am writing about them at all. All I can say is that they were wonderful days and were a natural lead up to my 'leaving all things'.

10

Leaving All Things

I finally reached the stage where I believed that success was possible and that I could achieve my dream to become a priest.

Whereas I had drifted, accepting failure as my way of life, I now deliberately set out on a road which would prove if I was a failure or not.

A number of things were happening at this time on a national, local and personal level. On the national level there was the massive Vocation Exhibition at Earls Court. There hadn't been the likes of it before and there hasn't been anything like it since. The fact that Religious Orders today are full of priests and nuns aged eighty and over is due to the overwhelming response to that Exhibition at Earls Court. Every Religious Order was represented and the atmosphere was just indescribable. To go around and see the priests and nuns in their different habits was a spiritual experience in itself. In those days each Order had its own distinctive habit (dress) and you could tell the sort of work they did by how they dressed. Not so today where all nuns wear a generalised habit or none as is the case of some male religious orders. Had I any doubts about my vocation before that exhibition I had absolutely none afterwards.

The effect of that national experience was reinforced by a book which came out around that time. *Elected Silence* was the autobiography of Thomas Merton. He was a journalist and had recently become a Catholic. His book spoke of his journey of faith and how from being a complete non-believer with the world at his feet he gave it all up and became a Trappist monk. His description of his spiritual journey was spellbinding and had a great effect on young men of my age. This book was quite instrumental in a number of people joining religious orders at that time.

At a personal level the CEG had had a great influence on me. In those days, I had little or no knowledge of Jesus Christ as a person and certainly no experience of him. But this changed one day while standing in the crowd and listening to the speaker. Quite suddenly a feeling came over me. I can only describe it as an awareness of Jesus Christ as a person with whom I could have a personal relationship. Until then my relationship with God had been purely structural and intellectual.

I knew the teachings of the church backwards and by this time there wasn't a question I couldn't answer. But there was another world opened to me that day. I stood there in awe and wonder and went home in a daze.

This experience was confirmed not long afterwards. There were many churches in Liverpool and the inner-city churches would have midday Masses for shoppers and city workers. I used to go from the Customs House to the Benedictine church of St Mary's, Highfield Street. The church was always full and one day I could only get a seat in the balcony. I attended Mass and at the end started to follow people out. I happened to look down at the altar and suddenly the world stood still. I shall never be able to describe it but it is as vivid in my mind today as it was then in 1951. It was as though a curtain, like on a stage, suddenly flashed open and I was encased in light. Then the curtains clashed to. That's all it was and took an instant of time but it was like a glimpse of eternity.

Back at the platform I was enthralled by the enthusiasm and inspiration of one of the speakers, Bernard Boardman. He always had a great crowd and it wasn't so much what he said as his absolute love of what he was teach-

ing. It was like watching and listening to Jesus Christ as I imagined him to be. Bernard was my age. He was also thinking of becoming a priest. He wanted to become a Diocesan priest as he thought that he would be put to teaching if he joined a religious order, his desire was for parish work. I had no fear on that score. With my academic record I knew I would never be asked to teach. I wanted to give missions and retreats and I knew that a Religious Order was the place for me. We both left Liverpool on the same day, he to the Archdiocesan Seminary and me to the Salvatorian Late Vocation College at Abbots Langley in Hertfordshire. He spent his priestly life in parish work and in the Apostleship of the Sea. But because of his great zeal he burnt himself out very early. He had strokes and heart attacks and eventually died in his fifties. Ironically, I was to spend most of my priestly life teaching and to this day I have never given a parish mission.

After saying goodbye to each other that day in Liverpool years were to pass before we met again. You won't believe it but the next time we met was in the Pope's private chapel. I mentioned earlier that the Salvatorian Renewal Directors had been invited to say Mass with the Pope. His is a very small chapel but there were some seats vacant at the back and Bernard, who was visiting the English College at the time, managed to get an invitation. I am sure he is in heaven now enjoying his reward.

And at a personal level things were hotting up. I was approaching twenty-six and I thought that if I didn't go soon I would never go. Twenty-six was old to be going off to study in those days. My sister, Winnie, had gone off to be a nurse some years before and Lily had gone off to be a nun so my money was needed at home. I also felt that I couldn't leave home while my parents' relationship was so bad. My mother leaned on me a lot emotionally and she now began to express concern about my going. I think she wanted me to be a priest but didn't want me to leave home. And I was scared. I had a good job with good prospects. What would happen if I came home? In those days to be a 'spoiled priest' as an ex-seminarian was called was a disgrace and brought shame on the family. Would I get my job back and so on?

I began to hate the thought of going away and went to priest after priest asking them if they thought I had a vocation. They all said yes—except one. I have forgotten who he was now but he said no. These priests were Jesuits of course. In fact I had only ever met one priest who wasn't and he was a chaplain in the Army. I remember the night this priest said no. I was over the moon and that night went out and celebrated. Foolishly, the next day I asked another one. When this priest told me he thought I had a vocation I remarked that I would hate to become a bad priest. I remember him saying, 'there is no such a thing as a bad priest', I presume he was speaking of the office of the priest rather than the person of the priest.

To priest or not to priest?

But you will never guess the de-

105

ciding factor in all these deliberations. It is true that God works in mysterious ways. I was in Ireland on holiday with my brother and two friends, Don Virgo and his brother. We were in Dublin and Bernie and I went into the public loo. We were standing fairly close to each other at the urinals. There was no one else there and suddenly Bernie said, right out of the blue, 'I'm thinking of becoming a priest.' My heart dropped like a stone. I thought if he goes I shall never be able to get away and, may God forgive me, that was what made my mind up. I had to go—now. I have felt rather guilty about that ever since. My guilt was assuaged somewhat years later when Bernie actually went off to become a Jesuit brother. My mother was going off to Rome for a fortnight's holiday and they both went off the same day. Bernie was back before my mother! Later he served my first Mass with great pride. He had a difficult life and in his later years his great pride and joy was to exercise the special Ministry of the Eucharist in St Cecilia's, Everton. He lived his whole life in Everton but was a rabid Liverpool supporter. He died suddenly, alone, aged sixty-eight, from deep vein thrombosis. I conducted his funeral with very mixed feelings thinking about that day in Dublin.

And so my mind was finally made up. I went to see Fr McDonald SJ. He was the priest whom I had helped in the House Library years before at the age of seven. I told him I wanted to be a Jesuit Brother still thinking I wouldn't be clever enough to be a priest. He advised against it telling me I would spend my life cleaning and scrubbing floors or cooking. So I decided to seek the priesthood. There was a college for 'elderly applicants' run by the Jesuits but which trained men for other orders and for the various Dioceses. It was called Osterly and was run by a Fr Clement Tiger, tiger by name and tiger by nature! I wrote to him and received a reply telling me to read the classics and apply the following year. I didn't know what the classics were but I was clever enough to read between the lines of that letter, 'Get lost, sunny boy'.

To this day I have never read a classic or watched one on television. I tried reading Scott once but never got past the fourth chapter. I did get through the Cloister and the Hearth by Charles Reade but that was hardly a classic.

106

At this time my mother used to organise coach trips to a college in Christleton near Chester. This was a Salvatorian Training College for their priests. The Society of the Divine Saviour (Salvatorians) specialised in late vocations as we oldies were called and seemed to take people from all classes. One of our parishioners, Frank Murdock, had joined them – hence the connection. He was one of the four priests I spoke of earlier who was ordained by the Archbishop of Liverpool. Anyway, I applied to the Salvatorians and was called for interview by the Provincial, Fr Kevin Kenny. Like magic the doors were opened to me and I was provisionally accepted.

I told my mother and she was thrilled but broken-hearted at the thought of losing me. My father was in the back yard cleaning up and I went out and told him. Without looking up, he said, 'If that's what you want to do with your life, go ahead.' He was a man of few words.

I told the Customs and Excise and, again with this terrible lack of confidence in myself, wrote to the Commissioners of Customs and Excise and asked if they would keep my job open for me in case I never made it and had to return. They congratulated me on my decision to go but kindly said they couldn't keep the job open but they would give a sympathetic hearing to my application should I return. I still have the letter just in case!!!

However, telling my parents and telling my colleagues in the Customs was nothing in terms of trauma compared to telling Eileen. Eileen was special and we had a beautiful relationship. So I went down to London to tell her my decision. She knew, of course, that I was thinking of taking this step as we had been very open with each other. She said that she took consolation from the fact that her rival was God and so we said goodbye and parted. I never heard from her after that. As I write this I have before me a picture card. Catholics call these cards 'Holy Pictures'. On the card there is a picture of Jesus Christ pointing to his heart. Beneath the picture is written, 'O Lord Jesus vouchsafe to fill with thy favours those of whom we confidently ask Thee.' On the reverse side is written, 'God bless you, always'. It is signed simply, 'Eileen' with the date, 13 September 1952. She gave me this as we said goodbye on Euston Station and she also gave me a small wooden crucifix mounted on a small stand. For years I took this with me wherever I went until one day the cross became loose and somewhere in my travels I lost it. I still have the base on which it was mounted which I keep with the 'Holy picture'.

So I made formal application to the Society of the Divine Saviour (SDS), known as Salvatorians and was called for interview at their Late Vocation College in Abbots Langley, the birthplace of the only English Pope, Adrian IV. Fr Anselm Slattery, the prefect of students greeted me and showed me around. He said that I must meet the Local Superior. He took me to the kitchen and the Superior, Fr Xavier Howard, was standing at the sink washing the dishes after the midday meal for twenty. No dishwashers in those days! If I had any doubts about joining the SDS they were dispelled at that moment. I was used to Jesuit Brothers doing the menial tasks while the priests got on with 'the real work' of saving souls. I thought, 'Fancy a Superior washing the dishes'.

Anyway I passed the interview and a date was fixed for my entry. All the major studies were to be in Latin and I was told that I would have to do a Candidacy of two years studying Latin and English. After that I would do a one-year Noviciate, two years of philosophy studies and then four years of theological studies. At various points along the way I would take the vows of poverty, chastity and obedience. The vows were taken in the first instance for one year and then there were two annual renewals and a year later they were taken for life. Until I took final vows

I could be asked to leave or I could leave of my own accord. Once a person had taken final vows they could not leave nor could they be expelled except without recourse to Rome.

So I made my farewells to family, friends, CEG and the Customs. I still have the letters and cards of farewell I received. The Customs Officers gave me a handsome cheque and the CEG gave me a book, which I still have on my shelf. It is inscribed:

> To Richard Sullivan, a faithful guildsman, wishing him every
> success in a higher apostolate. From grateful members of the
> Liverpool C.E.G.

On 13 September 1952, three months after my twenty-sixth birthday my father took me to the station and we said farewell. I smoked cigarettes in those days, Senior Service of course, and as the train pulled out I lit up. After a few minutes I thought, if I'm going to give my life to God, I might as well go the whole hog. So I threw it and what was left in the packet out of the window. The train stopped at Crewe twenty-five minutes later and I got out and bought another packet.

Such was the length of my commitment. And sadly, I have been doing the same ever since – giving and taking back. I pray that when my time comes I shall be in the giving stage and that on balance the giving will outweigh the taking.

PART THREE

Student Years 1952–1961

At last I set myself to achieving my lifelong ambition to the exclusion of everything else. I was to spend the next nine years doing nothing but working towards that goal.

But I had to do it in the company of others. My army experience came in useful in terms of communication with my fellow travellers but my strict and narrow spiritual upbringing became a barrier to integration.

Feelings of failure gave way to feelings of rejection and this became a pattern throughout my religious student life.

11

The Candidate

Abbots Langley 1952–1954

I entered the Society of the Divine Saviour (Salvatorians) 13 September 1952. We are called Salvatorians because the Latin title for the order is Societas Divini Salvatoris and we write SDS after our names for obvious reasons.

The Salvatorians were founded by a German priest called Fr Francis Jordan of the Cross in 1882. He was a man ahead of his time. He lived at a time in history when Europe was in turmoil because of certain movements, political and religious, which were having disastrous consequences on society. In Germany it was the time of Bismarck, the chancellor, who, as time passed, gained practically complete control of society. The new idea was that of 'liberalism' in which everyone was supposed to be free. As part of this 'freedom' he was determined to crush the restraining influence of the church, and the church was made to suffer. Dioceses came under state control, bishops were arrested or made to conform. Religious orders were disbanded and priests were persecuted and scattered. The old orders like the Benedictines and Franciscans and many others were pillaged or exiled, a move which robbed the poor of any support.

This was the world in which Francis lived and it was within this political atmosphere he founded the Salvatorians. Our mission statement states that we believe we are called to follow Christ, the Divine Saviour, by living as a community within the universal Church for apostolic service. This mission compels us to share our call to be apostles with people from all walks of life. We are expected to serve people everywhere, by all ways and means which the love of Christ inspires.

I think what attracted me to this particular religious order was those words, 'by all ways and means'. I didn't want to join a teaching order or a missionary order. Through the influence of the Jesuits I wanted an apostolate of preaching and giving retreats, i.e. courses on the spiritual life. The Salvatorians could obviously accommodate me in this and throughout my student years I prepared for this work. But man proposes and God disposes, as we say, but more about that later.

My first reaction as a candidate was one of disappointment. I expected a similar regime to that I had seen among the Jesuits at home. There were a number of candidates in 1952 and most of them had come from secular parishes, i.e. parishes run by secular priests. Secular priests are those who take one vow of celibacy and a promise of obedience to a bishop. They belong to a diocese run by a bishop and can only be moved between parishes within their chosen diocese. Priests belonging to religious orders can be moved by their superior to wherever there is a house belonging to the order anywhere in the world. As I have explained, I had come from a parish run by the religious orders of the Jesuits. Some orders are stricter than others and the Jesuits are considered to be among the strictest.

Mixing with the students from the secular parishes I began to think they hadn't a clue about religious life. Perhaps I was a spiritual snob but I felt very let down. The regime was kept strictly but it was not a very strict regime, I had expected a more rigorous life. Fr Anselm, our prefect, was very good and his talks on the spiritual life saved the day for me. At least he put before us a good model of religious life but I don't think the heart of too many were in it. I had to remember, of course, that we were only candidates and had yet to be introduced into the Salvatorian religious life proper. We were not yet fully paid-up members, and looking back it was to be expected that the regime should be flexible. We were, after all, learn-

ers. In spite of that I think I can say truthfully, fifty years later, that those two years were in fact the most fruitful in terms of spiritual formation.

But, in spite of all this, they were a happy two years. We studied Latin and English, French, Scripture and History. Those teaching us were not academics by any means and had probably been told to teach a subject unknown to them as I was many years later. This was the format in those days. There was a job to be done, there was a priest available so he did it. Whether he was qualified in that subject was immaterial. In an ideal world we would have been entered for 'O' levels at the end of the two years but this was considered unnecessary. This was sad as years later when I was asked to do a degree and had to have 'O' and 'A' levels for entrance requirements I didn't have any. I find it interesting looking back at the marks I received then. Either I had come into my own academically or the pass mark was very low. My marks went like this:

Over the two years, 1952 to1954 my lowest mark in Latin was 79 and my highest was 91

English Grammar	55	79
English Literature	72	87
French	80	96
Scripture	78	85
History	76	85

I laugh now when I think of getting 96 for French. It must have been all theoretical as I cannot ever remember being able to speak a word of

French.

But life was more than study. We had some very happy times out of the lecture theatre. Although the war had ended in 1945 the times were still influenced by the effects of the war. I remember we had to take our ration books with us when we entered the college and locally we were asked to help in Civil Defence by forming a Unit of the Local Defence Volunteers. I am not sure what we were about, except I have a photograph of the candidates dressed in army uniforms and steel helmets at the side of a vehicle of some sort or another. The irony of this was that some of the students were fervent Irishmen.

A strong companion of those days was a guest student, John Hood. He was destined for one of the strictest religious orders in the church, the Order of Cistercians of the Strict Observance. Like all of us he was a mature student and in his words, 'had toured and wallowed in all the flesh pots of Europe'. He had decided that it was time to put some real meaning into his life and so was off to Nunraw to join the Cistercians. These men are commonly known as Trappists and are famous for their vow of enclosure. They emerge from their monastery only for very serious purposes like visiting their parents should they be seriously ill. John left us for Nunraw in September 1952 and is still there over fifty years later.

H·R·H's

The Royal Weakness

As I said, Father Anselm tried to maintain a strict lifestyle and one of the rules that he expected us to

adhere to rigidly concerned the day off. From time to time we would be given a day off when we would go cycling or walking or whatever as the money allowed. We were not supported by the Order at this stage and we had to ration ourselves according to the amount we had brought with us. The big rule about the day off was that everybody had to be back by 9p.m. On one of these days I went into London with a candidate from Derry, Northern Ireland. We had a great day together and didn't notice the time passing at all. Gradually we realised that we would never be back in time. This was a capital offence. What could we do to save the situation? Now one of Father Anselm's weaknesses was the royal family. He was terribly English and worshipped anything connected to the Establishment such as royalty. Danny was very much a Northern Irishman with the passions that sadly exploded into all-out civil unrest in later years. But he was also a natural psychologist. Before we left London he bought a picture of the royal family. As we entered the portals of Breakspear College, as our college was called, there was Fr Anselm standing with his watch in his hand. 10p.m. Before the terribly disapproving look could be translated into words Danny pushed the picture into Father Anselm's hands and said, 'Sorry we're late, Father. We spent ages trying to find this picture for you.' What could he say?

Danny decided to become a brother rather than a priest and he spent many years on our mission in Africa. Eventually he felt called to the priesthood and the Order sent him to the Beda College in Rome. This was where older candidates did a short course for the priesthood—four years. While he was there I visited him one Christmas and together we went to the Pope's midnight Mass. Back home it was traditional in the community that we gathered after midnight Mass for port and mince pies. In the Mother house in Rome everybody just went to bed. So there was Danny and myself without port or mince pies. The nuns who did the cooking had long since locked the kitchen and we searched the very large refectory and the larders, etc., high and low for something with which to celebrate. Eventually we found one tea bag and a mince pie. We solemnly raised our teacups and wished each other a happy Christmas.

Danny was ordained priest and worked in England. When I left the parish of Ystradgynlais in Wales he succeeded me as parish priest. He was there for two years and did wonderful work in that time. One day one of the parishioners rang me up and said, 'Something terrible has happened. What do we do? Fr Danny is lying dead in the kitchen.' He had been sitting there with some parishioners and had asked for a glass of water. The lady went to the tap and when she turned around he had collapsed and died. A massive heart attack. All his Irish relatives came over for the funeral and he had a magnificent send-off. They took his body back to the Ireland he loved so much for his final resting-place. There is a stained glass window in the little Welsh church of Ystradgynlais in his memory. May he rest in peace!

Those two years punctuated by visits home for Christmas, Easter and the Summer holidays passed very quickly and by 1955 we were considered suitable to become Novices.

Merry Christmas

12

Christleton Hall, the Major Seminary

Noviciate and philosophy

Failure and success were put aside in the noviciate. I felt I belonged to a Religious Order.

But if there was no question of success or failure there was constant assessment of one's suitability for religious life. My strict upbringing and narrow set of values were strongly challenged when I thought they would be strengthened.

However, self-assessment and self-analysis took second place when we became actively engaged in the major study of philosophy. At last we were really studying for the priesthood first-hand.

I discovered a subject which wasn't religious as such but enthralled me even more than my personal study of theology had done in the army. It was the study of philosophy. It seemed everything took back place for me now. Who could be concerned about failure and success, not to mention rejection, in the presence of the Queen of Sciences. Philosophy became my passion.

At last I was being weaned from a life almost obsessed with matters religious and spiritual albeit within the structure of a mild religious life.

By the time our two years of candidacy was up a number had left or been asked to leave. Consequently when the time came for us to begin our noviciate year there were only four or five of us from Breakspear College. Another four joined us from the Junior Seminary at Sindlesham and another four came straight from our other college, or straight from 'civvy street'. So there were twelve of us, the largest number the British Province had ever had in a noviciate at any one time, before or since.

And so the time had come for us to begin our noviciate, a truly major step in our lives and certainly a turning point in mine. A noviciate is a time of testing. The religious order tests the novice and the novice tests the order. It lasts one year and the novice can leave at any time during that year without giving any explanation and, likewise, the novice can be told to go also without explanation.

The noviciate began with a ceremony of clothing when we were each given the habit. This is a full length black garment which is bound at the waist with a black girdle called a cingulum. The girdle is like the white rope you see the Franciscans wearing around their waist with two strands hanging down at the side. We had four knots in ours. There were three on one strand to remind us of the vows of Poverty, Chastity and Obedience and on the other strand there was one knot to remind us of our promise to work in the Apostolate. Worn suspended from the girdle is a very long Rosary. This was ostensibly used for prayer but when we were teaching boys the noise of it as the beads knocked against each other, or against the wall as we walked, was a dead give-away. The boys would hear us coming and quickly assume the form of angels!

At one point during the ceremony the would-be novices were presented with the habit. They would then leave the chapel to change and they would come back dressed in their habit. I remember how proud I felt changing from my ordinary clothes into the religious garb. At the cere-

119

mony we were then given a new name. This was in line with St Peter when Christ changed his name of Simon to Peter and also to remind us that we were adopting a new way of life. My name was to be Nicholas Owen. He was the Jesuit Lay Brother who made hiding holes for the priest during the Reformation. Somewhere along the line I had developed a great devotion to him alongside the great St Francis Xavier. After the ceremony the novices had to assemble in what was called the asceterium to meet the Novice Master. You have to remember at this point that this was 1954, long before the Second Vatican Council. The older among the novices had given up good jobs with good salaries and prospects and all of us had left home and all things, determined to give our lives to God. Think of that and what happened next. The Novice Master walked in and deliberately left the door open. We all sat down and his words to us on beginning our commitment to God were, 'You will notice that the door is open. You are all independent gentlemen and you are free to walk out that door anytime you like. And I am free to ask you to go.' Not a word of welcome. Then he proceeded to tell us the rules and regulations of the noviciate. I remember as I left the chapel to go to the asceterium somebody saying to me, 'Stick it out'. It was the most sound advice I have ever been given and was to be a mainstay on more than one occasion when I felt like walking through that door. But that night as I lay on my bed and looked at the habit hanging from the hook, I thought, 'the journey has begun'.

Novices were kept away from the professed members, i.e. those already in vows or ordained priests, and formed their own community. I never understood whether that was to prevent us contaminating them or vice versa. Our bedroom accommodation consisted of a large dormitory divided into twelve cubicles. In each cubicle was a bed, a small chest of drawers and a hook to hang our habit on. This type of accommodation was to be ours for the next six years until we became deacons, when we would be allowed our own rooms. In addition to bedroom accommodation we had the asceterium I spoke of. This was a large room with twelve classroom-type desks in it. Each of us had a desk. And that was it.

So what is a noviciate all about? Our Novice Master was an elderly priest who had been received into the order by the Founder himself, no less. He was a very saintly man who had been sent to England by the Founder to learn English prior to going to our mission in Assam. The First World War broke out preventing him from going and consequently he stayed in England and became virtually the Founder of the British Province. He had been Novice Master for many years and was in fact coming to the end of his active days in this role. We were his penultimate noviciate. In addition to being Novice Master he also lectured in Moral Theology to the scholastics, a role he was to continue until the Major Seminary closed. He was known affectionately throughout the Province as 'The Old Man'.

'Stick it out' was good advice because one day followed another with tedious repetition. Morning prayer was followed by an hour's meditation, and then house cleaning followed by breakfast. Each day there would be a talk by the Novice Master called for some reason 'a Chapter'. This talk would be about the Founder, the Order and the rules and regulations. It was important that we knew what we were about to undertake when we made our vows. Our meals were all taken in silence while we listened to one of the brethren reading a book to us. At lunchtimes this was from an adventure story and the evening meal was accompanied by a more serious religious book. The professed students had the privilege of reading and occasionally, to liven things up, a reader might add his own bits to the book. Of course, this lead to dire penalties when the culprit confessed it at the monthly Chapter of Faults.

Every First Friday we would have what was called the Chapter of Faults. Before the evening meal each member would have to go 'down in the Ref' and confess his transgressions of the rule during the previous month. It was sufficient to confess one transgression as it was really more a matter of exercising humility than asking for forgiveness. Going down in the Ref meant prostrating oneself on the floor of the Refectory in the presence of the whole community who stood solemnly at their places at table awaiting their turn.

The sort of things confessed would be breaking the 'magnum silentium' the great silence which took place from after recreation in the evening until after breakfast the next morning. This was a very strict rule and woebetide anyone caught breaking it. Other things confessed were transgressions against poverty such as breaking a plate, or being uncharitable. The Chapter was held in Latin and each culprit in turn would begin, 'Admodum Reverende Pater, accuso me ipsum quad contra ...' (Reverend Father, I accuse myself of ...). It would be quite boring until perhaps some wag to enliven the proceedings would 'accidentally' say contra castitatem (chastity) instead of caritatem (charity). Of course all the eyes would look up at this one! Penances given by the Superior who was the 'Admodum Reverende Pater' would range from doing various forms of manual work to perhaps taking one's meals at the punishment table. This was a table set aside for the 'sinners' and the latter would have to take their meals kneeling down. This had its advantages in that the servers would feel sorry for them and give them extra.

And so the year would go by, hopefully with the novice increasing in awareness of the rule but principally growing in sanctity. It is said that the noviciate year is the holiest year in the life of the monk. With the emphasis on prayer and the three vows and with hardly any distractions the atmosphere was conducive to sanctity. In fact the only distractions came from the four free days we were allowed in the year. On these days we would be allowed to go out for the day and we would be given one shilling (five new pence) to spend as we wished. Some went cycling and spent their money on food. Others might use the money to go somewhere by public transport. On our return we would have to give any change we hadn't spent to the bursar. They were good days and we really enjoyed them.

One major event singled out our noviciate from all others. During the year the noviciate house was discovered to have dry rot and of course it had to be repaired immediately. Canon Law stated then that novices had to remain in the same house for the year. But in view of the exceptional circumstances we were allowed to go to our Junior Seminary house in Sindlesham, Berksire for two weeks. This was real luxury. For some reason or other while we were there the Novice Master decided we could go to the pictures. A suitable film was chosen and he came with us. In choosing the film the old man had forgotten about the trailers. As we made our way to our seats there sprawled across the screen was the scantily clad body of

Marilyn Monroe, her film was to appear the following week. The old man's face was a picture in itself. I remember soon after that, rather mischievously asking one of our old priests who was eighty-two when did the temptations stop. He said quite seriously, 'Eighty-two'. That evening a young lady came to the house and he came back to me and said, 'Make that eighty-three!' Life in the old boy yet I thought.

One big advantage of the year was that there were no exams. There was no question of success or failure. It was a matter of continuous assessment on the part of the novice and the Novice Master of whether the novice had the vocation to become a Salvatorian, so whether he did or did not it was not success or failure but rather an indication of a person's suitability. If I remember correctly all of us were deemed suitable and on 11 October 1955 we bound ourselves to the vows of poverty, chastity and obedience for one year. If we considered ourselves, and were considered, suitable at the end of the year, we would renew our vows for a further year. This would happen twice and the following year we would take the vows for life. Until we had made that commitment we were free to leave at the end of each year or could be asked to leave. But after final vows it would require the authority of Rome to leave or to be dismissed.

And so with hope in our hearts on 11 October 1955 we became scholastics and began our major studies for the priesthood, beginning with the study of Thomistic Philosophy. We had to go back to Breakspear College in Abbots Langley for this as the numbers in those days were too great to be accommodated in the one house.

Here we were back in Abbots Langley but with a difference, a big difference. We were now members of the order, albeit for the time being. We were no longer novices—the lowest form of religious life—but fully fledged scholastics. Students for the Catholic Priesthood were called scholastics because it was the scholastic philosophy of Thomas Aquinas we now embarked upon. As this was the foundation of the theology we would study later we continued to be called scholastics until we were ordained

But what's in a name I hear you ask. Well, I would reply, everything, if it means the difference between a novice and a scholastic. A novice could be compared to a chrysalis with all the strictures of its confinement whereas the scholastic could be compared to the imago of the butterfly able to spread its wings and explore the environment. We were not quite as free as the butterfly in that we couldn't fly where we wished but they were two totally different lifestyles.

While the emphasis was still on spiritual growth we were back into the academic world of lectures, study and examinations—all in Latin.

Philosophy was a mystery to me and when we were told that it consisted of Logic, Cosmology, Ontology, Theodocy, Special Ethics, General Ethics and Psychology it became even more mysterious.

It was a two-year course and half the time was spent in translating the Latin text books before we got anywhere near an understanding of the subject. I was completely in the dark for the first six months and then one day it all clicked. It was almost like turning a bend in a dark tunnel and seeing the light before you. We had been told this would happen but of course we didn't believe it. Well from that day on I became enthralled with the subject. I had studied theology privately over the years but I had never heard of such subjects as logic, cosmology, etc. I fell in love with philosophy and to this day I would class it among my favourite subjects. We had been told it was the Queen of the Sciences and I truly believe it. Ironically, for one who later became somewhat of an expert in experimental psychology, I fell in love with the idealists summed up by Monsignor Ronald Knox in his famous little ditty:

> There once was a man who said, God
> Must find it exceedingly odd
> If he finds that this tree
> Continues to be
> When there's no one about in the quad.

It was not unexpected that I did well in the philosophy exams in

1957, now aged 31, gaining such marks as:

Logic:	Magna cum laude
Critic:	cum Laude
Ontology:	Magna cum laude
Cosmology:	Magna cum laude
Psychology:	Summa cum laude
Theodocy:	Magna cum laude
Special Ethics:	Magna cum laude
General Ethics:	Magna cum laude
Hist. of Philosophy:	Magna cum laude

I had begun to pass exams with the Customs and Excise and these were the first since then. I romped home and I thought I was home and dry. I was, until I began public exams again after ordination but that is a story for further on. Now I was in love with studies and would look forward to being examined on them.

The two-year course passed very quickly and along with my new-found discovery of philosophy I quickly discovered the meaning of the vow of poverty. And if I passed philosophy with distinction I failed miserably with my vow of poverty.

The vow hadn't touched me until one day I needed some clothing – underpants to be precise. We had been told that if we needed anything, all we had to do was go and see the bursar and he would provide it if we really needed what we asked for and providing the money was there. Well, in all innocence I went off to the bursar and asked for a new pair of underpants. He looked hard at me to see if I was joking. When I assured him I wasn't he said he would have to consider it. Well! Such rigmarole followed. I was called to the Superior to give an account of why I needed them and if this request was absolutely necessary. The Superior felt that this was too important a decision for him to make and so put it to the next meeting of the House Council. Eventually it was agreed that such an item was necessary and that the money had to be found from somewhere. I am not sure if they held a raffle but eventually I got my underwear in time for the winter months. As you can imagine the saga of Sullivan's underpants is told wherever Salvatorians gather.

But I wasn't the only one to suffer from over-zealous bursars. I mentioned that as novices we used to gather for a Chapter once a week. This continued during philosophy days when the Superior would address the community and after a ferverino he would deal with matters of discipline in general. There was always the question of television. It was still fairly new and heavily monitored in case our innocent minds were corrupted. Programmes which we were allowed to watch were marked and normally consisted of Panorama and the news. After the 9p.m. news the Superior would switch the television off and we would be expected to go to bed. It is not generally known that as structures of community life broke down after the Second Vatican Council members would always gather to watch the 9p.m. news on BBC. This took the place of the old community recreation. Then they would go to their rooms. This was true with most religious orders. The BBC didn't realise the havoc they caused when they changed the time of the late evening news.

But during one of the Chapters I was speaking about the Superior began to talk about furniture. He had noticed that an armchair had disappeared from the recreation room and was very puzzled as to its whereabouts. We looked at each other wondering who was the miscreant that had availed himself of an armchair at the community's expense. That night around midnight one of the students, who shall be nameless, could be seen furtively tiptoeing across the hall returning an armchair. Goodness knows how he thought he would get away with it. Depriving the community for one's own comfort was the 'mortal sin' of the day.

I think it was shortly after this that our 'class' of '55 became known as the 'scruffs', a nickname that has stuck with us through the years.

Then there was the matter of Christmas cards and gifts. Completely out of the question we were told BUT we were given a bottle of bleach between us and we were told to bleach out the signatures on the cards we received and then sign them ourselves and send them on. As for presents, that was when I learnt the true meaning of recycling. We were told that we could send gifts we received to others making sure that we didn't return them to the giver by mistake. We must have been the pioneers of recycling. We learnt very quickly not to ask for things and to learn the art of adaptation and improvisation.

These two years gave me an opportunity to redress an area of my life that had been sadly neglected, namely hobbies. At home my principle, if not the only, source of recreation was the cinema. There was no television of course and the wireless didn't interest me a great deal so virtually every night I would go to the cinema. I would walk home from work, calling in at the local church, have my tea and then go to one of the many cinemas that existed in the locality. In those days the programme was continuous so you could walk in at any time and stay and see the whole programme over and over again until the cinema closed. Hence the expression, 'this is where I came in'. It was on those occasions that I fell in love with Rita Hayworth and Betty Grable. We didn't have popcorn in those days but we always had an ice cream at the interval.

Now in religious life we had to spend an hour together at recreation after dinner and after supper. Well there is only so much you can say to each other as the days go by so we used the time to develop hobbies. I had always wanted to play a musical instrument and I thought this would be my chance. Way back as a boy my mother had sent me for piano lessons but the piano teacher either gave me up or I gave up myself. I can still read music a little from those days but that's as far as it got. Now I decided to try the guitar. It was in the days before the Beatles but chords were coming in as a means of accompaniment and I began to learn those. I thought that if I picked up a few tunes I would be the life and soul of the party, so to speak. We used to put on concerts for the community and I thought this would be my contribution. But where to get a guitar? The Order wasn't going to pay for one that was for sure. Well, I had brought my bike from home and still had that with me. I received permission to sell it and buy a guitar for the princely sum of £7.

As luck would have it, one of the students was a brilliant musician (pianist/organist) and he was horrified to hear me plucking away at the chords for an hour every day. My room was above the chapel and those visiting for private prayer at that time must have thought the angels were about. Though they could be forgiven if they thought it was from the other place. So he advised me to learn classical guitar. Stupidly, I listened and from then on it became a nightmare. Every day for an hour I would pluck away at the strings trying to learn 'home sweet home' and other so-called simple tunes. I was even persuaded to convert the instrument into a Hawaiian guitar and tried to play the boat song. Had I stuck with the chords I could have been the precursor of the Beatles. Next I decided I would try a wind instrument. So, again with permission, I sold the guitar and bought a clarinet. That was even worse. I could never blow a note out of the blessed thing and gave that up quickly. So what next. Would you believe that I sold the clarinet and bought? Yes, you've guessed it, a bike. And what joys that bike gave me all my student years after that.

However, I couldn't ride the bike around the recreation room so I had to develop something to occupy my time during recreation. I chose calligraphy and became a dab hand at illuminating addresses and inscriptions in books and so on. Other hobbies I tried at this time were photography, tennis and scrabble but with little or no success. The hobby I really took to and which gave great joy to myself and countless others was reading personality through graphology and body language but that came later when I began to study experimental psychology. Remind me to tell you about the time I was asked to speak to the Keele Psychological Society on the subject of graphology. It was one of my crowning moments.

Well the two years went by and we were introduced to such philosophers as Kant, Descart, Sartre and many others. Introduced is the right word for any philosopher other than Aristotle or Aquinas were quickly described and dismissed as adversaries in about three or four lines. We loved Aquinas not so much for his intellectual stature as his physical stature. He was known as the Dumb Ox. He was huge and had to have a semi-circular piece carved out of the table for him to have his meals.

We had pronounced our vows for one year and now, half-way through our philosophy course we renewed them for another year. We did this again at the end of the course one year later. Only one more year had to pass before we would hopefully be invited to take them for life. So with hope in our hearts we returned to Chester and Christleton Hall to begin life as senior students studying theology. We were more than half-way

13

Theology and Ordination

Emphasis on religious discipline increased as we came within sight of our goal. For most of our years of study emphasis on our own personal growth had been allowed to take second place and, for me, it had been a very dry period in terms of the spiritual life.

Fortunately, religious studies were tempered with manual work and I found myself involved with gardening and bee-keeping. My philosophy of life was approaching a balance without my being aware of it.

At last, ordination. My life-long ambition achieved. Now I presumed that I would practice my priesthood in a religious community developing my spiritual life and my relationship with God.

But no sooner had I achieved one ambition than another took its place. Just prior to ordination I received an instruction from the Provincial that was to change my way of life completely and produce the balance that had been lacking in me since those early years. During the next few years I turned 180 degrees in my attitude towards others and in terms of my own spiritual life.

The Provincial instructed me to get a degree in biology.

As novices and during the period of philosophy studies we had not been allowed home. We were allowed a visit or to send a letter once a month but not both. Letters had to be handed in to the Superior unsealed and letters coming in were opened by the Superior before being handed to us. It was said that the Superior never read the letters but just in case he did, we were always careful about what we said. We were constantly scared we would be thrown out. On the other hand, this did give us the opportunity to voice our complaints to whoever was reading it under the guise of writing to our dear mother or whoever. This regime continued throughout our student years.

So here we were back in dear old Christleton Hall as senior students studying theology. Only four years to go and we were becoming increasingly aware of Ordination looming ahead of us. Our study years, after our first profession, were punctuated with milestones such as renewal of vows, taking final vows and then as we got nearer to our goal, we began to receive 'Orders'. When we spoke of a person in Holy Orders in those days we referred to the seven orders which a person received before his final ordination ceremony. These were the minor Orders of Lector, Acolyte, Porter and Exorcist. Then came the major Orders of Subdeacon, Deacon and Priesthood. Being milestones they were always an occasion of assessment both by the individual and the Superior. Should I take this order? Should I renew my vows, and the inevitable, 'will I be allowed to?' And, of course there were always the exams, most of them still in Latin. Theology is a misnomer for those years for while theology itself consisted of Dogmatic, Ascetic and Moral theology we also had Sacred Scripture, Church History, Canon Law and Sacred Liturgy. We tended to have lectures in the morning and the afternoon would be spent gardening. In the evening we would review our morning lectures and write papers, etc. Added to this, at some time during the day we had to 'get in' our meditation, Divine Office, Rosary, Visit to the Blessed Sacrament and one quarter hour's spiritual reading. Is it any wonder the time went so quickly?

At a personal level it was at this time that I decided I would use the time for spiritual reading to read through the Bible once. Obviously, every day was interspersed with readings from Scripture during the Mass and the

Divine Office but I had never read the Bible from cover to cover. So I began and read every word and it took me just two years at fifteen minutes per day. On the first Friday of each month the time allotted for our spiritual reading had to be spent meditating on preparation for death—our own deaths. We would sit in the chapel looking very serious, trying to imagine ourselves on our deathbeds or even in our coffins. Often, if we really entered into it, we would almost frighten ourselves to death there and then.

Our gardening would take the form of two hours every afternoon and we would each be given the responsibility of a particular patch under the supervision of Brother Alphonsus and, later, Fr Leonard. We were told what to do with our patch and I remember I was given the job of growing celery—an awful job. But help was at hand. Nearby was an enclosed order of Benedictine nuns and one of them kept bees. The sister beekeeper very kindly died and there was no one to replace her. One of our priests, Fr Richard (not me) knew about bees so he offered to take them. We took five hives and had them in our kitchen garden. I don't know how it happened but I was asked to assist him and I must say, Big Dick, as Fr Richard was affectionately known, gave me a new lease of life. He opened a world to me that gave me tremendous joy and satisfaction. Eventually, when Christleton Hall became a Junior Seminary, I was given charge of them and I was given an assistant from the student body. I will talk about this period of my life a bit later but suffice it to say that it was a prestigious post and I think I grew a little in stature—in my own eyes at least and, dare I say it, at last.

And then there was the football—oh dear. You remember I told you that my mother had kept me away from all dangerous sports but, apart from this, I had no coordination whatever. I could see the ball coming, put my foot out but they would never connect. I was the same at school when I tried to play cricket. Never did I hit the ball with the bat, with my head, yes, or my leg but never with the bat. Every Wednesday afternoon we had to play football and we had no option until the day we were ordained deacons. I used to dread it, as did Joe Caldwell a fellow theologian. He was fortunate in that he had a physical presence and he would get the ball and charge down the field like a wild bull. Everyone would get out of his way but he hated it as much as I did. But what was a cause of great stress became a source of great delight, almost ecstasy, the day we were ordained deacons. We had our celebratory lunch, and then Joe and myself went and collected our football boots. We marched down to the big pond at the bottom of the grounds. We stood there in silence for a few moments, said a thanksgiving prayer and then with whoops of delight threw the boots in the pond where they disappeared without trace. What a moment to treasure that was. Actually they reappeared some years later. But that can wait.

Talking of Joe reminds me of many anecdotes that would fill a book. Perhaps they will keep for a sequel but I will just recall two here to give you a flavour of his character and indeed of all my fellow students at that time. I mentioned before that I was twenty-six years of age when I entered. By today's standards that was old. The normal age of entry was eighteen. So throughout my 'monkish' life I have always been the oldest in any group I've belonged to. Being the oldest among the students I was appointed prefect. The job of the prefect was to ensure that the other students did the jobs allotted to them. I forgot to mention that each of us had an area of responsibility in terms of keeping the house clean. I had to check this was done properly. One day during the winter I noticed the house was unduly cold and so I went down to check the boiler. Joe and another student, Jim Bradley, who later became Provincial Superior, had the responsibility of keeping the boiler going. They saw this task as an opportunity to sit by the boiler reading and occasionally look in to see the boiler was still going. When I got down to the boiler room there was no sign of Joe at all and Jim tried to distract me. I eventually managed to get a look into the boiler and inside there was Joe on his hands and knees blowing on some sticks of wood trying to get the boiler alight. They had let it go out.

Another story of those days is priceless. Joe and myself entered the same day and although he was very Irish and I was very English we struck up a deep friendship which lasted until Joe sadly died in his fifties. But like all friends we more than once really antagonised each other. He was the only person I have struck in my life when I punched his nose during our noviciate days. One particular day during our theology days he had antagonised me at recreation by throwing nuts at me one by one waiting for me to explode. By then, thanks to him, I had developed the art of patience to an eminent degree. But I decided to get my own back—such was my level of sanctity! I told you that we slept in individual cubicles in the one dormitory. A week or so before this incident I had received a tube of cheese from France. By this time it was smelling to high heaven and on this particular night I rubbed some of this cheese under Joe's bedstead before he came up to bed. All the other students knew of this but not Joe. We all settled down to sleep and then we heard Joe begin to sniff and sniff and sniff. Well, what a night and what antics with Joe getting up to try to find the source of the dreadful smell. Wherever Salvatorians meet the story is told again and again. I don't think Joe threw a single nut at me after that. As I said, Joe died early. He had spent his priestly life on the missions in Africa, Australia and Tasmania. He came home burnt out and one morning was found dead in his bed. It was as though he had laid himself out. He was found lying on his back with his hands across his chest clutching his crucifix. A tremendous character and a great priest! I remember the day we began our noviciate. Before going into the asceterium I mentioned ear-

lier, Joe and myself stood at the back door of the house and vowed we would become saints. I think he made it.

I could keep you here all week just recounting anecdotes from those days. But time moves on as did our theology days.

Our community consisted of a lot of scholastics at different stages of preparation and of course many priests who were responsible for our education, training and general well-being. Brother Cuthbert, a German, was the cook and he ruled the kitchen, quite literally, with a chopper. If you dared to go into the kitchen while he was preparing a meal he would chase you out with the chopper screaming, 'You get out of my kitchen'. He would start cooking the midday meal at about 8a.m. But he was well-meaning and would be a great person to talk to when we felt down. Brother Joseph took over from Cuthbert when the latter died. One of my responsibilities at one time was to assist him in the kitchen and I used to help him prepare the Christmas dinner. I learnt a lot about cooking from Joe especially how to cook his 'pièce de résistance' – Queen of Puddings. I knew how much Joe respected me when, on the day he retired, he solemnly presented me with the recipe book he had used in all his days of cooking. It has pride of place on my bookshelf and comes in useful for older recipes such as rabbit stew, etc.

Gradually the end of our nine-year course loomed in sight. We began the immediate preparations for our ordination. We were taught how to say the Tridentine Mass and how to hear confessions but we still had to get through our finals. We had been examined at the end of the philosophy course and now we were to be examined at the end of the four-year course of theology. Can you imagine it?

I don't know if I told you that from the day I entered religious life and spent at least eight years doing exams I never failed one. In fact I was normally at the top of the class, reaching my summit one year by getting 100 per cent for Canon Law. So I had no fear of the finals. I had studied hard, I knew the subjects backwards and felt I could respond to the most searching question they could ask. It was an oral exam and five priests sat at the table. I went in for the Dogmatic Theology exam full of confidence. It will give you an idea of the seriousness of this exam if I tell you about an incident that happened during the very first lecture I attended on this subject four years previously. In the two years of philosophy that had just elapsed we were encouraged to ask questions of the lecturer. I loved philosophy and was avid for clarification on anything I couldn't understand. This was seen to be good and a very positive aspect of the student. I went into the theology lecture with the same zeal and asked my first question. The lecturer, who shall be nameless and has since gone to God, glared at me and there was a moment of frozen silence that felt like hours. He said nothing at first and then asked who was I that dared to question the teaching of the church. I felt that I was about to be excommunicated. I realised then that one did not question theology but accepted it blindly in toto. It was the days before the Vatican Council of course when even scholarly research was frowned upon, if not forbidden. It was the days of the Index, which was a list of books Catholics were not allowed to read under pain of mortal sin. I had always thought this list would contain the titles of 'dirty books' but in fact it was a list of philosophical and theological tomes that people like me wouldn't read anyway. We wouldn't have understood them. This reminds me of another ban in force at that time. Priests and nuns were not allowed to attend live theatre. We could go and see any blue movie but it was forbidden to go to the theatre. I think it stemmed from the days of Vaudeville when some of the shows were blue to say the least. The church hadn't caught on to the filth contained in many films at this time. But I remember when the ban was lifted soon after my ordination there was a Gilbert and Sullivan Operetta being staged in nearby Liverpool so the community went to see it. The theatre was packed with priests and nuns taking advantage of their newly found freedom. They were in their 'dog collars' and religious habits of course, we were not allowed to go anywhere dressed differently. I was sitting next to a layman and he couldn't understand it, 'Is there a religious convention in town?' he asked innocently.

So I went into my exam. The five priests looked at me very seriously and the chairman asked me to sit down. This I did and waited for the first question, eager to show off my knowledge. 'What is the First Commandment?' asked the first priest. I looked at him and laughed. I didn't think he was serious. But he wasn't even smiling. He asked again, 'What is the First Commandment?' Would you believe it? I couldn't think what it was and laughed again, a bit more nervously this time. 'This is no laughing matter, Frater', he said. We were called Frater in those days, Latin for Brother. To this day if somebody asks me that question I can't think of the answer. Well, he passed it over and we went into more 'serious' questions which I could answer with flying colours. I passed what I believe was the most important exam in my life and I was almost through to the priesthood.

There was one more to go, that of what is called the Faculty exam. This was an examination in Moral Theology and as priests we would not be allowed to hear confessions if we failed. I mentioned before that the Old Man lectured in 'Moral' as it was called and he was the examiner. I went into his room and sat down. Without a moment's hesitation he got up from his chair, knelt down at the side of me and said, 'Bless me Father for I have sinned.' Blimey, I thought. Even with my experience of the army and Customs I had never heard of some of the sins he came out with. Of course it was a pretend confession and I was judged on the responses and the guidance I gave.

I should have mentioned that there were two books that were lifesavers for examinees. The four years of dogma were summed up in a book called *The Fundamentals of Catholic Dogma* by Ludwig Ott. It was in English. The four years moral theology was summed up in a book called *Moral Theology*, by Herbert Jone, also in English. It contains every sin that has been committed or could be committed and would be a bestseller if it was published commercially. It too was in English. They were the sort of 'crammer' books you see around these days. If any two people deserve to be canonised it is Jone and Ott.

So I passed this exam and the road was clear for ordination. This was to take place a few months ahead and meanwhile, it was a question of what were we going to do as priests. We all knew what we wanted to do. I had always had my heart and mind set on giving retreats and preaching missions in this country. I knew that there were good courses on this in Rome and I asked permission to attend one. 'You're not clever enough to study in Rome' I was told by the then Prefect of Scholastics (Déjà vous, I thought). But that didn't deter me and when the Provincial summoned me to his room I felt confident he would give me permission to do this work without the 'Rome experience'. My exam results throughout my nine years belied the words of the Prefect.

I sat down before the Provincial and waited for him to ask me what I would like to do. He didn't ask me. He looked at me and said, 'I want you to teach biology'. I nearly fell off the chair. Two years Latin and English, two years philosophy, four years theology and he said, 'I want you to teach biology'.

'I beg your pardon', I said, absolutely dumbfounded. He repeated, 'I want you to teach biology'. And then he uttered the magic words that changed my life – yet again. 'I want you to get a degree, a science degree'.

14

Christleton Hall, the Junior Seminary

After our ordination, Christleton Hall was converted to a junior seminary where boys of eleven years of age and upwards, who had expressed the desire to be priests, were educated. I was told to teach 'O' level biology and at the same time get a degree.

Never had the thought crossed my mind that I would be given this opportunity. For the next seven years I taught biology and the natural sciences part time and studied for my degree full time.

In the course of time all the boys I taught passed their 'O' level biology and I obtained a science degree in zoology and psychology.

From time to time a few words have changed the course of history. Chamberlain springs to mind when he waved that piece of paper after Munich and said 'peace in our time' only to say a few months later, 'we are now at war with Germany'; a man to a woman saying for the first time, 'I love you'; a cardinal announcing the election of a new Pope with the words, 'Habemus Papam' and so on. But, you know, none of these words had half the impact as the Provincial's words to me that morning, 'I want you to get a degree'.

Can you imagine it? Me! With my background of constant failure and low self-esteem, I could hardly qualify for night school let alone for a university. But here I was being told by my lawful superior to go to university and get a degree in biology. One of my fellow pupils at SFX, who had been in the 'A' stream but whose family knew ours was now teaching at Liverpool University. So, I thought, no problem, he will see to it all. I wrote to him and told him I had to go to university to get a science degree. 'Would you arrange it for me please.' In my innocence I thought it was as simple as that. But I was to be very disillusioned when he wrote back and said that I needed at least five 'O' levels and two 'A' levels before I could even be considered. Moreover one of the 'O's had to be in maths and another in a foreign language. I hadn't a single 'O' level to my name never mind maths or a language. What was I to do? I knew I had passed one or two subjects from the College of Preceptors on my way to the Customs and Excise and I discovered they didn't count. But looking through my file of past academic results, mostly 'Fs', I came across a letter with the heading of 'The Institute of Army Education'. The letter stated, 'this to certify that Sgt Sullivan sat for the Forces Preliminary Examination. His results are as follows: English, Mathematics, General Knowledge—all credit. History—pass'. I had completely forgotten these exams and I wrote immediately to my friend in Liverpool. He made enquiries and told me that the credit subjects qualified but not the pass. And, of course, there was no language. So I went to the Provincial and told him the sad news.

Now in my euphoria at hearing him telling me to get a degree I had completely forgotten the next thing he had told me. 'Here is £20', he had said, 'start a laboratory.' Did any saint have more confidence in God than did our Provincial in those days? And when I told him about the exams I needed to get into university all he said was, 'No problem. Go to night school and get them.'

You may be wondering why I was asked to teach and why I needed to start a lab? You will remember that up to this point Christleton Hall was what is called a major seminary, i.e. a college for students pursuing major studies for the priesthood. Christleton Hall had been such since the 1930s but now the present Provincial wanted to change that. In those days religious orders trained their own men for the priesthood but this tied up priests who might be better employed in other apostolates. Moreover, our Provincial had negotiated with the Jesuits to allow other orders to send their students to them. This guaranteed them an education of the highest order and, at the same time, released our men to do other work.

In those days junior seminaries were in vogue. These were colleges where boys of eleven years of age who had expressed the wish to be priests were sent to do their secondary education. It had been decided by the powers that be that Christleton Hall would be converted into a junior seminary not just for students for the Salvatorians but for other orders and dioceses as well. Thus teachers were needed for this and I was one of the chosen ones!!! You will remember that the last thing I wanted was to become a teacher.

So here I was a few months off ordination with my vow of obedience and told to get into the local technical college to do science 'O' levels and then science 'A' levels, but that was at night school. During the day I would teach what I had been taught the previous evening.

All that was forgotten as the great day of ordination approached. Out of the twelve that started the course eight remained. The time for our immediate preparation dawned when we went into retreat for eight days. I could hardly believe we were so close. I must say that the thoughts of teaching and getting that degree intruded into my immediate preparation and I was getting up at 4a.m. to begin the study of the secular subjects that would eventually lead to my getting the degree. It is ironic that having studied philosophy and theology for six years, here was I studying biology as the great day approached.

Years later I was walking with my father to the pub and I asked him what was the greatest happiness in his life. I was very moved when he said, 'The day of your ordination.' I was moved because on the day itself the rift between my parents was evident. After the ordination ceremony the newly ordained priest gives his first blessing to his parents. Traditionally the mother receives it first. Eight of us lined the altar rails and waited for our parents to come forward. Mine were seated in different parts of the chapel and I could see them making for the altar rails, I prayed to God that my mother would reach me first as my father was not aware of the tradition. My mother was of course. Well, as luck would have it my father reached me first and I had to ask him to wait. I knew it would break my mother's heart not to receive my first blessing. But my father took it in good stead though I knew he was disappointed. In fact he walked home alone to Liverpool that day, a distance of thirty miles. Of course, none of us drove in those days and I expect the rest of the family went by train.

It was traditional that the newly ordained priest celebrated his first Mass in his home parish church and this is what I did. It was a wonderful day and all my friends and many of the parishioners attended. My whole family were there apart from my sister who is a nun. Her order was very strict in those days and she had been given permission to attend the ordination or my first Mass but not both. She had chosen the ordination. However, the day after my first Mass I went to Leeds to her convent and said my second Mass there. I remember they gave me a gold pyx which is a little vessel for taking Communion to the sick, I am using it to this day.

It was nine years since I had left home to study and I was given a week's holiday. After that I had to report back to assist getting this junior seminary off the ground before the first boys came along. Fr Adrian, who had been ordained with me, had also been appointed to the seminary. He was to be Prefect of Students and teach music. The old Community had been dispersed and the new one, which was to conduct the junior seminary, was in place. Being the junior members we got all the menial tasks and we spent the first few weeks after our ordination washing down walls, assembling more than thirty beds rescued from a nearby disused army camp and bumpering and polishing all the floors of the house. It was the first Saturday of September 1961 as Adrian and myself were finishing off the bumpering that the first boys began to arrive.

In between these chores Adrian would practice and prepare his music lessons and I set about building a laboratory with my £20. After ordination I was told that not only was I to teach biology to 'O' level standard but general chemistry and physics as well. I hadn't a clue about science. I spent the money on a book called, *Teach Yourself Biology*, and a number of test tubes. An old classroom was put at my disposal and I set it up to make it look as much like a lab as possible. I found some large glass bottles and I put different coloured water into each and wrote a chemical formula on them. These I put on shelves to make the place look 'scientific'. Then came a great blessing. As I said in an earlier chapter, I used to help out an elderly priest at weekends in Meols on the Wirral and I told him what I had been asked to do. He was a scientist as well as a priest and in his spare time, almost as a hobby, he had engaged in research in textiles for the local ICI. His eyesight was beginning to fade so he had had to resign from this work He had two ancient brass binocular microscopes and he gave them to me with some slides. What a Godsend! For the next six years the boys would queue to look down those microscopes at various specimens I had bought or fished from the pond in the grounds. Every boy in that college passed their biology 'O' level. I still have one of those microscopes. It is dated 1876 and is in perfect condition.

I enrolled at the Chester College of Further Education and began the study of biology, chemistry, physics and geography. Somewhere along the line I took up Latin again as I needed the 'O' level pass for entrance to university. The Latin I had studied as a candidate was very general and simply prepared us for the studies ahead. It was examined internally and so didn't count. The 'O' level course was designed for one year and it won't come as any surprise when I tell you I failed all subjects at the end of that year. I took them again as I was wont to do and passed them all at the end of the second year. My first students took their 'O' levels one year after me and they all passed. Any questions they asked me by day I would put to my tutor in the evening and respond to my students the next day.

After I passed the 'O' levels I signed up for chemistry, zoology and botany 'A' levels. During the zoology classes we had to dissect animals and to keep the costs down we worked in pairs. I will never forget dissecting the nervous system of the dogfish with my partner who turned out to be a very beautiful female student. It didn't do my nervous system any good I can tell you. I must tell you about one dissection we did together. It was the nervous system of the same dogfish, which is all we ever seemed to dissect, except the venous or arterial system of the frog. I never knew one from the other and I remember in the practical finals for my degree doing a perfect dissection of the venous system. Of course the exam question was for the arterial system. Anyway, this young lady and myself spent hours teasing out the system. We looked at the textbook, which told us what to find where. But either our fish was disabled or the book was wrong. Eventually we called over the demonstrator and pointed out the difference between the book and our dissection. To his credit and our honour he said, 'believe the fish'.

Again this was a one-year course which I failed miserably. The next year, 1965, I passed botany at grade C and zoology at grade D. That year I also passed Latin 'O' level after four unsuccessful attempts. I was eligible for university. By this time I realised that my friend would not be able to 'get me in' as UCCA was now in place. I applied to four universities and received rejection slips from Leicester and Bangor. I was put on the waiting list at Liverpool and offered a place at Manchester. I couldn't believe my luck

The next chapter will reveal how I got on at university, but let's stay at Christleton Hall for a while.

I had never taught in my life apart from the platform of the Catholic Evidence Guild and I had little or no knowledge of the subject I was about to teach. On that first morning I stood outside the classroom listening to the noise of the boys within wondering how on earth I was going to control them. I am sure any teacher reading this will remember her/his first classroom experience. As I was about to walk in the Headmaster passed by. He was a very experienced teacher and had come from being Head of a large secondary school in London. He saw my state and simply said, 'Go in there and treat them like animals.' You could have knocked me down with a feather. I had been ordained less than three months and was full of apostolic zeal. These lads were supposedly training for the priesthood and

I felt so proud at having been chosen to help them on their way to the goal I had fought so tenaciously to achieve. 'Treat them as animals!'. I was still under the impression that there was no such thing as a bad boy. I ignored the Headmaster's advice and went in to begin my apostolic life feeling a bit like Daniel must have felt when he went into the lion's den.

I owe that teacher a great debt for within days I was treating the boys as animals, albeit of the human species. And I was almost qualified to do this. Wasn't I studying for a degree in zoology?

However, in fairness to the boys they were just boys. The fact that they were training for the priesthood didn't alter their behaviour at that age. Admittedly we ran the school on seminary lines with a strict rule of life as the backbone to their education. Up early, Mass would begin the day. At mealtimes one of the boys would read a holy book from the lectern in the Refectory. There would be evening prayers and so on. They were closely supervised but that didn't stop them from 'breaking out' from time to time. Who will forget the huge explosion in the grounds one November evening. A student had packed a bottle with fireworks and gun powder, screwed on the lid and lit a fuse. The effect was dramatic. The lid embedded in a tree is now grown over but the whole college was shaken to its foundations by the blast. Then there was the evening when the Superior discovered the Community car was missing. A quick check-up on the number of boys present in the college revealed three were missing. They had taken the car and were out joyriding. Fortunately, I was not involved in those events as that was the lot of Fr Adrian, the Prefect of Discipline. Besides, I had enough troubles of my own keeping discipline in the lab.

I thought that if I made the subject interesting it would keep them occupied. But I was an innocent abroad. Showing them how sodium lights up and whizzes around on water was fine until the lit sodium left the bowl of water and nearly set the lab on fire. Then there was the day when I was demonstrating the power of hydrogen and nearly blew up the college never mind the lab.

I formed a Dissecting Club which would meet during the evenings. Boys would hunt for dead animals in the grounds and get great glee from opening them up. The boys were ecstatic when one of the cows died and we could really go to work. I remember we had terrible trouble trying to expose the brain without damaging it. We sawed through the head and one of the Nuns on the staff got to one side and I got to the other and we virtually tore it apart. But that brain became a prize exhibit in the lab from then on. As you can imagine, my coloured water bottles had been replaced by the real thing by now and I actually had a real lab, purpose built to my own design complete with Bunsen burners, bell jars and specimens preserved in formaldehyde.

Another 'interesting thing' I dreamed up was to dissect the pond. We had done a similar thing to this in fieldwork during my degree course. We spent twenty-four hours in a boat on Lake Bala taking specimens from various areas and depths at different times. So I thought, no problem! We built a raft. Relationships between the boys and myself must have improved for they named the raft 'Old Nick'. Remember my name in religious life was Nicholas Owen. Little did I know that they had every intention of sinking this raft with me on it. Now there were not only plankton and fish of various sorts in that pond, and one day when some of the boys used the raft to do a spot of fishing, they hooked a really big one. Can you guess what sort? Absolutely right – a pair of long-forgotten football boots.

I tried credit lines. Do you remember my telling you that the Jesuits gave us white bills when we were to be punished. These had the number of strokes we were to receive. They also gave us red bills if we did something really good. These also had a number on them and we could exchange a red bill for a white bill. The punishment I used for misbehaviour was writing out lines. So, using the Jesuit system of reward and punishment I would give credit lines for good behaviour and they could exchange these.

I even tried bees to keep the discipline. Actually, I had accidentally introduced the bees to the boys one Wednesday afternoon when they were playing cricket. It was a beautiful day and I decided to use the afternoon to work with my bees. For some reason one colony was not too happy and when I took the lid off the hive they 'hived off' in one great body to the cricket pitch, there to wreck havoc with the game, not to mention the boys and Fr Edmund. To this day I feel sure the boys thought I did this deliberately. I was not known as a great lover of cricket. Anyway, back to the classroom. I would take my pet bee safely ensconced in a matchbox with holes in it into the classroom. I would threaten to release it if they didn't behave. Of course, they didn't know a lot about bees and I made sure my 'pet bee' was a drone which was perfectly harmless. Drones don't sting.

The crux came one day when they hadn't done the work given to them, they weren't paying attention and they took no notice whatever of my 'threats'. So I said to them, 'Right, if you won't work, neither shall I. I am going to my room and I intend to stay there until you come and apologise and ask me to teach you again.' A teacher couldn't do this in today's world of course but this was in the early sixties. Two days went by and I prayed and prayed that they would come and apologise. If they didn't I would have to eat humble pie and teach them of course. On the third day my prayers were answered when a piece of blue paper was slipped under my door. On it was written:

> 'Dear Fr Nicholas, we are writing as a form, firstly to apologise for any wrong we have done you, secondly to ask for your friendship once more. Yours, Form 1V.'

Each student had signed it. One had changed his mind and

scratched out his name before delivery but that didn't matter. I had been vindicated. So as a gesture to them I took them for a camping weekend to the Llanberis Pass in Snowdonia, North Wales. The weather was foul but we pitched our tents and I slept in one while the boys slept in another. We did everything together, cooking, eating, hill-walking, climbing Snowdon but I think what won the day for me was that I slept in puddles just as they did. We became great friends after that. I even let them polish my Territorial Army uniform buttons and blanco my equipment. But more about the TA later.

Boys came and went. As they grew older a number of them realised it was unreal for them to pursue a priestly vocation and so left and went into the secular professions. Others went on and became priests of our order or the different Dioceses. One became a canon and two actually became bishops. I wrote to them after their episcopal ordination to congratulate them. I said that there are two bishops in the hierarchy who might not know a lot of theology but they can certainly dissect a frog. Very useful if they ever entertain French Bishops!

A number of those boys are still in touch over forty years later. In fact not long ago a boy, now fifty, came to see me and brought his biology exercise books with him, those I had marked. With a serious look on his face he said, 'I would like these to be looked at and re-marked again please.' So I did and marked them down!!!

They were very happy days once we had got our act together and I had visions of spending all my priestly life in the lab training boys for the priesthood. But the days of junior seminaries were coming to an end. It was realised eleven years of age was too young for boys to commit themselves to seminary and religious life and they began to close all around the country. Ours was to close in 1970.

My new-found knowledge of biology came in very useful one day when I went to say Mass in a local convent. It doesn't happen now but in those days when a priest said Mass in a convent he was always asked what he would like for breakfast. The sisters were wonderful and would cook whatever the priest wanted. But you could guarantee that whatever you asked for on that first day you would get every time you went there to say Mass. I asked for the full English breakfast and I got it. However, the sausages were never fully cooked throughout. I had been teaching my students about the tapeworm and how one of their stages of growth takes place in undercooked sausages. What could I do? To leave them on the side of the plate would be unthinkable in a convent. Fortunately, my handkerchief came to the rescue. They didn't have doggy bags in those days. So thereafter whenever I visited that convent I would take an extra handkerchief with me. Another item for the Sullivan folklore book.

I had gone to university in 1965 and for the first two years I continued to teach, this time giving the boys evening classes after returning from Manchester. For my final year I was allowed to attend university full time and I took up residence in the Jesuit Catholic Chaplaincy – where else?

After nine years study for the priesthood and seven to get my science degree the Provincial of the day came to see me. There was a different Provincial in office now. He congratulated me on my degree which was in zoology and psychology and said, 'I want you to go to our school in Wealdstone and teach religious education.'

That incident was interesting actually because in my first few weeks at university a student had confronted me coming out of a lecture and shouted at the top of his voice, 'I don't believe in heaven.' Without thinking I replied, 'Well go to hell.' I thought of this when the Provincial asked me to teach RE. Was God getting his own back?

15

BSc, Dip.Ed.G, MEd

My student years in the major seminary took place in an atmosphere of calm and tranquillity, almost a protective atmosphere. There was no competition and little challenge. It almost seemed as though I was pursuing these studies while I waited for ordination. I learnt little new during the theology years and I must say that I never felt the presence of a spiritual life during that time. Perhaps this was what the spiritual writers call the dark night of the senses. If so it had lasted and was to last for a very long time.

Back to studying secular subjects in a secular world I suddenly became alive again. From the day I went to night school to study science 'O' levels I was up against challenge in every direction and from top thinkers – undergraduates, postgraduates, lecturers and professors. All I had ever learned in theology was questioned and I was well able to defend my corner. The study of zoology and psychology challenged everything I believed in.

The most dramatic effect on my life at this time came through my studying non-judgemental client centred counselling. This caused me to question my own attitudes to others and began the 180 degrees turn around in my life.

Add to this my experience in the Territorial Army which I joined at this time and the stage was set for my personal renaissance.

As I have described, I eventually had the necessary qualifications to apply for university entrance. By that time I was more knowledgeable about the ways of university entrance and so I went through UCCA, as it was then. Liverpool gave me a conditional acceptance; Leeds and Leicester rejected me. (In fact I gave a lecture there in later years so they regretted not taking me I can tell you!) But Manchester invited me for an interview. I had applied to do zoology as I had seen some marine fish in an aquarium somewhere and I felt I would like to get to know them better. I knew absolutely nothing about botany in spite of now being the proud owner of a botany 'A' level. And, of course, the Provincial had said, etc. Off I went for my interview. I won't mention names but the interviewer, God bless him, was obviously concerned about my religious life interfering with my zoological life. His first question was, 'If I asked you to write to the Pope to request being excused saying Mass during your course would you do so?' He was a little taken aback when I said absolutely not. I hadn't slaved over textbooks in philosophy and theology for nine years and in Latin to give it up to study the innards of a few animals. Then he asked my age and that was the clincher I think. It was politically correct, though that expression had not been thought of in those days, to take a few oldies to add a little maturity and common sense to the undergraduate world. But of course there was a snag. Isn't there always? You're too old, he said to do an honours degree but we will accept you on the ordinary course. You will have to do three subjects in your first year and then specialise in two. My heart burst with pride. I knew nothing about the difference between honours and ordinaries, but I did know I was about to achieve an impossible dream, in fact to be honest, I had never even dreamed of it. This little lad from Everton became an undergraduate at the age of thirty-nine and sat with the best of them listening to wonderful and learned lectures by the most eminent scholars. For my three subjects I did zoology, psychology and chemistry. I didn't understand half of them of course but that's neither here nor there. Of course there was the usual problem of having to teach daily as well as study. Each day I would travel from Chester to Manchester, attend lectures and practicals, travel home and then teach biology 'O' level in the evenings. At first I was allowed the use of the house scooter and then gradually the Superior gave me twenty-five pounds to buy a car. Every time I went out in it I would have to call the RAC. It reached the point where, on one occasion, I rang up the RAC and I heard one man say to the other at the end of the phone, 'It's that reverend gentleman again'. Eventually my Superior relented and let me get another car for thirty pounds. This was really living, apart from the fact that whenever I opened the door it would fall off, and have you ever tried leaning out the car window in the pouring rain to clean the windscreen by hand. This car had no windscreen wipers.

Well, there I was at university a full-fledged undergraduate, a priest of thirty-nine years of age sitting with youngsters of eighteen. I had to wear my clerical collar of course in those days but I have to say those fellow undergraduates were marvellous. They supported 'the old monk' and we used to have great discussions about science and religion over coffee or lunch in the university refectory (It took our minds off the food!). I won't bore you with the details of my academic career, at least, not yet. But talking about science and religion reminds me of the field trip we went on to Roscoff, Brittany. We had three field trips during our course. One was to Betws-y-coed, known to Liverpudlians as Betsy co-ed, in North Wales for terrestrial fauna, one to the Gower Peninsula for marine fauna and one to Roscoff. This was the big one—two weeks on the Brittany coast—can you imagine it. As I said before, I was now doing an ordinary degree and, as like is attracted to like, I discovered another three on the course who had been dropped from honours to ordinary. Of course we had nothing to lose. The honours undergraduates, in search of a first, spent every waking moment looking for rare specimens and writing up an account of their particular research, which they had to present at the end of the fortnight. Well, we did too but we were considered fairly harmless and so there wasn't much pressure. So quite nonchalantly we would comb the beaches, a bottle of Sauterne in our pockets looking for interesting French specimens.

believe it or not the biggest specimen we got was the oil tanker, the Torre Canyon. A huge oil tanker came apart and leaked oil on to the sea around Roscoff. This was the first oil tanker to leak oil and so knowledge of what to do to rescue the beaches and the wildlife was minimal. As a zoological party from England we were called to help. The lecturers might have made a big contribution but all we lesser mortals did was to attach balloons to ropes and try to keep the oil away. The headlines in the local papers that night was, 'oil experts sent from England to rescue Roscoff beaches'. Fame at last. I was almost famous for another specimen collected during that fortnight. I discovered a very white sponge-like material, which I took back to the lab for identification. I couldn't identify it so I took it to the honours students who, likewise, couldn't identify it, then the lecturers failed until, eventually, in desperation we took it to the professor. By this stage my stock had risen considerably and these first-class honours hunters were wild with envy at my discovering what seemed to be a rare specimen of sponge. The professor looked at it, measured it, looked up some identification books and eventually smelt it. He then proudly identified it. It was a piece of orange peel bleached by the sea. To this day they think I did it deliberately. Fame gave place to infamy and for the most part has stayed.

But I mentioned that we used to have great discussions over science and religion and these reached their climax in Roscoff when at night-time we would sit into the night and discuss the difference. Being the priest I was looked upon to defend the Catholic position on a number of things and I must

IF IT'S NOT A BANANA, IT MUST BE AN..... ...APPLE!!!

(ACADEMY FOR GIFTED PRIMATES)

confess I felt much more at home being a priest than being a zoologist. But I held my own so to speak. The upshot of these discussions was that I was invited to address the Manchester University Biological Society on this subject. However, I knew my limits. The knowledge and experience in dialogue gained at the Catholic Evidence Guild was not sufficient to take on real experts in their own field. But I knew a Jesuit priest who had a doctorate in theology and a doctorate in science. I invited him to do it, which he did with great eloquence, knowledge and wisdom. He was a great success and was actually invited to the senior common room after the evening drew to a close to continue the debate in more informal surroundings. It was one of those evenings to savour.

After two years of travelling back and forth from Chester to Manchester and teaching in the evenings my superiors gave me permission to study full time. I took up residence in the Manchester University Catholic Chaplaincy, once again coming under the influence of the Jesuits. From here I did my final year but the damage had been done in terms of academic achievement. At the end of my first year, not understanding much about organic chemistry I had decided to do psychology and zoology for my finals. I did very well in zoology, so much so that the Prof said that if I could keep this up the following year I could transfer to Honours. I hadn't done very well in psychology. I remember going up to Manchester for the exam and finding a student breaking her heart crying with stress and anxiety. Being a gentleman I used my precious last-minute revision time comforting her. We went into the exam. She passed and I failed. I spent a lot of time in the second year catching up on psychology. In doing so I neglected the zoology. During the exam there was a huge dog racing around the exam hall with the invigilator after it. That was a bit distracting but I can't really use it as an excuse for doing badly. Anyway the question of doing Honours was out. I came out with the lowest degree possible, namely a second-class ordinary degree. But had I gone on to the Honours course I would have missed out on the student world later not to mention enjoying my university days so much.

Getting any sort of a degree was a major achievement for me and the second-class ordinary has been a Godsend when I have had to counsel students with poor degrees. And in spite of it I have lectured professors, heard the confessions of Generals and eventually reached the stage of Visiting Lecturer at Aston University. But to this day, when I think of my performance during the final practical examination, I think the zoology department created a second-class ordinary degree to enable me to graduate. I was preparing the heart of a snail in order to pass through an electrical current when the invigilator came up to me and said, 'For goodness sake put the knife down, you're making us all nervous.' One great thing about that exam will always hold a special place in my memory. It was a sweltering day and the exam lasted eight hours. According to the rules of the church I was dressed in my black suit and clerical (dog) collar. Half way through the exam the professor came in and gave everybody an ice cream. 'When I did my finals, my professor did this for us so I am handing on a tradition', said the worthy professor. I could have kissed him— but I restrained myself.

My mother and sister came to the graduation ceremony and I am not sure who was the proudest of the three of us. The conferment of degrees had been going on all week and ours happened to be the last on the Friday afternoon. As my name began with an S and it was the zoology department conferring the degrees I was the last of the whole week to mount the dais. To this day I would like to think the cheers that went up were for this old fellow tottering up the steps to get his second-class ordinary degree rather than the fact that, at last, the weeks of conferring degrees were finally over.

During this final year and the next year I did supply work at the Salford Cathedral. There, I was given the opportunity to begin my preaching career if I may call it that. It is a grand cathedral and in those days we were still mounting the pulpit to preach. I have always been extremely nervous before speaking in public.

There is a nice little story about what happened one day when I preached at Mass in the Chew Valley. It was the normal Sunday Mass. Afterwards one of the parishioners brought their child of five to me and said Anne would like to know if you are still growing. I wondered at this and asked her what she meant. The father explained that she had seen me standing on my toes when I was preaching. She thought it was because I couldn't see over the lectern. I am so nervous that all my energy goes down to my toes whenever I speak publicly. Recently a chiropodist told me that this is why my feet now need his attention. Isn't it a funny old world?

But at the Cathedral in Salford it gave me a great feeling to mount the steps and see such a huge congregation waiting for me to start. Obviously I had become interested in public speaking during my time with the Catholic Evidence Guild and I think it must have been in those days that I acquired a gift for preaching which has given me so much fulfilment over the last forty years. I have been very fortunate in having the gift of communication and I think preaching is a product of this. Certainly I have never had trouble thinking up a sermon and my time with the Guild helped me to utilise this gift in terms of voice projection, timing and so on. Standing on a platform having to draw your congregation purely by dint of your own speaking skills is the best preparation anybody could have for preaching.

One Sunday I was preaching in Salford Cathedral and preached what I thought was a reasonable sermon. As I was getting unvested in the sacristy after Mass a lady came in and asked to speak to me. In those days we were not allowed to go to the back of the church to greet parishioners as they left so she had come in to see me in the sacristy. She began, 'Father, that was the most beautiful sermon I have ever heard.' I think I grew in stature as she talked. I was just about to thank her when she added, 'I am just going home to write to the Queen and tell her about it.' My balloon burst. The poor soul was a little demented but over the years when people have told me I preach well I think of that lady and my head stays the same size. I owe her a great deal.

I stayed at the Manchester chaplaincy for two years. After graduation I enrolled to do a diploma in educational guidance, a pseudonym for school counselling. You will remember that I had been teaching biology during the time I was studying for the degree. The object of taking the degree was to give me knowledge of the subject and also to qualify as a teacher of science. I expected to go back to Chester to teach full time once I graduated. However it took me so long to get this degree, four years at the tech and three at the university that another person had become Provincial. As I said earlier, he came to see me and after congratulating me on my modest achievement said he wanted me to go to our school in Wealdstone to teach religious education. The Second Vatican Council was over by now and a great change had come over religious orders. Previously I would have had to say, 'yes Father' and gone. But now we were allowed to discuss decisions such as this. So I told him about an idea I had been brewing over during the last few months.

Virtually all my life people of all ages have come to me with their problems. I suspect I learnt my real counselling skills at my mother's knee trying to keep peace between my parents, sadly without success, but I found it easy to listen and to empathise with most. There was a diploma course in Educational Guidance (school counselling) just starting at Manchester and I thought it would be very useful to have a qualification in counselling if people were going to continue to come to me seeking help.

When I finally got my famous second-class ordinary degree the university offered me a bursary to enable me to do this diploma course in counselling. So when the Provincial asked me to teach religious education, I used my skills of persuasion to get him to change his mind. He didn't and I was called for an interview with the school. During the interview the head teacher who was a layman asked me why I wanted the job. I told him I didn't and I told him what I wanted to do. Fortunately, school counselling was all the rage at this time having been introduced into England from America by Peter Dawes, and Keele University was the mecca for those wanting to get a qualification in this subject. The head teacher spoke to the Provincial and I was allowed to go back to Manchester.

Counselling as it is now was in its infancy, indeed, in those days priests were the principle counsellors and lay counsellor specialists in bereavement and suchlike were unheard of. People went to their priest for help. In fact, I remember a psychiatrist saying to me what great therapeutic value the confessional had. Now as the numbers of priests have decreased and the media has rubbished them for the most part lay counsellors are the secular priests of the day. But this was back in 1968 and counselling as such was new to this country. In fact I was the first Catholic priest to become qualified in school counselling. The Education Department ran the course and, for some reason unknown to me, I was awarded that bursary to enable me to pursue the course. The lecturer in charge was a member of the Department and an expert in Piaget, the mega philosopher of education. We thought our man was an expert in client-centred counselling which was in vogue at that time and was the principle theory taught on our course. We admired him for his skill in keeping quiet in order to get others to talk, as befits the theory. At the end of the course and after we had won our colours we congratulated him on this. Imagine our disillusionment when he said he had kept quiet because he hadn't known what to say. He was an expert in his field but had been asked to run this course to get it off the ground. Every day he sported a red tie and I wore my clerical collar. You can imagine the great discussion we had when it came down to client-centred therapy versus absolute values. Many a red line underscored my essays. 'Too authoritative' was a common comment.

I have to say that what I learnt during the course did not improve my natural counselling skills but I did find the supervised school placements of great value. In fact I still find myself referring to them mentally in counselling situations to this day.

There was one case of a boy playing truant. I was asked to go and visit his parents to see what the problem was. Fortunately we had been drilled in the necessity of involving relevant experts in every case in which we were involved. So I accompanied a social worker to this house, and what a good thing I did. As we stood outside waiting for someone to open the door, she said to me, 'When you go in, whatever you do don't stand on the mat.' I thought this was rather strange but did as she said. We went in. The young mother was watching TV and smoking cigarettes. She was dressed very smartly and when we asked her why her son wasn't at school she simply replied, 'we can't afford the clothes for him'. When we got outside I asked the social worker about the mat and why we didn't stand on it. She told me that on her first visit to that particular house she had stood on the mat. When she got home she found herself covered in lice. It could have been a matter of 'fools rush in where angels fear to tread'. Since that day I have always had a healthy respect for the professionals. In all my counselling experience I have always called in the experts as soon as I have felt they were needed.

The experience I gained in those Manchester schools was invaluable when I began to train counsellors at Aston University many years later.

When the Provincial gave me permission to continue at Manchester I suspect he had planned for my appointment to Wealdstone College as School Counsellor. But yet again, God had different ideas.

Little did I realise as I mounted that dais to receive my degree from the zoology department that I would hardly ever teach the subject in my life. Henceforth I was to be a 'psychologist' and would begin my professional educational career as a lecturer in education psychology. How this came about is related in the account of my days at Mary Ward College in the next chapter. But it is relevant to mention it here because the appointment led to my deciding to follow my diploma with a course leading to the MEd.

Now this is a saga of epic proportions. Are you sitting comfortably? Then I'll begin.

I had a phone call from a very old friend—a Jesuit of all people and not only that but one of those who actually taught me at SFX. Well into his eighties now, he is still working as chaplain to a Retreat Centre. He rang me 'for a chat between two old buddies'. I told him that I was putting him into this diary and he asked me why. I told him it was because he was one of the only two priests in that college that I could remember with kindness. There was him and the priest who gave me the 'red bill' I spoke about earlier. Fr Bulbeck is one of those rare people who make you feel you are of value and that you have something others need. I told him that I had mentioned Fr Ryland Whittaker who was on the parish at the time

Fr Bulbeck was in the college and immediately he said, 'Wasn't he a wonderful man?' And it is true. I have been very fortunate in meeting some wonderful people who have offset completely those I remember with rancour. And they were not all priests by any means. Nor were they all Catholic. One such was Mary Kirkman who was a receptionist at Mary Ward College during my time there. She was one of those people who always had that bit of spare time to do whatever you wanted even though she had plenty of work to do herself. I was into my second year MEd when I met her and if it hadn't been for her this chapter could never have been written.

Let me explain: academia is addictive. There were professors at Keele University who had been there since they had got their first degree. They had never known any other world but academia. I almost caught this addiction after I got my diploma. Fortunately there were no grades given in the Diploma world other than a 'distinction' and that was a very rare award. So, when we qualified as counsellors believing that we were all worthy of distinctions but somehow or other had been overlooked, we all said, what next? Well it was obvious. We all decided to apply for the master's degree. To gain admission to the course one had to be in possession of a first degree and/or a diploma as long as we could pay for the necessary tuition fees. My good superiors by this time had resigned themselves to my not teaching religious education at Wealdstone and were happy for me to return to Christleton Hall to take up the 'Chair of Science'. I was head of science and all the staff of the science department rolled into one. I knew I would be pushing my luck if I asked for another year off to take an MEd but I discovered that there were part-time courses. I was well used to studying by day and teaching at night so it was no hardship to do a part-time course while working full time in another position. So, in for a penny in for a pound, I enrolled for a two-year part-time course which would be examined by thesis. The student had to attend two evening lectures a week, attend tutorials by arrangement and eventually submit a thesis to qualify for the degree. This did not seem too bad as I was living in Chester at the time and it was only an hour's drive away. But little did I know that the college at Christleton Hall was going to close the next year and I was destined for Mary Ward College in Nottingham, two and a half hours' away. Still, I thought it would be only one year of travelling for the lectures and I could arrange the tutorials to fit in with the days of the lectures. After the student completed the lecture course he was allowed one year to complete the thesis. Would you believe it? Of course you would. It took me eight years from start to finish.

One of the most difficult parts of a thesis course is deciding what research a person is going to do and the title of the thesis. This was not too pressing while I was doing the lecture course but there was a date given not only for handing in the title of the thesis but also an outline of the research. I hadn't a clue. I was assigned to a gentle, elderly tutor in the Education Department and fortunately he was a Catholic. So I think it was as much for the reputation of the church as for me that he was determined that I would get through.

Again fortunately for me by the time I had to hand in my title I had moved to Mary Ward College and it was a gold mine for the research I came up with. I was lecturing in educational psychology and had to go out and observe students on their teaching practice. At assessment meetings with the staff the criteria for what makes an effective teacher was discussed at great length. These were the days of pupil-centred learning and open-space classrooms. It was the era of first schools and middle schools. So if a teacher could not control the children in the classroom, no matter how good a teacher she was, the end result was chaos. So I saw my opportunity. I decided to try and find out what was needed in a person to make an effective teacher in the middle school. With the aid of my tutor I came up with the title, 'Authoritarian Attitudes and Divergent Thinking as Related to Rated Teacher Effectiveness in the Middle School'. What a mouthful! I am not going to bore you with the details of the research here except to say that the result was, 'The research has revealed that religious minded people, who according to previous research, tend to be authoritarian, need to change their method of teaching in the pupil-centred world of today's middle school in order to be effective'. Should the reader be interested in reading the thesis there is a copy in the library of Manchester University Education Department.

BSc, Dip.Ed.G, MEd.

The students, all Catholics and all females, at Mary Ward College lent themselves to the research and willingly became guinea pigs for me. They filled in copious questionnaires and answered a multitude of questions over those years. And although I did the research during term time it was only during the holidays that I was able to write it up. Regularly, every month, I drove from Nottingham to Manchester over the Snake Pass to see my tutor who somehow or other on more than one occasion was himself at another meeting on the other side of Manchester.

I have always been a great believer in rewarding oneself for doing something over and above the call of duty. And I remember with great nostalgia stopping at a chippy on the edge of the Snake Pass and getting pie and chips with gravy. I did this on every return trip and would place the little tray on the passenger seat and dip into it all the way over the Pass. I have travelled the world since then and dined in the best restaurants but nothing can replace the pie, chips and gravy with onions of that chippy. Someday I must go back and see if it is still there.

Time passed, again, and I was given an ultimatum: 'Get the thesis in this year or else forget it.' One of my problems was that the computer had just been discovered and lecturers were all talking about relative coefficients. I think that was all the computer could do in those days but I had little or no knowledge of what a relative coefficient was. Fortunately my tutor translated these long pages the computer spewed out and eventually I was ready to write up the thesis. And this is where Mary Kirkman came in. She offered to type my thesis for me in her spare time as a labour of love. Amstrad had not got their act together by this time and so it was a question of the typewriter with all that that involved. Night after night she would labour, unravelling my handwriting before she could type a word. Eventually it was done, typed and bound with beautiful gold lettering on the front announcing the title. On the spine was my name and date of the thesis also in gold. Imagine my pride driving over the Snake Pass with the book on the passenger seat beside me.

I handed it in and returned to Nottingham indulging in what I thought was my last opportunity for pie, chips and gravy with onions.

With bated breath I watched the post each morning waiting for the letter informing me I was now a Master of Education. Eventually it came but not with the news I expected. As you know I have never passed a public exam first time in my life so I don't know what possessed me to think it would be different this time. I had to resubmit having made various alterations. But the worst thing of all was that I found the external examiner who had rejected my great work was none other than my red tie 'friend' of my diploma days. Not being a stranger to repeats I set to work, did what was asked of me and Mary, God bless her, typed it all again. It had to be at the binders the next day to catch the deadline given to me by the university. Around 1a.m. she finished and there it was ready for the binder. We sat back and relaxed and decided to have a cup of coffee. Can you imagine what happened next? You're right. We spilt the wretched stuff all over the thesis, forty pages ruined. Back to the typewriter and Mary finished it at 4a.m. The binder did his job and off I went again with it sitting in the passenger seat. I was in plenty of time so I decided to stop at a transport café for a cup of tea. Back in the car I took a look with great admiration at my thesis. I looked again. The binder had got all the pages mixed up and none of it made sense.

Back to Nottingham, I found the binder who sorted it all out and eventually I handed it in with a minute to spare.

I waited and wondered. Would I get it? At last the letter came. I had been awarded the degree of Master of Education. It was 1977. I had begun my Bachelor's degree in 1965. I should have mentioned that three copies of the thesis had to be handed in. One went to the Archives, another to the Departmental Library and the fortunate graduate was given back his copy. I had decided to graduate in absentia. I went up to the university and collected my copy of the thesis. I toured each building of the university which I had frequented during my time there and said a positive goodbye. I swore that the university would never see me again. I have never returned to this day. However, I must say that I owe a great debt to the staff and my fellow students at Manchester University. They helped me to fulfil an almost impossible dream.

I took my thesis home with me. It was the culmination of twenty-five years study. I had begun, you will remember, at Abbots Langley in 1952 with Latin and English. I went back home to my bungalow. I built a bonfire in the back garden. I set my copy of the thesis on the top of it and set the fire alight. I had the happiest two hours of my life as I watched it burn.

Mary was horrified and rightly so after all she had done. With shame I borrowed the copy from the library and had it photocopied. So sitting on my bookshelf at this moment is a photocopy of the thesis. I don't often look at it but I do look at the certificate proving I am a Master of Education. In fact it is on my bedroom wall, a reminder that I am not altogether dim. Thank you, Mary.

Second Interlude

The Territorial Army

Taking up a lectureship at Mary Ward College meant I would have to live outside my community and live alone. Again God stepped in. By joining the Territorial Army I received the finest training for what is called the individual apostolate, i.e. working alone.

Back in 1961 when I was told that I couldn't do missions and retreats, I asked the Provincial of the day if I could go into the army as a chaplain. During the four years in the army as a soldier I only ever came across one army Catholic chaplain. I thought I had the skills for this role and that it would be a very fulfilling apostolate. He assured me that I was needed to teach and that he couldn't release me for the army but he gave me permission to join the Territorial Army. This simply involved one night a week at the local Territorial Army barracks, one weekend a month and fifteen days camp each year. For the next fourteen years I used that fortnight as my annual holiday. We went to many places, many of which were in Germany. It was in Bielefeld that the incident occurred that prepared me for the necessary change in my lifestyle if I was to take up the position of lecturer at the College of Education. I was sent to do my 'camp' at a British Army of the Rhine camp in Bielefeld. My assignment was to help the local army padres so that they could take a break

In the Salvatorian religious life the emphasis is on community. We lived very closely together, we ate together, we worked together, in what is called common apostolates. Few Salvatorians lived alone or worked on an individual apostolate which the new constitutions allowed reluctantly. The nearest community house to Mary Ward College was 150 miles away in Chester and so to take up the lectureship it was necessary for me to move out of the community. The nuns who ran the college had offered me a flat over the chapel where I could live until I found more suitable accommodation and this is where Monsignor McMillan and the army came in. Wherever I went for my army camp in the first few years I would take over the chaplain's quarters. These were normally well furnished and kitted-out one-man flats suitable for a person of captain's rank. The officer could dine in the Officers' Mess but normally because of the flexible nature of his work the man would look after himself. He had to be independent to do his work properly. Thus I began to ease my way out of community living to living on my own. Apart from brief spells during holidays I have continued to do this to this very day. Though belonging to a community with strong ties and regular visits, most, if not all, of my apostolic works have been in the field of individual apostolates. That I have been able to do this I owe to Don McMillan who was the first person to show me how.

It took me over two years to become a Local Acting Unpaid Lance Corporal when I was a soldier. When I was accepted for the Territoral Army I was commissioned Chaplain 4th Class Royal Army Chaplains' Department (RAChD) with the rank of Captain immediately. Six years later without any effort on my part I was promoted to Chaplain 3rd Class with the rank of Major—Field Officer rank if you please. I was entitled to wear 'scrambled egg' on the peak of my cap and wear a crown on my shoulder. I served fourteen wonderful years in the TA and met some wonderful people. In the RAChD I met some really genuine holy men of all denominations whose sole concern was their love of God and the welfare of the men and women in their care.

Nothing in my experience as a chaplain in the TA could have been more different to the nine years I had just spent as a student priest. But my experience as an 'OR' (Other Rank) in the war years was the finest preparation for being in the Terriers with officer status. Many were the experiences we suffered and enjoyed and many the incidents embedded in my memory.

There was the night in Germany when I was called out to visit somebody who was to have an emergency operation thirty miles away, yes, thirty miles away and it was three o'clock in the morning. There was a business conference of some sort and an Englishman attending it had suddenly been taken ill. I was the only English-speaking priest in a very wide area and I was asked to go and see this man. He had been told there was a fifty-fifty chance of recovery and he was terrified of dying. I had no transport of my own and so I called out the duty driver. He was none too pleased, especially when he discovered I was the Catholic padre and we were going thirty miles to attend another Catholic. This driver was a regular soldier and he had just come back from service in Northern Ireland where he had seen all the troubles there first hand. To him all Catholics were pigs or 'tegs' as I think they were called. He spent the journey telling me what he thought about them in no uncertain manner. I said nothing as to say anything more would have been to add fuel to the fire.

We arrived at the hospital and the patient was waiting for us. He was obviously in a terrified state and was walking up and down just waiting for me. The driver saw this and saw me take the man into a waiting room. I heard the man's confession and gave him the sacrament of the sick, the sacrament that used to be known as the last rites, and had a good chat with him. After about fifteen minutes he was very calm and serene and ready to accept whatever was to happen to him. The driver saw him as he came out of the room and he couldn't believe his eyes. The patient was smiling and seemed a different person all together. 'What on earth did you do to him', he asked me as we drove off. I told him about the sacrament of the sick and the sacrament of reconciliation (confession), and all the way home we talked about the acceptable face of Catholicism. God knows, he had seen the unacceptable face. As I left him and thanked him for taking me over he simply said 'I shall have to rethink all my thoughts about the Catholic Church.' So that was a good night's work done.

And then there was Popsie. This story should carry a Government health warning. I was at an annual camp with a particular Unit which shall be nameless, for reasons which will become obvious. Midway through the first week two of the junior officers came to see me. They were obviously a little nervous and became more so as they began to speak. They told me that they wanted me to know that the Commanding Officer would be having his popsie visiting him at the weekend. This was before the days when having a 'partner' is seen as acceptable by some.

They wanted me to know so as to avoid embarrassment should I meet her. This didn't disturb me too much as there was going to be little or no scandal in such an environment—jealousy perhaps but not scandal!

Well, on the Friday the Commanding Officer came to see me. He too was looking nervous. He began with, 'the other officers don't know anything about this, Padre, but my popsie is visiting me this weekend. I hope you don't mind.' It was good of them all to be concerned about my feelings but I had got so used to nefarious activities of all sorts by this time that this almost seemed respectable. She duly arrived in a nice little red mini (I refer to her car!) and I was introduced to her. In fact, I was invited to drinks with the Commanding Officer and the lady before they went off to discuss whatever Commanding Officers and their popsies discuss. Oh, by the way, did I tell you that the Commanding Officer was married?

A year went by and I was at a dinner night when I happened to be seated very close to, guess who? The popsie of course! There was no male in attendance and after the dinner I spoke to her. She was in tears. During the course of the year she had been ditched, evicted from the flat she had been living in and the car taken back. I have to say she was a lovely person and didn't deserve such treatment. BUT, popsies everywhere beware!

On another occasion I was attached to an Engineering Unit and our annual camp was at Blaenau Ffestiniog. The Unit took over the single-track railway that had been restored by amateur railway enthusiasts and was in action during the summer months mainly for the use of tourists. This was great training for the Unit and there was a Church of England padre attached to them along with me. We had little to do during the days when the men were training so we volunteered our services. We discussed what our respective roles should be and just by chance almost, it was decided he might be best suited to stoking just in case his future destination might require this and I stood on the footplate blowing the whistle – giving warning to people. That was one of the occasions when the padres got on really well and there wasn't the slightest tension the whole fortnight. It wasn't always so, sadly. I mentioned before that padres always had officer status and we received the King's Commission. But though we carried the rank we were not 'real officers' in the strict sense. We were priests given the rank so that we could gain access to all ranks be they privates or generals. Most of the time we were highly respected. This respect was earned for modern chaplains by Fr Willie Doyle. During the First World War he had thrown himself on a hand grenade to save the lives of the nearby troops. Of course he was killed on the spot.

It is interesting that in the army traditions are born from simple incidents which become legends and are incorporated into the particular regiment's folklore. There is the well-known story of the regiment that drinks from finger bowls before their meal on their dinner nights. This tradition goes back to the dinner attended by King George VI. It is said that he was at dinner with this regiment on one occasion. Finger bowls were handed around after one of the courses and one of the junior officers thought it was for drinking from. As he put the bowl to his lips everybody looked at the King to see his reaction to such unseemly behaviour. The King, aware of this, and to save the young officer from later censure took up his finger bowl and drank from it. Thus the tradition was born.

In a similar way the action of Fr Willie Doyle inspired respect among the troops which is still evident to this day. I have walked into an Officers Mess lounge and seen the general stand up to greet me. Naturally all the other officers followed suit. But sadly some padres forget they are priests and expect by right the respect due to an officer of field rank. There was one I knew, who would report a soldier for not saluting him. But such padres are rare.

And it wasn't only the officers who showed respect. I went into the NAAFI once and sat at table with some squaddies as the other ranks were sometimes called. I was in uniform but without my clerical collar. We got talking and the language was colourful at times. After a while we reached the stage of, 'what mob are you with?' I told the chap next to me I was a padre. There was a hush and he turned to his mates and said, 'Eh, watch your language, he's an effin' padre.'

Talking of generals I remember one who was the guest of honour on one of our dinner nights. Guests of honour were always treated with great respect and the freedom of the bar was theirs for as long as they stayed. On this particular night the guest of honour was a really friendly person and happened to be a Catholic. It was a Saturday night and I was drinking G and Ts with him as one does with generals when he asked me what time Mass was in the morning. I told him it was at 8a.m. followed by breakfast. 'I'll be there, Padre', he said in a general's accent and off I went to bed. I could see he was settling in for the night with his G and Ts and I doubted very much if he would be up for Mass. Sure enough 8a.m. came on Sunday morning and we were all ready for Mass. But no sign of the general! I waited a little while and I thought, would I wait any longer for a corporal. I decided I wouldn't so why wait for a general and I began Mass. I was sitting in the mess enjoying my full English breakfast though it wasn't called that in those days—just a 'fry-up' —when I heard a bellow. 'Where's the padre?' I got up and he said, 'I thought you were saying Mass at 9a.m. Padre.' 'No,' I told him, '8a.m. and I've just finished.' I don't know if he expected me to say another just for him but he accepted it. And that was the beauty of it. The more senior the rank, the less privileges they expected from the padre. Rather they were great allies in helping the troops.

I remember another general who was guest of honour on one Saturday night. It was considered highly disrespectful to leave before the principal guest at the end of the evening but this good man looked as though he was settling in for the whole night—remember free drinks, etc. Well, I knew I had to be up for Mass in the morning and so around 2a.m. I went to the Commanding Officer and asked to be excused. He refused but I exercised my right as a padre and said I had Mass in the morning and that I was leaving. I went and excused myself from the general and he understood as one would expect. So I went to bed and enjoyed a trouble-free night. Not so junior officers if they left before the principal guest. I remember one lieutenant who went to bed and the other junior officers went and lifted the bed with him in it and brought him back to the mess and dumped him in front of the general. There was a lot of horseplay at those dinner nights but thankfully I was able to maintain a dignified distance.

Every camp brought its own memories, some joyful and some sad. There was one where a really tough-looking sapper was breaking his heart crying. He was missing his boyfriend back home. This was before the modern-day attitudes towards such behaviour. It reminded me of the time when I was on guard as a soldier with rifle and fixed bayonet during the war. One night about midnight a civilian who was working at the camp came to visit me with a mug of steaming tea. It was delicious until he started asking me if I was lonely 'out here on your own'. It suddenly dawned on me that I was being solicited. I must confess that every time I see Dad's Army and Corporal Jones with his fixed bayonet, I think of that night. 'They don't like it ...'

Padres were normally attached to a brigade and would go to camp with the units of that brigade. Eventually all padres were posted to Military Hospitals. Each Unit not only had its share of highly qualified consultants but also the highly qualified nurses of the Queen Alexandria Nursing Corp. (QA). This meant that all the camps had their share of males and females. It certainly enlivened the Mess and dinner nights were much more respectable in terms of conversation—until the port was served and the senior female officer would get up and lead the ladies to the drawing room. That's when the dirty stories, as I have mentioned earlier, were told. But I used to attend one unit where there was a particular female officer who would goad me at the bar about my religion. She was quite a senior nurse in her own hospital. She was an atheist and would throw question after question at me. My time with the Catholic Evidence Guild came in very handy and I was able to bat them without too much difficulty.

For a while I didn't come across her for some reason or other and then one day I received a letter from her asking if we could talk at the next camp.

We got together and she said out of the blue, 'What do you have to do to become a Catholic?' Talk about St Paul on the road to Damascus! I found the address of her local church and she went there for instruction. I only met her at camps and lived on the other side of the country from her so I couldn't do it. It was a long time before I heard from her again and one day I received another letter from her inviting me to receive her into the church. She had received all the required instruction and she became an ardent Catholic. She played a large part in her local church and even began to give talks on medical ethics. She even gave such a talk to a group of bishops. As they say, it doesn't do to play around with God. Let him into your life in any way and he has a habit of staying around.

In addition to the compulsory attendance required to retain membership of the TA, there were opportunities to serve over and above the call of duty. Sometimes the regular chaplains would take advantage of this and use the TA padres as supply priests if such were free. It enabled them to go on leave knowing that their people were in the hands of experienced padres. This was of mutual advantage as it meant the TA man getting a paid holiday in beautiful parts of the world. I used to supply for chaplains in Germany when Donald McMillan was the Senior Chaplain. I mentioned him earlier in that he trained me more or less to live on my own outside community. I would occupy his flat while he went away. The first time I did this he met me at the airport with two other chaplains and they gave me a great welcome. They showed me the ropes, introduced me to people who would be of assistance to me and in general I was made to feel I was really wanted. Remember, they were regular full-time padres. Father McMillan belonged to the Clifton Diocese and the other priests were from Liverpool. One of them wanted to be a Para Padre and spent all the hours God sent to train for this. He eventually qualified and served with the Paras in Northern Ireland. One day back in Aldershot he went to his car, opened the door and was blown to bits. The other priest was taking a car to a mission station in Africa and was killed in a simple car accident. Fr McMillan went on to become a Senior Chaplain to the army with the rank of Monsignor and died naturally just a year or so ago. Heroes, all three of them!

It was on one of these supplies that I discovered I could speak German. It was a beautiful summer's afternoon and Donald's secretary, Christine, invited me to her home in Bielefeld for the afternoon. There I met her husband and we sat on the veranda in the blazing sun drinking beer and raspberry flavoured schnapps. He couldn't speak English and I couldn't speak German, or so we thought, but you know, as the level of schnapps in the bottle dropped and the crate of beer seemed to empty we began to communicate freely with each other—I think in each other's language.

As I mentioned earlier, before we became attached to the RAMC and the Military Medical Hospitals, padres were normally attached to a brigade and went to camp with different units each year. So one year it might be the infantry, another the engineers or the signals, etc. A great ally to the padres at these camps was the medic, the doctor. Like the padre he tended to be a spare part until some emergency or other and we had to devise ways to avoid having to go on the exercises with the troops. So we would have a so-called 'support services conference' which usually meant a drink at the local pub or some such which. However, sometimes we got caught out. I had made friends with a psychiatrist on one camp and we were having one such conference one afternoon. After a drink the psychiatrist stretched out on a stretcher in the ambulance we had with us and decided to have a 'kip'. Suddenly there was a clamour as two medical orderlies rushed to the ambulance, there was a pretend emergency on the exercise. The two men dived into the front seats, started the ambulance and drove off at high speed. The psychiatrist hadn't closed the back door and you can imagine what happened. The ambulance whizzed forward and the stretcher whizzed backward with the psychiatrist on it. He came an awful cropper on the hard ground. But we had a good laugh that day, I don't suppose he has forgotten it any more than I have.

But the laugh was on me on another occasion. I was with my own unit now and we were practising evacuating casualties from the battlefield by helicopter. Pretend casualties on stretchers were strapped on the landing blades of the helicopter and off it took with the blades above whizzing around. I was watching this nonchalantly when I noticed people were looking at me. They had run out of 'casualties' and were waiting for me to volunteer. I was about to find something to pray for or a sermon to prepare or even conjure up a war wound when I noticed some of the QA nurses were volunteering. Well, what could a man do? For King and country not to mention self respect I volunteered and was strapped to the stretcher and then strapped to the outside of the helicopter. Just as we were about to be lifted up to heaven knows where the sergeant said to me, 'keep your eyes closed, there's a lot of grit whirling about'. 'Stupid man', I thought. What ever made him think I was even going to blink. The things we priests do for the Faith!!!

I wonder if the medics thought I was getting my own back the day I attended one of their high-powered conferences. They used to have these sort of in-service training conferences and I went to them as a gesture of goodwill. I would sit in the auditorium smoking my pipe and, in general, looking interested though rarely did I understand what was being said. On one of these occasions my pipe had gone out and I took my matches out to light it. There were no ashtrays about so when I had lit my pipe I blew the match out and put it back in the matchbox. A few seconds passed and suddenly there was a whoosh and a burst of light. The match had not gone out and the box was on fire. A number came to me afterwards and thanked me for the welcome diversion. I seem to be prone to 'not putting fires out' as you will see when I come to talk about my time at Ystradgynlais.

Time moved on and I had served fourteen years with the required number of camps and I was entitled to receive the Territorial Decoration, a prized medal. It was one of those treasured moments when I read in the London Gazette that this had been awarded to me and I have it among my treasures in my glass cabinet for all to see. A padre was only allowed to serve up to a certain age. He was expected to be as fit as the fittest man for padres were expected to be able to go into the front line at a moments notice. My time was up but I managed to get three annual extensions until finally I got the extension which was endorsed, 'for the last time'.

A dinner was given in my honour by my unit as indeed was given to all retiring officers. I remember Beef Wellington on the menu. The Commanding Officer made a speech and he said they had intended presenting me with a silver plate as was the custom. 'However,' he said, 'being a priest you would probably have used it to take a collection.' Instead I was presented with a pewter chalice-shaped mug inscribed:

Dick Sullivan
from
THE OFFICERS MESS '202'
1977

PART FOUR

Working in the Field

It was as though everything I had experienced in my life up to this stage was a preparation for working in the field apart from one thing—my lack of knowledge of women. Mary Ward was a Baptism of Fire in the fields of lecturing, of counselling and of working with women.

Time spent at Mary Ward College was a period in my life where success followed success and the pattern of my future apostolic life was determined in a relaxed and caring environment. From Lecturer I became Senior Lecturer, from counselling to teaching counselling, and my skills in preaching were really put to the test in preaching week in and week out to a totally female congregation all with intelligence above the average.

Previously, on a visit to Ireland I had kissed the Blarney Stone and was given a certificate proclaiming I was being sent forth with the gift of eloquence. At Mary Ward College I was given a certificate from the Students Union proclaiming me an honorary woman.

The time at Mary Ward was the happiest time of my life. It was also the time when I began my journey which would lead to the office of Provincial by being elected to the Provincial Council.

16

Mary Ward College

How did it all begin? I have mentioned that I had received permission to resign from Christleton Hall to continue my degree course full time. I was about to start my final year. I have already described my poor results on the BSc course where I was limping along from one year to the next. Little did I know that the Professor of Zoology had it in mind to advise me that unless I gave up my teaching work I wouldn't get my degree. Another example of God moving in mysterious ways!

It happened like this. You remember that I was living in the Manchester University Jesuit Chaplaincy. An assistant chaplain there would sometimes join a team of priests and give three-day residential retreats to young sixth-form ladies from a nearby convent school. They would go away to Nottingham to a College of Education belonging to the sisters and there they would make the retreat together. On one of these occasions the assistant chaplain was ill and had to back out. He asked me to go in his place, which I did. I had never related to girls in my life before. Apart from asking two girls out before I entered religious life I had hardly spoken to women. I had never given retreats in my life. The team gave me a few tips and within twenty-four hours I had taken to it like a duck to water. Ever since then most of my pastoral work has been among women.

In fact, resulting from that retreat came requests to do a number of three-day residential retreats for sixth-form girls and often these would lead to counselling face-to-face during the retreat and by correspondence afterwards. On my wall there is a painting of a boat out at sea sailing along peacefully and calmly. It's not a particularly good painting but the reverse side is more interesting. It is just plain hardboard and is dated September 1976. It is inscribed 'With best wishes from Advanced 6, Loreto College' and is signed by thirty-two girls. Just think, they will be in their early fifties now. I stand in front of it sometimes and wonder what has happened to them over the years. What a wonderful book that would make. But I am digressing.

One evening I was chatting to the principal of the college and she was telling me about her students and the life of the college. I told her about my background, mentioning in passing that I had a degree in zoology and psychology. The next day she came to me and told me there was a vacancy in the college for a lecturer in educational psychology and would I be interested. Well, is the Pope a Catholic? I contacted the Provincial and received his permission to apply. On 1 September 1970 this black sheep in the family of white ones was appointed lecturer of educational psychology at Mary Ward College. Thus I was seen as psychologist and it was here during the following year that I was made an honorary woman, but more about that later.

I think I mentioned that when Christleton Hall closed the priests in the community were scattered to other houses and some were sent to open a new house in Birkenhead. The province didn't want to lose touch with our Liverpool friends and benefactors who had been so good to us over the years. Part of our Rule is that if a member is engaged on an individual apostolate, he continues to belong to a Community. So I

remained with what was left of the Christleton Community as they moved to Birkenhead. But it was not long before I was to pack my bags, leave the security of the Community and take up residence in a flat above the Mary Ward College Chapel. By this time I had graduated and received my Diploma. I was raring to go.

Mary Ward College had been purpose-built as a College of Education in response to what was thought the likelihood of an increasing population. Colleges of Education, formerly called Training Colleges, were going up all over the place and ours was in the beautiful countryside of Keyworth between Nottingham and Leicester. Many a time I would sit with a colleague outside a pub in Melton Mowbray with a pie, onion rings and a pint and watch the hunt go by.

It was a Catholic college, called Mary Ward after the founder of the Loreto Sisters. There were approximately 550 female student teachers, though occasionally a man would get in. In fact, by the time it closed in 1977 the male population had risen to four. What would have happened had the college continued in existence, the Lord only knows. Most of the students came from Loreto schools in the UK and Ireland and from the Sisters' Colleges in Mauritius and Gibraltar. Loreto schools were so called because they came under the jurisdiction of the religious order known as the Loreto Sisters. This was one of the three religious orders founded by Mary Ward over 400 years before. The student population was approximately fifty per cent English and fifty per cent Irish. The latter came from the south and the north of Ireland. It was a time of great hostility between Northern Ireland and England and

The power of an onion

180

this was to make itself felt in the college from time to time as we shall see later. Members of the academic staff were all professionals and varied male and female to about fifty per cent of each.

The College had all the usual amenities but being a Catholic college the focus of the campus was the College Chapel, a magnificent building that formed the gateway to the college as a whole. In addition to the library, the gym, lecture halls, tutorial rooms, etc. there were a number of halls of residence on the campus. A Student Union building guaranteed an excellent social life and it is a credit to the sisters that there was invariably an atmosphere of harmony all round. Disruption came from time to time through students having men in their rooms after 11p.m., the biggest sin a student could commit. Regularly at 11p.m. a member of staff, usually a nun, lay staff safely at home by then, would go around checking. An observer could see men jumping out of windows to escape the wrath of the good sister. On one occasion a nun caught a man racing across the campus and thought; great, 'Where have you come from?' she asked hoping to find the name of the recalcitrant student. 'Sheffield, Sister', the man answered as he ran away leaving a very perplexed nun behind.

I have often been asked what was the happiest period in my life. I have been very fortunate in having made friends in all my varied apostolates. While they have all been very fulfilling in terms of my priesthood, I have to say that I have never been so happy in my life as the days I spent at Mary Ward, as we affectionately called the college. I lived with 550 girls for seven years. I worked with them, ate with them, listened to them and counselled them. Eventually some asked me to officiate at their weddings.

Talking of their weddings reminds me of the day when I went on a honeymoon. It was in Ireland. Where else? It was soon after my ordination when a friend whom I had worked with before entering religious life asked me to do his wedding. The Nuptial Mass was to take place in Belfast so I thought I would make a holiday of it and go on to Dublin after the wedding. It so happened the bride and groom were to spend their honeymoon in Dublin and when he heard of my plans the groom offered me a lift. He absolutely insisted on it so after the reception and speeches were over, the couple got into the front of their car and I slipped into the back covered with confetti. Fate had decreed that we should be spending the night in the same hotel. I was sitting having my breakfast the next morning when down from the nuptial suite came the groom. His first words were, 'Well that's finished my chance of becoming a priest.' We had worked together in HM Customs and Excise before I entered and we used to talk long and hard about vocations. At one time he had toyed with the idea of becoming a Trappist monk but he settled for marriage instead – sensible fellow.

And so I entered the world of women, a brand new lecturer in psychology and a student counsellor to boot I had the world at my feet, not to mention 550 young ladies. My first perk, so to speak, was the acquisition of a brand new car. Can you imagine it? Brand new. My superior realised I was on a very good salary which would go to the order and that it would increase annually. He also realised that I would have to tour Nottingham and the local countryside visiting schools on teaching practice and so would need wheels, as they say today. My nephew worked in the motor industry at this time and he was able to get me a discount on a mini, a brand new,

MOTHER RICHARD SULLIVAN

green mini. What joy, what rapture. As I've said, I lived in a small flat above the chapel situated on the campus and so was easily available to the student population, most of whom lived on campus. I would have my lunch in the common re-fectory with the staff and students, separate tables of course in those days, but I would cook for myself in the evenings. My reputation as a cook spread very quickly and quite by accident. My kitchen was next to the stairway that joined the chapel to the balcony. One evening I was frying an onion when one of the sisters went by. She smelt the onion and must have been very hungry for she thought I was cooking a fantastic meal. She quickly spread the news that the new priest was a terrific cook. My reputation was built on an onion. I'm still living off that onion. Whenever I entertain guests to dinner I fry an onion before they arrive. Invariably they say as they come into the house, 'Gosh the food smells good' —the psychology of cooking!

There were three priests on the staff, two in the theology department and myself in the education department. In return for providing a chaplaincy each of us had a beautiful bungalow. I will never be able to thank the Loreto Sisters for the opportunity they gave me, for, from the day I started at Mary Ward in 1970, I have been associated with students in one form or another. As I said, I have taught them, counselled them, married them, baptised their children and in some cases given First Holy Communion to their children. Sadly, from time to time I was called upon to bury them. Thankfully only a few.

But let me go back to the beginning when I arrived full of enthusiasm in my brand new car. The staff were fantastic especially in the Education Department. They had never had a priest in their ranks and although the Department was the largest in the college, after all, every student had to belong to it, it was seen as the poor relation by the professional academics. They took me under their wing and taught me the ropes. There was another lecturer starting with me in the Education Department, a nun, and we very quickly became aware of the 'in group' among the lecturers. Doesn't every organisation have them? But this nun was very clever. She and a few others quickly formed an 'out-group' and thus survived the day.

It was Sister Mary Anthony who continued my education on the subject of the mysteries of the 'gentle sex', begun all those years ago by Pat Mackrell. The Education Department was very proud to have a priest in their ranks—theology had two and they were only a small department compared to education. Every student had to join the Education Department whereas theology was an option. Obviously it was the largest staffed department. Sr Anthony, one of the staff, took me under her wing and showed me all the ropes, not to mention the pitfalls, of working in a college of education and a female one at that. She was one of those sisters with a heart of gold but the appearance of a matriarch of the forbidding kind. Students were very wary of crossing swords with her. But only God, to whom she went some years ago, knew the number of girls she helped on a one-to-one relationship. Secretly she was worshipped but no one dare show it. Essays were always due in by midnight on certain days. Now why midnight was the closing time I shall never know for there was never a tutor who would be around to receive those handed in at the last minute. They were normally surreptitiously pushed into pigeonholes the following morning—except those destined for Sr Anthony. On a day when a particular education essay was due in she would walk around the campus well into the night and early morning and note whose light was still on. Noting the room number she would be watching for the relevant essay the following morning wanting to know what time it had been handed in. I remember the first and perhaps most valuable bit of information she gave me. It was to do with the marking of essays. She told me to watch for the student who would burst into tears if you had to chide her about a particular piece of work. They will play on you, she would say, and plead all sorts of female illness, which, you being a man, will not understand. Armed with such guidance I awaited my first student whose essay was poor to say the least. I sat there telling her what I thought of it and, sure enough, she burst into tears and began to tell me that she had not been well. From a great height, after all I was a lecturer, I said, 'Oh yes, I have been told about students like you, it won't make any difference.' Would you believe it, she had been seriously ill and had only recently returned to the college. She ran out of the room shouting, 'I was told about you. Students either love you or hate you, and I hate you.' And she was a nun! Actually I met her recently and she is now on a priests' assessment team – getting her own back no doubt. Thankfully, the reputation didn't last long for I was quick to learn. In fact, partially due to that incident and the guidance of Sr Anthony, I became one of a very rare group—an expert on women. The Student Executive endorsed this one night in the Union bar over a drink. So impressed were they with my expertise they solemnly elected me to be a woman— 'honoris causa'.

But that was still to come. My 'induction course' by Sister Anthony reminded me somewhat of my battle inoculation course in the army and approaching the lecture hall to give my first lecture reminded me of the time I stood outside the Fourth Form classroom dreading my first lesson. But this was so much different. They were GIRLS. They were students and all over eighteen and here was I about to lecture on a subject I hardly knew anything about—again! This was 'Individual Differences', sometimes called 'personality theory'. I stood outside the Lecture Hall, took a deep breath and thought of Nellie Lemon. Nellie (she always wore a yellow beret, hence her name) had been one of my regular hecklers at the Pier Head in Liverpool. I thought none of these could be as bad as her. I was right. They gave me a great reception and applauded my lecture. Before very long some of the 'wags' in the front row would be holding up mini placards with numbers of approval on them as I was actually lecturing, like they do announcing the scores in skating. We became great friends and I think I had an advantage over the lay lecturers in that as a priest I had more than one role. I was lecturer, counsellor and chaplain. There was never role conflict, quite the reverse.

So as they got used to me and saw that I was fairly harmless, a social life developed around the bungalow. Each week I would invite a group of students round for dinner, and curry would normally be on the menu. In fact I became quite an adept at making curry. I used an old army recipe and we had many a happy evening in that bungalow. Sometimes the girls would bring me flowers and I dreaded walking to the campus the next morning. I would see one or two gardens which were conspicuous by the absence of flowers!! Then there was the night as they were leaving, one of them stood outside the bungalow and shouted up to the bedroom, 'goodnight Mary' for all the neighbours to hear. Of course, there would be no Mary, or Joan, or Eileen or anybody else for that matter.

Being ladies and aware of social skills I would be invited to their residences in return. I remember the first one when six nuns who were students invited me to supper. I suppose we were all a bit nervous but they were especially so and I wondered why. Towards the end of the evening they got very fidgety and gradually drew from under the bed a large parcel which they asked me to accept. In all my years with students I have received many gifts. My many homes have been full of them and I have never thrown one away. On my mantelpiece is a little rubber tortoise playing a guitar, it is about one inch in height and is now about forty years old. A little girl of three years of age gave it to me when I was an undergraduate in Manchester. If I get depressed, I walk around the house and look at all the artefacts and they give me so much comfort. Well, this one from the nuns was the very first. I opened it and it must have been the first flat pack as well. It was a coffee table. The four legs had to be screwed on and when it was assembled it proved to have a decorated tiled top. They had made it themselves and it has sat at the side of my bed from that day to this. Remind me to tell you of the present of a bike I received at Keele University when we get there.

There was another occasion when I was sitting happily in a student's room having dinner with her and her friends and the door burst violently open, a wild-eyed student stormed in and stood in front of me, 'You're supposed to be having dinner with us' she shouted. Oh dear, I had double-booked. This happened to me years later when I double-booked an appointment at Keele. I got home to find my dinner on the doorstep. They didn't do things by half at Keele.

One evening at a curry supper we were talking about the social life at Mary Ward and it was felt not enough happened in the way of outdoor pursuits. My ears pricked up and I immediately thought of Brede and the Bunk House. These students were going to be teachers and I thought how wonderful it would be if they could be trained to take children up the mountains, so I contacted Brede in Dieniollen in Snowdonia and we organised outdoor-pursuit courses. Students would go for a week and be introduced into rock climbing and abseiling, etc. At the end of the week they would be given a certificate to confirm they had done the course. Brede had become a professional mountain guide by this time and, of course, the Government paid for the courses. Now I could keep you here all day with stories from those courses. But what I want to tell you is that as a result of those courses my trips to Snowdon began again, only this time with adults.

But we went further. On two occasions I took more than thirty students to Switzerland, each time with a member of staff. On the first occasion I made the mistake of asking Brede to come with us as our guide. She nearly killed half of us the way she strode up those mountains in avalanche conditions thinking we were as strong and skilled as she was. There was one day when a student disappeared up to her neck in the snow. I was smaller than she was so I couldn't go to her rescue so two or three of the taller girls had to go and drag her out. The next year I took over the guiding and we walked gently up the slopes of the Matterhorn — and I have a photograph to prove it. Just before we leave the mountains let me tell you about Brede. She and her husband are both mountain climbers and Brede in fact has become a Himalayan guide. She took part in the all-female expedition up Annapurna, a mountain almost as high as Everest. She has eight children and would guide even in her eighth month of pregnancy. Now she guides in Europe and the Himalayas. Each year she takes children referred to her by the courts up Everest to Base Camp with the hope they will discover a way of life different to the one that got them into difficulties and ended them up in court.

Looking back, which is what this book is all about, I am amazed at how quickly I settled in at Mary Ward. But I nearly blotted my copybook early in the very first term.

As you can imagine I wanted to ingratiate myself with the staff, such learned people, and one day I asked a member of our department to lunch. I asked this particular person around to lunch because he talked posh and had a very commanding appearance. Only later, in fact, last year here in the heart of the Chew Valley did I learn that all the people in the South West speak posh – well with a Somerset accent which seems posh to Evertonians. I first learnt to cook in the army when I used to open a tin of bully beef and serve it with water biscuits to my officer. Then, as I have mentioned earlier, during my days at Christleton Hall I would assist Brother Joseph in the kitchen when sometimes he would cook for as many as forty at one time. Of course I also had the story of the onion to boost my confidence. So it was with a certain amount of confidence that I invited this good man around for lunch. I decided to make a pork-pie salad using only the best of pork pies—Melton Mowbray of course. We lived in Melton Mowbray territory and were able to get the real thing. He was a good guest and ate everything before him, thanked me, and left rather hurriedly I thought. The next day he was nowhere to be seen. He was off with stomach trouble. Nobody had told me that you don't warm pork pies. Thankfully he recovered and we still laugh about that meal when we meet, alas all too seldom.

This time it was the staff who were forgiving and I was able to settle down to a long and happy association with them culminating in my being elected President of the Senior Common Room for three years running.

Many are the stories I could quote about my time at Mary Ward. Before I move on to Aston let me recall just two more.

The college had a very good drama group and each year they would put on a particular play, sometimes light hearted like a musical, sometimes, rather serious like a Greek tragedy. There was normally a three-line whip for everybody to attend these plays and on one occasion, when a Greek tragedy was being performed I was sitting at the back with some students. We were not terribly into Greek tragedies and rather softly, so we thought, we were having a bit of a laugh at the actors' and playwright's expense. Little did we know that the Principal of the college was sitting behind us taking in every word we said. The next morning both lecturer and student were summoned to what was known as the 'bridge of sighs' on which was an office where the Principal reigned supreme. We were called upon to give an account of our behaviour.

Actually, that student wasn't very particular about going to Mass on Sundays but the night before the finals she could be seen in the chapel fervently praying for success. One 'good' girl went up to her and said, 'You don't think He's going to listen to you now do you?' But he did and she passed. What about that for mercy!

My last story concerns Bernadette Devlin who was a Member of Parliament at the time and a great orator in the House. Her sister, Sister Mary was a student and while she was at Mary Ward the time came for her to take her final vows. She asked me if I would officiate at the ceremony and I said I would. The night before the event Sister Mary casually mentioned her family would be coming over for the ceremony among which, of course, was Bernadette. You could have knocked me down with a feather. She had just recently given a speech in the House which was considered to be the finest since Disraeli or William Pitt and she was only twenty-one. I had my tuppeny-ha'penny of a sermon ready to give in her presence. Well, I did it and, fair enough, Bernadette was a trouper. She came to me afterwards and said what a good sermon it was, praise indeed, eh?

It was while I was serving at Mary Ward College that I began to take part in the politics of my religious order. For some reason I was beginning to get noticed for my outspoken views at Community meetings principally on the subject of the Second Vatican Council's call to renewal. Like all societies there was a governing body which in the case of our Province consisted of the Provincial and four Provincial Consulters who assisted him. The Provincial and his Council were elected for a period of three years which could be extended to another three if the members so wished. In 1971 I was nominated for the office of Provincial but I felt I was not ready for such a responsible position and declined. However, I was elected to the Council with responsibility for renewal. In 1974 I was short-listed for Provincial but failed to get elected. Instead I was re-elected to the Council. In 1975, while I was still at Mary Ward College the priest who had been elected Provincial was elected to the General Council in Rome. Another election had to take place in the Province to elect his successor. I led the short list this time but was pipped at the post by six votes. Again I was re-elected to the Council. Later in my story I shall tell you more about religious politics but at this stage in my life, fourteen years after being ordained priest I had served on the Provincial Council for seven years.

But back to the College! We, staff and students alike, were devastated one morning to be told that the college was to close. The Government must have underestimated the popularity of the pill because the population was falling not rising and all these newly founded colleges of education were now no longer needed. It became the policy of the government to gradually close the colleges or amalgamate them with local universities. I am not sure if there was a policy of last-in first-out but our college was among the first to close. Princess Anne had opened it in 1970 and we received notice of closure in 1974. We were allowed to run down and in fact the doors closed for the last time in 1977. We protested and even got our young recently elected MP to support our cause. He asked a question in the House but to no avail. However, it didn't do our MP any harm. He eventually became Chancellor of the Exchequer, the one and only Kenneth Clarke.

I have described elsewhere the personal tragedies which hit the now redundant lecturers. Each solved their own in their own way. I was now a Senior Lecturer and I thought I would have no difficulty in being accepted for a position, tailor made for me, being advertised by a college of education in Newcastle. How wrong can you be?

17

Aston University and Birmingham Polytechnic

If ever there was an illustration of a stark contrast between two institutions it was that between Mary Ward College and Aston University. From a Campus college of 500 female Catholics I found myself in a population of 17,000 students of different nationalities and different faiths. At a time of great student unrest I became a student chaplain at Aston University and the Birmingham Polytechnic and eventually also a visiting lecturer at Aston.

Success continued in that I found myself lecturing in human communication on the Counselling Diploma course, the BSc course and even the MEd course and I was consulted by members of staff on theological issues.

At the same time I was employed by the student body giving me access 'by right' to all the students.

My 'light' was beginning to shine in the SDS Province when I began to appear regularly on the short list for the election of a new Provincial.

My education continued. I learnt a lot about the different

cultures of our former Empire and became aware of a world outside Europe.

Sadly, the unpleasant side of ecumenism reared its head during this time. A team of two Anglicans, one Methodist and myself did not see eye to eye on the most fundamental theological matters and our work among the students was hampered as a result.

This period ended with my being appointed to a Salvatorian parish and a return to the Community. I presumed I had left the secular student world behind.

It was Father Malachy, the Provincial of the time, who saved the day for me. Christleton Hall had by now been sold and Mary Ward was soon to follow its fate. It was not a matter of one or two redundancies. The whole staff had to go. That the college was allowed to run down gradually gave a breathing space for staff to find other employment. Ironically, staff and students were competing with each other for the same vacancies in the schools and it was the students who had the advantage. For the salary a school would have to pay for a redundant lecturer it could employ virtually three probationers. Some at the peak of their careers with children in private schools suddenly found themselves unemployed with little hope of finding employment in education, their chosen profession. Some tried transferring their skills to other professions such as running a sub-post office, founding a rare-books business or even in one case starting a frozen fish and chips business – from his garage!

I must have been the most rare species in the country at that time—a redundant priest. I answered a couple of advertisements for other colleges which seemed to be safe from the axe. I remember one in the North of England, the vacancy was exactly for the position I had had at Mary Ward. There was another applicant being interviewed with me. I knew I would not get the post when he bustled in, full of enthusiastic energy, and asked if he could wait in the library, the implication being he could continue his reading while waiting. He had on a pink waistcoat and a multi-coloured jacket and was really clued in. Interview technique had not been heard of then but he seemed to have a good idea about it. A few days after the interview I received a letter from the Sister Principal informing me that they had given the position to the pink waistcoat, 'not without looking over our shoulders and wishing we had two posts to offer'. The letter reminded me of the rejection slip of a Chinese publishing house that returned a manuscript to its author explaining:

We have perused your manuscript with exceptional relish. We fear, however, that if we were to publish your outstanding work, it would be quite impossible for us to ever again publish another work that would not come up to its standard. And we cannot imagine how any other work will be its equal in the next hundred years. So, to our deepest regret, we are compelled to return your incredible composition. And we beg you a thousand times over to pardon our short-sightedness and faintheartedness.

In my simplicity I had presumed that a simple priest who happened to be a senior lecturer with a psychology degree and a diploma would have been snapped up. How little I knew and how much I had to learn. I had worked so hard to get my qualifications as per the Provincial's instructions and here was I at the age of fifty, an unemployed priest. It was 1976 and the college had one year left. Staff were being made redundant gradually and now it was my turn. And it was just at that point I received what proved to be a life-saving letter from Father Malachy.

'The Archbishop of Birmingham would like you to go and see him. He might have something for you.' That was the gist of the letter. I rang the Archbishop's secretary and I was invited to tea. George Patrick, as the Archbishop was affectionately known, was President of the Hierarchy at that time. Cardinal Heenan had recently died and Cardinal Hume had yet to be appointed. George Patrick Dwyer was a character in his own right. His greatest claim to fame was winning the spitting competition in his schooldays. A man after my own heart, I really enjoyed that tea with him watching him spitting out the crumbs from the rock cake he was eating. It occurred to me how awful it would be if he did that when taking tea with the queen. As President of the Hierarchy of England and Wales, it was part of his duties to meet with Her Majesty from time to time. We hit it off the moment we met, the Archbishop, not the queen! And I like to think we became good friends over the few years left for him to live. In fact he resigned the Archdiocese in the same year as I was to leave it to go to London. Sadly, he died soon afterwards.

So we were sitting there having our tea, he happily spitting crumbs all over the carpet, when out of the blue, he said, 'I am looking for somebody to go to Aston University.' He had obviously heard that I was available. He asked me if I would be interested in taking up the chaplaincy there. At that time the chaplain also looked after the Birmingham Polytechnic. Altogether, there were 17,000 students from 74 different countries. There was no mention of lecturing at this time. He told me about the unusual nature of gaining admission into Aston and what I would have to undergo to be accepted. Aston was a declared secular university so Christian chaplains

as such had no place within the structure. The Students' Union realised the value of chaplains as cheap counsellors, if nothing else, and so 'employed' them as part of the student support service. To be appointed one had to submit to a rigorous interview by eleven students and a member of staff appointed by the Union. It was a non-denominational appointment so the priest was not allowed to call himself a Catholic chaplain. In fact, from the first, the Students' Union had let it be known that they did not want denominational chaplains, or indeed a Catholic chaplaincy or Chapel. To say Mass the chaplain had to hire a room on the various university and polytechnic sites, this meant that he said Mass at a different Mass centre each day. The university and the poly between them were centred on ten different sites. The system was that the Students Union appointed the chaplain for a four-year period (the first being probationary) and followed up with two-yearly interviews to extend or curtail the post. They decided the 'job description' but paid no salary. They usually liked more than one Catholic chaplain to choose from at the interviews. Of course, not all priests get on with students and few would have tolerated the interview procedure. So it was virtually impossible for the Archbishop to find more than one priest to go for the interview. What happened in practice was that a genuine applicant would apply and the Archbishop would ask one or two others to go for the interview intent on failing. Sometimes the Student's Union would get wind of this and deliberately appoint the 'wrong person' and actually reject the real applicant.

Once a chaplain was accepted at Aston the Archbishop then appointed him to the chaplaincy of the polytechnic. This was the appointments system for the polytechnic. So the one priest became chaplain to Aston University and the Birmingham Polytechnic. The Archbishop told me all this and I agreed to go for the interview being encouraged by his concluding words, 'Go for the interview but take no notice of the b...s.' The Archbishop had had to deal with the Birmingham bombings and the scandal caused by one of his priests supporting the IRA so I expect he felt that students were small fry.

I should have seen the signs from the very beginning when one of the interviewing panel asked me how I felt about changing sides, the implication being, of course, that as I had been a lecturer at Mary Ward College I would now be a member of the Student's Union. Remember these were the days of the student unrest. Another member of the panel dropped a real clanger at that interview by asking me where I got my Doctor of Theology. He obviously hadn't done his homework nor read my CV. The TD after my name stands for Territorial Decoration, a prized award for doing more than twelve years continuous service in the Territorial Army. And it was fairly obvious that more than those two members of the panel knew very little if nothing about the work of the chaplain. 'Are you prepared to take part in the cut and thrust of intellectual debate', one of them asked me. I remember being at a Chaplain's Conference once and somebody, a new boy, asked what exactly is a chaplain and what does he do. In fact this is one of the greatest mysteries of life. A chaplain of some experience stood up and said a chaplain is like a piece of grit inside the oyster of the university. He sits there as life passes over him and through him hoping one day he will form a pearl. As regards being able for the cut and thrust of intellectual debate I discovered that most of my life as a chaplain was spent helping young ladies, 'How do I get a fellow, how do I get rid of a fellow, etc.', not to forget the poor men who actually tried to understand the women and came a real cropper. I remember writing a paper during my time at Aston called, 'The predatory aspects of the male and how they fall into the trap'. Experience has proved that University work is about ninety per cent relationships and ten per cent intellectual debate. Fortunately, in answer to the student's question I was able to assure him that I was well capable, having by now a BSc in psychology and zoology, a Diploma in educational guidance and was halfway towards obtaining a Master's degree, not to mention being an honorary woman.

They must have been satisfied with me for they appointed me, and my 'sleeping partner' heaved a sigh of relief and went back to his very comfortable parish.

Although Aston was not a campus university they did have a residential campus out at Handsworth. Some of the accommodation there was reserved for staff and the Archbishop bought one of their flats. I moved in on my fiftieth birthday, 2 June 1976 and began what proved to be the most difficult apostolate I had ever experienced or would experience to this day. Read on.

In point of fact there was a moment when I thought I would never start the Birmingham phase of my life. The Arch, as an archbishop is affectionately called, God bless him, was well aware of the difficulty of a chaplain's life at Aston and made it his business to see to the chaplain's welfare. On one occasion he decided to show me around Handsworth Campus, the flat I was to occupy, the chapel in the grounds, students' quarters and so on. I met him at the Cathedral and his secretary drove us to the Campus. We had a lovely day and I was very impressed with the fatherliness of the archbishop, 'any time you feel alone or lonely just call in for a cup of tea'. And he meant it. On our return journey we were chatting away merrily when suddenly the car screeched to a sudden halt, skewed to the middle of the road and nearly turned over. My first thought was, my goodness, I can't go wrong. To arrive at the pearly gates in such distinguished company is bound to be a winner. Straight in, I thought. My second thought was what will the headlines be tonight. We had been driving along keeping to the Highway Code and the car in front of us stopped dead without any warning. He had been approaching traffic lights too quickly when they changed colour and he had done an emergency stop. Our driver never expected this and swerved suddenly to avoid running into him thereby veering to the middle of the road and in fact nearly hitting the traffic lights. It says a lot for the skill of the archbishop's secretary that the three of us were not killed. The archbishop was very calm and understanding about it, and the secretary? He is now bishop of one of our larger diocese.

But start I did, moving into the flat soon after this little escapade. It was a completely new flat totally unfurnished. Nobody told me where to get furniture or even gave me the money to get any. There wasn't even a bed. Fortunately I was still attached to Mary Ward College as I was to continue my contribution to the BEd course that had been started the previous year. I mentioned that the sisters had provided each of the three chaplains with a completely furnished bungalow. Now, they were to sell them and when they heard of my predicament the Principal told me to take anything I needed from the bungalow which I had been inhabiting. I took the lot. The Principal, God bless her, said that it was very comforting to the sisters to know that I would have around me the things which had contributed to my being so happy in my previous post. It sort of provided a continuity. Now twenty-seven years later I still have some of that furniture with me. This was a Godsend because there was very little money attached to my 'job'. The Students Union gave no salary but the Provincial had negotiated with the archbishop a remuneration for my services. This went into my Community as did the redundancy money I was beginning to receive from Mary Ward. Add to this the stipend from Mary Ward for continuing with the lectures. So my Superior was very generous with me and I lacked for nothing that I needed. I still belonged to the Christleton Community though this had now moved to Birkenhead. I had my own room there and I would repair to it for the Christmas, Easter and Summer breaks. I loved returning because it was such a change from the almost hostile environment of Aston and the Poly.

The student population I was about to serve was the complete antithesis to the Mary Ward population. There were 17,000 to begin with from seventy-odd different countries. They were from all sorts of religions and none, and of course male and female. At Mary Ward there had been 500 females all Catholic from about five or six countries. I mentioned above that strictly speaking I was a student chaplain available to all the students. There were four chaplains in fact, two Anglicans, one Methodist and myself. We were funded and supported by our own denominations so we tended to give our own 'flock' priority without neglecting others who might need and want our services. So my first concern was to find the Catholic student community. I looked for the Cath Soc. There had been no such thing at Mary Ward as it was one big Catholic Society. I am not sure if the Cath Soc found me or if I found it. In fact I wouldn't ever have known there was such an organisation had it not been for my own student experience at Manchester—another example of God preparing me for what lay ahead perhaps? Anyway I was told where to find them. I knocked on their door expecting to be met by droves of students and all I found were two girls on the floor making posters about times and places of Masses. They introduced themselves to me as the presidents of the Aston Cath Soc and the Poly Cath Soc. I had forgotten there would be two. I discovered the two Cath Socs did everything together and pooled resources. But for student grants and suchlike they had to have two separate identities with two executive bodies. Sue and Karen were wonderful. They explained Catholic student life on the two campuses and how they operated. They organised events and even the Masses and the priest was invited along as their guest. Remember I wasn't strictly 'their chaplain'. I helped them with the posters and then drove them to the various sites to put them up. I learnt there were quite a few sites between both institutions and that I would be travelling to a different one every day with my Mass kit to say Mass. At some sites there would be quite a few at Mass. At others there might be one. The posters we put up were to advertise Mass times and venues and then the most important event for me in the academic year—Freshers' Fair.

Freshers' Fair was a bit like a market. A huge hall with stalls and advertising bunting all over the place. Students standing on tables, chairs or whatever, calling for the freshers to join their society, free gifts offered, etc. Every society in the university was on display, each assuring the unsuspecting fresher that it was the best one to join. Some had no problem attracting students, such as the sports societies. Others looked as though they had been smitten with the plague. Such tended to be the religious societies at first. But gradually, after students had joined the obvious societies they would wander around and some would bump into the religious societies by default. The more attractive the stall and the more extrovert-type students running it the more likely they were to attract the unsuspecting fresher. It was a unique opportunity for putting your wares on display.

This was my first experience of a Freshers' Fair and I was really impressed by the enthusiasm of the Catholic students to get members into their society. It was very difficult to attract students into the society after Freshers' Fair as they would have already joined other societies. We had the advantage of advertising the society at Mass for those who had missed the opportunity before. Again we had two Freshers' Fairs to attend, one at the university and the other at the poly. Thank God we did very well and in my first year the very few already in the society attracted a good few to their number. One difficulty we had was lack of premises. To say Mass on Sundays I had to use the Methodist chapel on the Handsworth Campus at nine o'clock and then travel five miles or so into the University Campus at Gosta Green for a twelve o'clock Mass. Thank God, Chris Blakely, a town-planning student, would meet me and help me to carry all the paraphernalia needed to say Mass including about forty hymn books. I used the Martin Luther King (MLK) centre for this. The MLK was a hall used for a variety of student purposes and we had to book it well in advance. I remember one morning I went in and found it being used by a group practising yoga. In the evening I would say Mass at the College of Education in Edgebaston. This was very difficult for I was totally dependent on a room being available. I remember one Sunday evening the only room I could use was the utility room and the only table for an altar was an ironing board—with the iron chained to it. Housekeeper's trust in students! As the iron was obviously on view to all the congregation I thought I'd better bring it into my sermon and I spoke about Mary doing the ironing. Some really wise student came to me afterwards and reminded me that 'they didn't have irons in those days, Father'.

I said it was difficult having to use borrowed halls and rooms for our Masses. Some students were used to the traditional church and preferred to go to Mass in local churches rather than come to the student Mass. So I never knew the Catholic population at any one time. And there was always the problem of transporting the Mass kit and hymn books around Birmingham. I have to say that if it wasn't for the Cath Socs at Aston and

the Birmingham Poly we could never have achieved all we did in the five years I was there. From those two students I met on my first day our societies grew into quite a large group and they would travel across Birmingham sometimes using two buses to get to social events which I held from to time in my flat on the Handsworth Campus. And not only that but Catholic students brought their non-Catholic friends.

Let me tell you a bit about my homemade pastoral psychology of those

200

days to increase the numbers at Mass. On the Handsworth Campus there was a beautiful Methodist Chapel. I don't know whether it was built as part of the Campus or that the Campus was built around it. I suspect the latter. We had an early morning Mass there on Sunday and for my first Mass there the congregation numbered seven. God knows how many hundreds of students were asleep in the nearby blocks of flats. I thought this wouldn't do. Now being a very observant fifty-year-old I noticed that in that congregation was a very lovely young lady with long red hair. Also there was a very handsome adonis sort of man. Well, I was already spoken for but I discovered that these two were unattached and also very popular in the community. So on my 'rounds' I sort of let it be known that these two would be at Mass on Sunday mornings. Incidentally, I told them I was doing this. Would you believe it before I left Handsworth there were more than forty students at Mass each Sunday. I think our organist secretly believed that it was her playing that did it but I didn't let on. (Actually she was probably right.) Our organist, Kathleen Hermole, was a

polytechnic member of staff who taught music and she was unstinting in the help she gave me with the services. In passing I might add that as the years passed I married the lady with the beautiful red hair and the handsome man but not to each other!

The MLK was a different ball game. As I said, this was an ecumenical hall used by various denominations and other groups for serious discussion or services. It was the main venue for the Catholic Mass on Sundays. The Cath Soc Committee would get the hall ready and we had a small folk group which would prepare the liturgy in terms of what hymns to sing and so on. More often than not the hall would be full and it was really comforting to see quite a lot of students at Mass without anybody watching to see if they were going or even reminding them to go. It is useful to mention here that often a parent would ring me up or write to me to see if I knew if her child was practising. Needless to say such a parent was referred to her/his own child. I remember one year when a mother brought her daughter up to begin her course. She introduced the girl to me and said, 'I have shown her where to go for confession in the Cathedral, Father, now I want you to show her where to go to Mass.' I took the girl aside and told her about the Mass times and so on but I also told her I would not be checking to see if she was there or not. I said to her, 'I'll see you when I see you.' The next time I did see her was three years later on her graduation day as she trooped across the stage to graduate. That reminds me of a nice story about a mother who was very distressed because her three children would not go to Mass. She cajoled them, begged them, even bribed them. She prayed hard but still they wouldn't go. In desperation one morning she got down on her knees and prayed, 'Dear Lord, I beg of you, please remove whatever it is that holds back my children from going to Mass.' There was a long pause, then, suddenly there was a big puff of smoke—and the woman vanished.

So as I was saying, the two Cath Soc Committees would get together and organise a common programme for the term. Each year the chair of this joint committee would alternate between the poly and the uni. It worked very well and the programme would include student dinners at my flat, outings of various sorts starting in freshers' week with a visit to Stratford-upon-Avon. There we would visit the Dirty Duck for lunch. I remember a couple of us eating our sandwiches with a pint on the terrace outside the pub. The Barmaid came out and very sharply said, 'You can't eat your own sandwiches here.' So we thanked her for this information and swapped them with each other! Early in the first term we would organise a 'rough weekend' to Snowdonia, sleep in an old bunkhouse and climb Snowdon. You will remember I began this in Christleton days and I continued it until the end of my days with students. It was in Llanberis that I met Brede and her family. I must have called at her house for water or something. When she discovered I was a Catholic priest she invited me in. She told me she was an Irish Catholic and anytime I wanted to say Mass in her house I could use her kitchen. I took advantage of that many times over the next few years.

By the time I reached Aston, Brede had moved up into Dieniollen, a little village on the side of Mount Snowdon and it was her bunkhouse that we used each year. It was very rough but ideal for new students to get to know each other, many a relationship was formed on Mount Snowdon and not a few weddings took place in later years. Brede keeps cropping up in my story as there was never a year since I took those fourth formers to Llanberis that I did not take students of one age or another up the mountain. We shall meet Brede again when I tell you about my time at Keele University.

Talking of Snowdon though reminds me of one occasion when we were climbing and a mist suddenly came down. I had warned the students about this. You could be climbing in good weather without a cloud in the sky and a mist would appear almost from nowhere. I instructed the students that if such a thing happened they were to remain exactly were they were until the mist lifted. To walk on in the mist was to court serious danger. Well on this occasion I was walking with a student when a mist came down. We stopped, sat down and began to talk. The student was not a Catholic and he began to tell me his problems. We were alone and he unburdened himself of very confidential matters. After a while the mist lifted and we discovered to his dismay that we were surrounded by the other students who had taken my advice and stopped. To this day we don't know how much they heard.

There were many outings and dinners on the Cath Soc programmes and many a story I could tell you about those days. There was the time when after a function in the Students' Union, three students were going home to their Hall when they noticed a branch had fallen off a tree and was lying in the main road obstructing traffic. Being publicly minded citizens they stopped and dragged it on to the grass verge. Just as they were doing that a police car happened to pass by. They stopped and went over to the students. Of course the students had been drinking and the police arrested them for carrying an offensive weapon, namely the branch of the tree. I had to go to court to give a character reference. While waiting for their case to come up I sat listening to a case concerning a lady who had stolen a TV set. The magistrate reached across the bench and asked her in an almost patronising voice, 'Tell me, Madam, why did you steal it?' She didn't seem put out at all and replied calmly, 'Because I didn't have one.' Sounded fair enough to me but then I come from Liverpool!

I think the culmination of the Cath Soc programme during my time was when we actually managed to 'man' a float in the Rag Day procession. You can guess the subject of the float of course, Vicar and Tarts.

Chaplains get some strange jobs. I suppose it showed the measure of one student's trust in me when she asked me to help her out one St Valentine's day. She had been engaged to this person but it hadn't worked out so they split up. But she had begun to have second thoughts and wanted to convey this to him. St Valentine's day seemed to provide the right opportunity and I agreed to help, little realising what I was letting myself in for. That morning at 6.30a.m. there was I carrying this huge panda across the Handsworth Campus to deliver it to the lucky man. Thank God nobody saw me or my reputation would really have been in ribbons. Past students of those days will forgive me for not including all the stories, all the wonderful memories of those days here. Time and space prevents it but they are ever present in my mind.

Sadly the memories are not always pleasant. There was the day when one student was found in bed with first degree burns having spontaneously combusted. He had gone to bed at night and suddenly burst into flames. Research has been done since then on the phenomenon of spontaneous combustion but then it was a complete mystery. Various theories were put forward about this incident, one being that he had washed his feet in potassium permanganate to harden them before going to bed. It was thought that this had reacted with the nylon sheets and created a spark. There were a number of attempted suicides each with their own story. Hardly a day passed without somebody trying to solve her/his problems with a razor blade or drugs. Thankfully most of them were attention-seeking exercises and there were very few successful suicides when you think of the number of students—17,000 from seventy different countries. Occasionally we could laugh together, the potential suicide and his/her saviour, after the attempt had gone wrong.

I have stressed the role of Cath Soc in my settling down and working out a modus operandi at the poly and the uni, but most mornings I could be found in my office in the Aston Student's Union. I must say that the Student's Exec could not be faulted in their care for the chaplains. They gave us office space, indeed an office each, and a large room were we could hold our meetings within the Union. While this proved very difficult for a priest accustomed to his own chapel and premises it served a very valuable purpose. We were seen by the students to be one of them rather than one of the staff. As long as we didn't try to adopt their lifestyle but maintained the role of chaplain we were accepted and more than just Catholics would visit me in my office with one problem or another. We were included in all things happening in the Union and there was a great esprit de corps between the elected members of the Union and the permanent staff. Many a drink we would have together and counsel each other bemoaning our lot.

I had a base at the Polytechnic North Centre which was their main site and I would appear there for some time at least once a week and by appointment on other days. Although the population of the polytechnic was much greater than the university there was less work to do at the polytechnic. Most of the students lived at home and were what could almost

be described as day students. There was no community as such though this has been rectified since and now there are polytechnic Halls of Residence. In fact as I write this the poly is now the University of Central England with its own full-time chaplain and independent Cath Soc.

Before I leave the students I must tell you about the weekly Mass we had at the University Students' Union. I would say Mass at noon in this big room next door to my office, there would be a goodly number attending, and afterwards they would come into my office and eat their lunch. I don't know how it began but spontaneously, at some time we began to talk about religious issues and the teaching of the church on particular subjects. It would develop into a debate with a member of staff who attended regularly, playing the devil's advocate to my orthodox teaching. We had some very interesting debates which would go on well beyond the lunch hour and sometimes students would miss their lectures, so interested were they. At times there were subjects other than religious discussed, such as the latest relationship, and those staying behind were by no means saints. I remember one occasion when a girl wearing a very flimsy dress complained about the cold. Immediately another lashed out, 'You wouldn't feel the cold if you had some clothes on.' God bless them – saints and sinners alike.

I think what constituted the biggest difficulty at Aston was the ecumenical scene. There were four 'student' chaplains: an Anglican lady, an Anglican priest (this was before the ordination of women in the Anglican church), a male Methodist and myself. I had worked with an ecumenical team in the army but there it was more a matter of live and let live and let each get on with his own flock sort of thing. I had met some wonderful men, and some not so wonderful, in the Royal Army Chaplains' Department. But this was totally different. We were expected to work together irrespective of denominations. Moreover we were not described as Christian chaplains by the Union and we were expected to take on board visiting Muslim and Jewish Ministers. It would have worked if the Christian chaplains were united but sadly we were not. The lady and myself worked very well together and our theology was orthodox and almost uniform. She was a great support to me when I first joined the team and we are still good friends.

My first intimation of trouble ahead came when I was informed that the chaplains had a working weekend away when they could enjoy each other's company away from the scene and catch up on latest developments in theology. This seemed OK until I discovered that the book we were to discuss on my first weekend away was going to be *The Myth of God Incarnate*. The very title sent a shudder down my spine and I can honestly say that that weekend was one of the unhappiest I have ever spent. One of our chaplains described himself as a non-theist Christian and another was very much into transcendental meditation which was becoming all the rage. From the discussions of that weekend I began to fear that two of my colleagues had a very different approach to Christianity than myself and I could see a lot of trouble ahead. My fears were borne out when a member of the Christian Union (CU) came to the lady and myself and wanted to know if all the chaplains were atheists. I have to say that the other two were good and sincere men and apart from our respective roles we were good friends. But as a team we couldn't find much in common and we virtually went our own way. And of course the student body suffered as a consequence. I had a very strong Catholic Society which gave me great comfort and support and there was an Anglican Society which supported the lady. But there were the groups outside of the 'official pale'. The Christian Union grew strong because of the divisive nature of the chaplaincy team and they more or less disassociated themselves from us. From to time we would meet and, depending who was on their Executive at any one time, we got on with them or we didn't. The crux came for me when two of them came and told me that I was a Satanist and urged me to pray with them to be saved. I had given a tongue-in-cheek talk on astrology to the Cath Soc and their vicar at home had given them a list of scriptural texts condemning me. I still have the letter with the texts. They were first-year students eighteen years old and I admired their courage to come and tackle someone who had been on the road a long time. When they said I must pray with them I invited them to Mass. A year later these two young ladies came to see me again and apologised. They told me that during the year they had grown up. I was very impressed with them and I invited them to tea and we became good friends. One of them married an Anglican vicar eventually.

Then there was the lovely Zulu Anglican. She was tiny and when she was introduced to me as a Zulu I said to her that I thought Zulus were huge. She took it in good form and in fact got her own back not much later. Her name, shall we say, was Dorothy. I met her in the street and mistakenly said, 'Hello Joan.' Quick as a flash she replied 'Hello Robert.' I told her my name was Richard and she responded, 'You whites look all the same to me.' We too became good friends. She is now a politician back in her own country.

So 'on the ground' the students of all denominations worked, prayed and played together. The discordance was in the team, which was a scandal.

University is about balance

And so time moved on. During my time at Aston, I was invited by a Northern bishop to investigate a claim that a house was being haunted. Time prevents recounting the details but it was alleged that 'Spirits had appeared in this house'. I decided to take a few students with me to see their reaction. One of them was the man who attracted the good ladies to Mass earlier in my story. He agreed to come and with bravado proclaimed that the only spirit he would see would come out of a bottle. But on the morning we were to leave he cried off.

It was also about this time that a past overseas student invited me to his homeland for a holiday. I declined at first but after a few such invitations he actually sent me the air ticket. I went and had a memorable week with him in the sunny climes. On the day of departure my host arranged for us to leave for the airport at a certain time.

I like to get to an airport in plenty of time and the time suggested that morning seemed rather close to take-off time. I put this to him and he told me not to worry, 'I have never missed a plane in my life', he said. But I was still anxious and he could see this. This time he said to me, 'You will be alright, I know people at the airport.' But this was not good enough for 'doubting Thomas' and I asked him again if we could leave earlier. Exasperated, he almost shouted at me, 'Will you stop worrying. I own the airline!' And he did. He had certainly done well! I half hoped then that I might miss the plane and get a private jet home.

I mentioned at the beginning of this chapter that when I was appointed as chaplain there was no mention of my being given an opportunity to lecture. I loved lecturing and missed it very much. After about six months I went to see the person in charge of the Counselling Diploma course that the university offered, and asked him what was the chance of my helping him out. I was prepared to do it purely for the love of lecturing. However he pointed out that I didn't have a Master's degree and was not qualified to teach. Moreover, there was no vacancy in the team. As you know I was working on my Master's and when I was awarded the degree I toddled off to him and proudly showed it to him. Fair do's, he said he could use me but there was no money to pay for an extra lecturer. We compromised and he paid me in book tokens. This was better for me than money. I would have had to hand the money to my community but with the tokens I was allowed to buy professional books and so build up a good library. I will tell you a little later how I fared giving lectures and conducting tutorials on the BSc course, the Diploma in Education course and the Master's course. But first let's have a respite and I'll tell you about my battle with the university sexologist.

This good man first came to my notice at the Freshers Induction at Aston. Each of the support team were asked to address the new students and tell them of the help available should they have any problems. I was speaking for the chaplains on this day, the University Counsellor was there and various representatives of the numerous support services available. Each one would begin, 'I am so-and-so and if you have a problem on such a subject go and see…' In fact there were so many, one student stood up and asked, 'Whom do we go to see if we haven't got any problems?' The point was well taken. Anyway the University Doctor was on last and he told them about the forms to fill in and where the clinic was, etc. And then he went on to tell them that he was a sexologist and if they had any sexual problems to go and see him. He then proceeded to give advice to the first years on various sex problems they might encounter. When he got down from the podium I went over to him. 'I didn't think they needed a priest here until I just heard you speak,' I said to him. 'Who are you?' he asked with some exasperation. 'I'm the Catholic Chaplain', I said to him with great pride. 'Hum,' says he, 'I might have guessed.' Thus began a relationship which lasted until I left the university. Once I began working on the counselling diploma course I was asked to join the official university counselling team. Of course, the Doctor was the Chair of this and he wasn't at all keen on my joining. He was convinced that I would be bringing all my Catholic ethics into the counselling suite and that I would be giving advice rather than practising the client-centred counselling that was in vogue at that time. He reluctantly agreed but he could find nothing to complain about though I understood his fears. I had given a day's course on counselling to Catholic priests in the recent past and had great difficulty getting them to accept the client-centred approach to counselling. Priests are trained in a moral system based on absolute values and Karl Rogers theories seemed to militate against this system wholeheartedly. I won't take up your time here giving you an account of his theories but rumour had it that he had in fact embraced absolute values himself before he died.

And so back to my academic work. You may have wondered why I am writing predominantly about the university and giving little acknowledgement to the polytechnic. From what I can remember I said Mass each day on a different site of the poly and spent one morning a week in the North Centre in case students wanted to see me. Apart from that the only contact I had was with the poly Cath Soc and that was in conjunction with the university Cath Soc. Nearly all of my non-student-contact time was spent at the university in a variety of roles. One of these was as a visiting lecturer. Mr Richard Nelson Jones and Dr Windy Dryden ran the counselling course between them and I was invited to join to teach communication skills, I did this on the BSc course to small groups and found great satisfaction in it. I taught the same subject to the counselling diploma course students. I was more involved with these students because we used to practice the skills in a role-playing situation. I also taught communication skills to those taking their Masters degree in educational technology. One day I was giving a lecture and there was a student in the back row of the lecture theatre talking. I looked over and realised he was a student I had taught as a boy at Christleton. I almost instinctively shouted 'take a hundred lines' when it dawned on me we were all a lot older than in those days and students of that calibre don't do lines. He came to me after the lecture and said to me, 'We both did very well didn't we?' Flippin' cheek!

I served five years at Aston and the poly. There was no fixed term of service but at Aston it was a four-year term and then the possibility of two two-year terms. I was into my fifth year when a letter came from the Provincial suggesting a move. Looking back it is incredible how much we did and how varied our work was. I have passed over my trip across the States at this time, my time as a guest at the Moscow French Embassy courtesy of a past Aston French student, the May Balls, my visits on supply to Norfolk where one day a parishioner was to save my life by noticing how ill I looked, and so many other things. Perhaps one day I shall write a book featuring Aston and the poly alone. I have enough material and memories to fill a few volumes.

18

Parish of the Precious Blood, Borough, London

I was appointed parish priest, local Superior and Prefect of students and was given a colleague to assist me. In the event it transpired that the house would take a long time to be transformed into a house of studies and during my time at the Borough my role consisted of parish priest only.

I found myself back in my own working-class environment helping the poorest of the poor in their journey through life.

We were inundated with ladies and gentlemen of the road, each with their own heart-breaking but, at times, breathtaking stories of life. I was to meet many who had succumbed to their failings and become failures, rejected people who had allowed themselves to become rejects.

I may have left the student world but they didn't leave me. A number of past students began to call and this trend has continued ever since to this very day. They were a great support at a time when things began to go askew for me.

I was not happy at the Borough for a variety or reasons and asked permission of the Provincial to return to the student world. Eventually, after twenty months, I left the Borough to take on another parish in Wales. Though the Borough people were wonderful it was a dark patch in my personal life.

It must have been about midnight towards the end of my first week at the Borough that I got my first sick call. At least I thought it was a sick call, in fact my first parish one ever, and so with great apostolic zeal I jumped out of bed, picked up my sickroom set, already prepared for such an emergency, and set off hoping I would be in time before she died. She lived about one quarter of a mile away so I arrived about 12.30a.m.

The lady who had rung opened the door to me. Fully dressed with a large whisky in her hand and a cigarette in her mouth she invited me in. I asked her what was the matter. Expecting her to want to go to confession and Communion I was flabbergasted when she said, 'Faver, I want to be a Jew.' That's why she had called me out at midnight. She wanted to be a Jew. I told her she wanted a rabbi, not a priest and offered to get her one the next day. She was in fact a Catholic though not too regular. Well, a few days passed and I got another call from her, again at midnight. This time I wasn't too enthusiastic. After all, I had been a parish priest for a week now and was very experienced. But I went and sure enough she had her double whisky and cigarette. So I asked her what she wanted this time and she began, 'Faver, I don't want to be a Jew now.' I asked her why and she replied, 'The rabbi keeps office hours'. The rabbi in question had obviously far more experience than me. Anyway this lady and I became good friends. My associate, Fr Charles and I would go and see her with a bottle of wine and we would have many a happy hour together. She was an incredible woman. She was a real rough diamond but as honest as the day is long—so I thought. I told her about the burglaries that were happening in the presbytery. When I visited her a few days later she told me not to worry about any more burglaries. 'I've told the boys to lay off the presbytery, Faver', she said. She had been to school with the Cray twins and McVicar and was in the know about who was doing what in the underworld. She would warn me when to watch for forged notes for she knew when they were coming on the market. And once, in a burst of confidence she told me that all her family had got to the top. She had just taken the wrong way. In fact her brother was a Savile Row tailor.

My happiest memory of her was when she called in at the presbytery one evening. She said she had one of those luxury artificial Christmas trees with all the decorations and would like to present it to the presbytery. You didn't look a gift horse in the mouth in the Borough so I gracefully accepted. When it was all up that Christmas, I invited her in to see how lovely it was. As we gazed on it in admiration she said to me, 'Faver, I think I should tell you, it's all nicked.' I should have expected it. She had started coming back to Mass but from time to time she would walk out during the sermon. She would ring me up afterwards and say, 'You got too near the bone that time, Faver. I couldn't take it.' She once told me that she would come to confession but, 'if a man knocked at the door tonight, Faver I would be in bed with him in a flash'. I left the tree up and she made me promise that I would take it with me wherever I went. It is with me to this day and every Christmas I put it up in my sitting room in her memory. She dreaded the thought of becoming fifty and soon before her fiftieth birthday she was diagnosed as having cancer. She went to Lourdes and wrote to me saying she had never been happier in her life. She wrote a poem about the Blessed Sacrament, which I publish in my newsletter every year around the feast of Corpus Christi. Here it is:

> I came late to the faith
> A stranger, searching
> From sorrow seeking
> Solace where it hid.
> An outsider, face pressed
> Against the window
> Looking in.
> And it seemed that I was bade,
> 'Enter and be still,'
> And in the celebration
> of the Blessed bread and
> wine, I saw a hand of friendship, and I heard
> 'In this sweet oasis of
> comfort, take your fill.'

This lady, and she was a real lady, died soon after coming home from Lourdes. Not all the saints in heaven are canonised.

I was to discover that the Borough was full of such characters of one moral persuasion or another, but let me go back to the beginning.

By 1981 I was beginning to feel the effects of the constant differences and tensions between the chaplains and their modus operandi at Aston. I was half hoping that the Provincial would contact me offering me another post. In fact I did get such an offer but it came from our own Salvatorian students rather than the Provincial. There were eight of them and

it was in mind for them to move to a house of studies in London from Abbots Langley. The Archbishop of Southwark and the Provincial had agreed a deal covering a very large presbytery in the parish of the Precious Blood in the Borough. This was the original Borough of London and full of history. The parish began at London Bridge, and included the Clink, the Globe, Dickens' 'playground' and, more recently, the Wobbly Bridge, Tate Modern and the Vinopolis and so on. The parish had been run for the past twenty-seven years by a Mgr Reynolds who was well-loved by his people. But the area was very run down and parishioners were leaving to find fortune elsewhere. As the parish numbers decreased so did the need for more than one priest and the presbytery had become too big to house that one priest. So our offer to the Archbishop came just at the right time. And, indeed, it came just at the right time for the students as they began to take up their studies at Mill Hill College and Heythrop, the Jesuit College of London University.

The presbytery needed a lot doing to it to make it habitable for a parish priest, his assistant and eight students. It was a three-storey house with a basement and those living on the second floor could watch the trains going past as they left Canon St Station for the south. In fact at one point the railway almost came into the church. We were not to know then that the Jubilee Line of the underground would be routed underneath the church. So it is now what you might call, 'a Railway Butty'. The quarters of the parish priest was the responsibility of the Archbishop and the quarters for his assistant and the students that of the Salvatorians. An assistant was needed because one priest could not fulfil the three roles of parish priest, Prefect of students and Superior of the community. So an arrangement was worked out between the archbishop and ourselves as to who would pay what and a contract was drawn up.

So, yours truly was chosen by the Provincial at the request of our students to be Superior, parish priest and Prefect of students. Fr Charles was chosen to be my associate. As it was still term time when we took over the parish I wasn't able to take up my appointment at the Borough until the September so Charles was the first Salvatorian there and ran the parish with the aid of a student, Brother Alexander McAllister. Charles had great experience in parish work and had spent many years on the missions so he was well able for this and when I tell you that Alexander became General Secretary of our Order later and I became Provincial it shows the calibre of the men who began this new venture.

BUT, and it is a big but, apart from Alex none of our student's took up residence during my time there. Plans had to be drawn up concerning the restructuring of the house and it was such a venture that when I left twenty months later nothing had been started. So for Charles and myself we ran a parish and were not called upon to fulfil other roles.

I took up my appointment on 8 September 1981. This was the feast day of Our Lady, and the birthday of our Order. Prior to taking over I decided to move my chattels down in advance and hired a van for this purpose. Some students came with me and I remember there was a lecturer as well, he who had helped out at the lunchtime discussion groups I mentioned earlier. We arrived about lunchtime and with great pomp I rang the doorbell expecting to be greeted royally. A lady opened the door a fraction, looked me up and down and then said, 'We don't want any more tramps today.' Honest. My first experience of parish work and my first response was, 'She'll have to go.' We eventually got in and deposited my luggage.

Rarely do I learn from experience. I duly arrived to take up the post on 8 September. I decided to arrive in the evening thinking the parishioners

217

would want to be there to greet me. I even expected there to be bunting. How stupid can a person get? I rang the doorbell and this time an African priest opened the door. When I introduced myself, he said, 'Oh yes, I was asked to wait for you to let you in. Father Charles is away on holiday.' Very soon after, he left and I was there in this huge empty house alone on my first evening in my very own parish. But help was at hand. About an hour after my arrival the doorbell went and to my joy opened it to find the archbishop himself standing there. He said he had called to welcome me to the parish. He stayed a little while and then left to attend an appointment. I learned afterwards that in fact it was as he was passing on his way to that appointment that he realised I was arriving that day and so called in. He told me this himself. But he did call and that was the main thing.

And so Charles and myself settled down to parish life. I had a lot to learn and thank God Charles was there to teach me.

Let me tell you about it and the wonderful people I met in that parish. My visit to Mary that night was the beginning of a real eye-opening chapter in my life. The burglaries had begun soon after Charles arrived and continued on a weekly basis for quite a while. In fact it was only when I told Mary about them that they stopped. 'I have told the boys to lay off the presbytery, Faver', and sure enough 'the boys' did. But we still had the occasional daylight burglary, as when out of the four bins I put out for the 'bin men' each week, two of them disappeared. The next morning a man came to me and asked me if I would like to buy a couple of bins – cheap. They were my own. On another occasion a 'visitor' came calling looking for money. We had a policy with the callers. We would give them food and tea and if they needed a bed for the night, we would give them a token to take to the local Salvation Army hostel. They would put them up and we would pay. This particular morning we gave this man his tea and sandwiches. In an alleyway next to our house there were a lot of leaves, it was Autumn, and he said, 'If you like to give me a shovel, Father, I'll collect the leaves for you.' Well, we thought this was very generous of the man and we gave him the shovel. A short while later I went out to see how he was getting on and there were the sandwiches on a pile of leaves and he had gone – with the shovel. And then the 'gentlemen and ladies of the road' began to call in earnest.

I opened the door one day to find Elvis Presley there. At least there was this man dressed exactly like Elvis, his hairstyle absolutely the same and his guitar over his shoulder. 'I'm Elvis Presley', he said. I looked at him and said, 'I'm Bing Crosby, come in.' He became a regular visitor but quite different than another who came in dressed in leather. As I said, I had no experience in parish work and I foolishly invited this man into the presbytery. He asked for money. I refused because of our policy of tea and sand-

wiches. We never gave money because there was a wine shop around the corner. Invariably if we did give money it would disappear into the wine shop almost immediately. I told this man our policy and offered him food and tea. He quickly drew out a knife and demanded money. As you can imagine, just as quickly I gave him some. Then there was the man who used to come on crutches and gratefully accepted what we had to offer. I followed him one day to find him tucking his crutches under his arm as he hastened to go to the next presbytery for whatever they had to offer. But the best of all had to be the lady who came looking for the fare to Newcastle-upon-Tyne. Those who came looking for money normally told the story that they had to get to Newcastle to see their mother or other relative before they died. It was always Newcastle for some reason. Well this lady wanted the money to go to Newcastle to bury her baby who had just died. I was at a meeting so a couple of students visiting at the time invited her in. She told them her story and showed them a picture of her baby in its coffin. They listened and shared a cigarette with her. She agreed to come back and see me as they couldn't give her anything. When she had gone they discovered their packet of cigarettes had gone with her. She came the next day to see me and showed me the photograph and asked for the money. I smiled at her and offered her tea and sandwiches. She smiled back and went on her way. She knew she had been rumbled. In fact, not only was she a lady of the road but also a lady of the night.

But these people were wonderful in their own way and they had lived. The stories they were able to tell about themselves were often spellbinding and one could only marvel at their stamina.

My goodness, the Borough was full of characters and in its time must have been one of the most active parishes in London. We had the Borough Pipe Band, Tommy Johnson, our own Pearly King who in fact became the Pearly King of Bow, the John Gerard Club and even our own primary school. I want to tell you more about these but first I must tell you about our Legion of Mary.

One of the parishioners, a lady I came to admire very much, was not too pleased when she heard that a university chaplain was coming to take over the parish. They had loved their parish priest as only Catholics can do and they were heartbroken when he left. Imagine after twenty-seven years to have a young long-haired university chaplain possibly with earrings and a ponytail thrust upon them! Well! They were not going to stand for that and this good lady wrote to the bishop to protest. Can you imagine her relief when, instead of a long-haired young priest with earrings and ponytail along came this fifty-five-year-old balding, harmless individual with not an earring in sight. She came to see me and said, 'We're so relieved Father.' She was Irish and didn't speak cockney. Two weeks later she came to see me and said, 'We don't know what we're going to do about you Father.' I had upset the Legion of Mary. These were a group of very strong Catholics any parish priest would give his right arm for. One day I asked this lady, the same who had written to the bishop, rather facetiously what the Legion did. I knew full well but I was having her on. 'Well, Father', she said, 'we are at the discretion of the parish priest.' So I said to her, 'Do you mean you will do what I ask you to do?' 'Certainly', she said. 'What would you like?' Again, having her on and I shouldn't have done, I said to her, 'I want you to disband.' Well, you could have knocked her down with a feather. But the real test of our relationship came when we were preparing for the outdoor procession of the Blessed Sacrament. I went down into the church the morning before to see if all that we needed was ready when I saw the Legion decorating the statue of Our Lady. I asked them why they were doing that and she told me that it was for the procession the next day. I reminded them that since the second Vatican Council no statues or pictures of Our Lady were allowed in procession or devotions to the Blessed Sacrament and consequently they were wasting their time. The emphasis had to be on the Blessed Sacrament and nothing else. They were most irate. I could see them thinking it over and then one came to me and said, 'Father, if Our Lady doesn't go, we don't go.' What do you think of that? Industrial action!

Being a male and weak before the gentle sex—they didn't know that I was an honorary woman—we reached a compromise. I agreed to Our Lady going as long as she was at the end of the procession. All was agreed. On the day of the procession I went out of the church carrying the Blessed Sacrament to join the procession already formed up in front of the church. Before the canopy which would cover the Blessed Sacrament the school-children were waiting—all four of them. Two of them disappeared a short while later when we passed a sweet shop. Behind the canopy was a van equipped with Tannoy system leading the Rosary and behind that at the end of the procession was Our Lady with all the parishioners. They had won.

Another winner was the lady who was unemployed and needed a job desperately. One day she came to see me to tell me she had been offered a job but she didn't know if she could accept it. The job was cleaning in a sex shop in Soho. She asked me if she could take it. She was a woman of great faith with a great love of God. Had I told her it was a sin to do such work she would have turned the job down, even though she needed it so much. I asked what she did in the sex shop. 'I dust these things, Faver', she told me. I asked her what she thought about when she dusted these things. She replied, 'I larf, Father.' 'Well', I said, 'I think it must be a very meritorious

221

thing to clean up a sex shop.' She went off happily. But what I didn't tell her was that I knew the shop she had been talking about. I had been there! Don't jump to conclusions now but read on. A Chinese student whom I had been counselling at Aston came to see me. He was a compulsive gambler and he had just moved to London. I asked him to show me the casinos where he gambled thinking it might help me in terms of background. We went to two casinos in Soho and when we came out around midnight, I asked him what he normally did after that. He said, 'I go to a sex shop.' 'Well,' I thought, 'in for a penny in for a pound,' so I went and saw the shop he visited. It was the very same shop in which this parishioner of mine was to be offered a job. Who says God doesn't prepare his priests for the trials ahead!!!!

Sadly it wasn't all sweet and honey. The John Gerard Club caused me many a headache. I began in the parish thinking to have such big premises in London was a Godsend and I had ideas of a youth club and all sorts of parish events happening there. There were some very happy and successful events such as the Monday Club when the elderly members of the parish met there for bingo and dancing on a Monday afternoon. There were also parish organised events which were very successful. It was at the club that I began to develop my very own parish priests' survival manual. Being the good people they were, the parishioners would want to buy me a drink whenever I was in the club and had I drank them all I would never have been sober. They knew I liked gin and tonic and they would ask the barman to set them up in front of me one after another. But they didn't know, and now it can be revealed, that I had an arrangement with the barman. Whenever he served me a gin and tonic he would put tonic only in the glass and put the gin in a bottle he hid under the counter. He would give me the gin to take home. Thus I remained sober and still had the gin later watching the telly. Sorry lads, but I did get what you ordered and paid for, God bless you. I developed other means of survival but I will tell you about them later.

But foolishly I organised a youth club without any experience whatsoever, it was for under-eighteens and we served soft drinks, etc. But unbeknown to myself the youth were smuggling in vodka which looked like water and had no smell. Riots broke out on occasions. On one such some youths had the club steward on the floor with an open razor at his throat. I was trying to keep the crowds of youth coming down the stairs to join in. I stood in the middle of the stairway with my hands on the banisters barring their path. They were screaming, 'Get out of the way, Vicar!' I knew then these were not parishioners but had just gate-crashed our club. Catholics would never call their priest 'Vicar', always, 'Father'. The police, eventually, asked me to close the youth club which I did.

19

Parish of the Sacred Heart, Ystradgynlais

The dark period continued when I found myself parish priest of a rural parish in the Swansea Valley. For the first time in my life I felt lonely and isolated. It didn't help that I had volunteered for this parish and it wasn't long before I began to think I had made a mistake. I had discovered at the Borough I was not given to parish work and now I began to long for the student world again.

The parish belonged to the Salvatorians so I was working in an officially approved Province apostolate but it was almost 100 miles to the nearest Salvatorian house.

Again the parishioners were wonderful and we did have a good community. This was overshadowed by the miners' strike of 1984, which caused long-lasting divisions in the Swansea Valley community.

Eventually I began to put out feelers about returning to the student world and one day I received a phone call from the Archbishop of Birmingham.

It was while I was at Ystradgynlais that my mother died.

'Mummy, there's a fire engine outside Fr Richard's house.' So cried my three-year-old friend who was very observant. In fact there were two and, I think, every fireman in the Swansea Valley. But they were not outside the house but rather the beautiful parish church. I had only been in the parish one week.

I never learn. Forgetting my Borough experience, I decided to arrive at the presbytery to take over my new parish at the weekend thinking people, off work, would gather in their hundreds to welcome me. It was Friday 15 April and I arranged to arrive at 5p.m. I was living at Birkenhead at this time, having spent the time since leaving the Borough giving retreats, and I set off in plenty of time. Of course, soon after leaving New Town I got lost. Can you imagine it? By the time I discovered the correct route it was dark and after a short while I got lost again. I was surrounded by black mountains, not a light in view and me trying to read a map by the light of a dying torch. I prayed to every saint I could think of except, looking back on it now, St David. Perhaps he was getting his own back, for I arrived at the presbytery hungry and weary at 10p.m. that night. There might not have been hundreds of parishioners waiting for me at 5p.m. but, at least, there had been a reception committee. By 7p.m. they presumed I was not coming and had gone home, except for two stalwarts of the parish, Gerry Geraghty and Eomen Durkan. I was to come to rely on those two good men in the months ahead in a parish the complete antithesis of the Borough parish.

Before I entered the Salvatorians I had never hard of Ystradgynlais and I was surprised how many knew of it when I began to tell people I was going there. In 1983 it was a real village on the River Tawe nestling in the Swansea Valley eighteen miles from Swansea and twenty from Brecon. My neighbours along the valley were the Danny Rogoff caves and the home of the late, great, opera singer Madelina Patti. By the time I arrived the latter's home had become a Cottage Hospital. Now the village has lost much of its character. The miners' strike in 1984 took its toll and the closure of the local branch of the Lucas factory caused many job losses. The advent of a supermarket built at the end of the village caused a number of local shops to lose their customers. However, the people are as warm-hearted and as welcoming as ever.

I was to live in the presbytery built next to a beautiful country church. The presbytery was a very big, two-storey house originally built as a community house. There were always two priests living there and still room for a visitor. Behind the house was a fairly big yard with a greenhouse and a huge, double, doorless garage. This had been used to garage a minibus which was used to ferry the children to the local Catholic school a few miles away at Clydach. Running along the back of the yard was a strip of a garden about sixty feet by six feet. Former parish priests had tended to be eccentric and one had returned from Tanzania after a very fruitful twenty-year stint. He, quite literally like missionaries of old, had gone into areas where no white man had ever trodden before. He was obviously used to being self supportive and he used this strip to grow his vegetables and also to grow his tobacco which he harvested, cured and smoked in his pipe,

Another parish priest, my immediate predecessor, emptied the greenhouse and whitewashed the glass. He installed a heater and, on his day

off, would take a flask of tea and sit there reading all day oblivious to phone calls and doorbells. Two great men, who appear again a bit later in this chapter.

So here I was, installed if not inducted, and slowly learnt the skills of a rural parish priest. In addition to the parish church there was a chapel in the village of Brynamon, up on the Black Mountain, where I used to go and say Mass

A new meaning to a house warming party

226

each Sunday. It was about five miles from the parish church and all uphill. Sometimes in the winter I would have to turn back unable to get the car up the icy roads. Local people, of course, had front-wheel-drive cars. En-route I was expected to collect people from such villages as Upper Cwmtwrch, Cwmcllynfell Brynamon, etc. I used to collect one lady who would stand at the side of the road waiting for me. She was a convert and some years earlier had undergone the required six months instruction before reception into the church. At reception she would have had to be baptised, make her confession, receive her First Holy Communion and the Sacrament of Confirmation. Her husband would have her breakfast ready for her every Sunday after Mass. One day he took ill and reached death's door. He asked to be received into the Catholic Church before he died. I received assurances from the nurse that he had little time to live. In such an emergency, once the priest has ensured the person wants to be a Catholic and knows what he is asking for, he can receive the person with the minimum of ritual. No instructions are required and the person is not required to confess his/her sins. They get the lot, so to speak, in a matter of minutes without any fuss. I received John into the Catholic Church, we prayed for a happy death and then he recovered!!! His wife was furious. She had had to go through the instructions and everything and here was her husband getting the lot in a few minutes. However, she wasn't furious really and was only too glad she still had him with her.

Apart from daily Mass and the Masses at the weekend there seemed to be hardly anything to do until the day I set the church on fire. Many years later the parish celebrated their Golden Jubilee and in the beautiful booklet they produced to commemorate the event, they included a list of former parish priests with a few notes of the contribution each had made to the parish. Next to my name was the note: 'He set the church on fire'. It is time to set the record straight.

One of my predecessors in the parish, the priest whom I mentioned had been on the missions, had obtained a lease on a bunkhouse up in the mountains and he would use this as a base for youth work, adventure weekends and so on. He leased it empty and so had appealed to the parishioners to help him furnish it with old sofas, armchairs, beds, etc. The people had rallied around but naturally had not given their best furniture. Consequently when the farmer recovered his lease the place was filled with what can only be described as junk furniture. My immediate predecessor, the 'glasshouse priest', had been given the task of emptying the bunkhouse before handing it back to the owner. He brought all the furniture from the bunkhouse and stored it in the large garage I mentioned earlier with a view to getting rid of it one day.

When I arrived I wanted to park my car in the garage so I decided to burn all this furniture in the yard bit by bit. One day I began and as the fire was burning brightly some friends arrived to stay for a few days. It was such a lovely day we decided to go to the Gower Peninsular and spend the day on the sands. I put the fire out and off we went. There was a small bridge near the presbytery across the Tawe and as we approached this on our return home in the evening, one of the children with us said, 'Look, there's a fire engine outside the church.' A wind had blown up and caught a spark in the fire I had supposedly put out. The spark had been blown into the garage and all the furniture was ablaze. We were fortunate. There was no natural gas on our side of the river so we had to use calor gas. There were a number of cylinders yards from the fire when the firemen arrived. Very quickly they grabbed them in spite of them being red hot and flung them into the river. Thank God the only damage to the church was smoke stains on the walls. One thing I learned from it was that if you want to meet all your parishioners in one fell swoop, start a fire. Everybody came out including the Chapel people and the non-believers– the whole village. The Church of Wales vicar flung his arms around me.

He was a lovely man who, with his wife and family, was a great support to me that night and we became good friends. And now back to the fire. Of course the insurance man came out and looked at what was left of the furniture and the garage. I told him the true story of the furniture but he said that it was second-hand furniture in storage and so we claimed for it. We received £1000—a fortune in a small country parish. There had been no parish newsletter of note in the parish so I bought a photocopier with the money and we launched a weekly newsletter under the name of—can you guess? Of course, *The Fireside*. The present parish newsletter is still called *The Fireside* but the paper is published in a different format. When I left Ystradgynlais I took *The Fireside* with me. It quickly became *The Matchmaker* at Keele and when I became Provincial it became *The Phoenix*. The reason for changes in the title will become obvious when I tell you about them in their proper place later on. Today in the Chew Valley it continues in the name of *The Lakeside*. And all because the fire had not gone out.

But it wasn't only the discovery of the fire engine for which I remember young Katy. She must have been about three at the time and we had been to the Gower as I said. At one point she wanted to be carried and as I was the only one not carrying anything I offered to do it. But nobody had told me what hips were for and I picked her up and carried her literally on my arm. Well, the next day I could hardly move. If I did anything involving my shoulder I reached screaming point. The locals told me I had the dreaded frozen shoulder and that I would be cursed with it for life. I went to the doctor and he gave me tablets which didn't ease the pain, then cortisone which added to the pain. In desperation he sent me to a physiotherapist. I was to come across this species later after my operation but Ystradgynlais was my first experience of them. They reminded me of the RAF Regiment we had training us in the RAF up in Arbroath. Lovely people, kind and understanding until they went to work on you. Then, my goodness, this good lady quite literally put me on the rack. By now they had decided that I had a trapped nerve and only traction would release it. I sat down and she put some sort of harness around my neck and then proceeded to add weights to it until my neck stretched. She didn't even smile when I told her that the English Martyrs got canonised for suffering the rack in Reformation times. But, 'fair dos' it worked. The next day almost miraculously that pain had gone. I was to come across the dear 'physios' a few years later when they forced me to walk up and down stairs after my operation. But without them I might still have a frozen shoulder and a 'broken heart'. They get little thanks for their work but without them many of us would have a much worse quality of life.

The people of Ystradgynlais continued to support me even though I had nearly destroyed their beautiful church. We had many a social evening in each other's houses and it was there I came across real ecumenism in action. A lot of the Catholics were married to non-Catholics and on Sundays the Catholics would go to Mass. During the summer months the non-Catholics would get the barbecues going in the yard so that we could all get together for a meal afterwards.

And, of course, past students of mine would inevitably appear. Parishioners made them very welcome and would arrange parties for them. There was one memorable occasion, without which any account of Ystradgynlais would be incomplete. Parishioners and students were all gathered together in the big parish room in the presbytery. We had had a good day on the mountain and the parishioners had put on food and drink for an evening soirée. We were sitting around, most of us on the floor, when after a few drinks one of the students stood up and began to hum the tune to 'Trishia the stripper'. One of the girls stood up and with a wiggle of her hips began to remove her blouse. Well! You could see the eyes of the villagers popping out of their heads. And I began to move out of the room, so embarrassed was I. What we did not know was that it was all a game. Trishia had about ten blouses on and never did remove them all or had the intention of doing so. Everybody had a good laugh except the wives who saw a different side of their husbands that night, or pretended to do so.

But, sadly, tragedy was to hit the valley in the form of the miner's strike of '84. There were many miners living in the parish and of course they were now out of work. There was a lot of poverty and feelings in the village were divided between those who supported the strike and those who didn't. It was a very difficult time for everybody and even to this day some of the wounds remain unhealed.

At times I would get very lonely in the valley. There was not a lot to do at nighttime and there was no night life other than homemade parties. I would sometimes visit a parishioner who I knew would cheer me up. Frances was paralysed from the neck down and only had the use of one hand. With a gadget in this hand she could open the door and turn on the TV, etc. I used to take her Holy Communion and I always felt refreshed when I came away. Never once did I hear her complain and if anybody had cause to she certainly had.

It was on one of those lonely nights when the phone rang and the person on the other end said, 'I'm afraid I have some bad news for you.' It wasn't about Frances. It was about my ninety-year-old mother. She had had to go into a nursing home about five months earlier and this was the Warden ringing to tell me she had just died in her sleep. She had always prayed for that grace and God had answered her prayers. May she rest in peace.

My father had already died in 1968 during the year I was doing my diploma course. As I have said earlier they both had very difficult lives, not helped by their inability to relate to each other and give each other the support each had a right to expect. Over the years my father took refuge in work, spending virtually all his waking hours there, and my mother found solace in her church activities. My father worked up to one week before he died at the age of seventy-seven. He had never been ill but he packed a lifetime of suffering into that one week. But if there is such a thing as a happy death that gift was given to him. My sister, Lily, a nun, was at one side of the bed; I, his son and a priest, at the other side; and at the head of the bed my other sister, Winnie, who was a senior nurse by this time, stood silently watching over him. I was reciting the night prayer of the church and as I said the words, 'Now thou can'st dismiss thy servant O Lord in peace', he died. I went to my mother who was in a neighbouring cubicle with Bernie and Flo and said to her, 'He's gone.' She was silent for a while and then said simply, 'he'll have peace at last'. The next night we were sitting around the fire and she said to me, 'if I only had him back for five minutes'. Now, when I give pre-marital instructions I tell the prospective bride and groom about them, to illustrate how important it is that the sun is not allowed to go down on one's anger.

I had been in the parish about twenty months when I received another unexpected phone call, this time from Archbishop Couve de Murville, Archbishop of Birmingham. I was sitting by the fire – this one was safely in the grate – minding my own business, and feeling very satisfied with life. Have you noticed how sometimes when the phone rings you get a premonition that you are not going to like this particular call. The ringing tone is the same but something puts you on the alert. I felt like this when I got up to answer it. As soon as I heard, 'Archbishop of Birmingham's secretary speaking', I knew I was right. I had known the Archbishop when we were both university chaplains. We had met at conferences. So when the secretary said the Archbishop would like me to come to dinner I felt in my bones that his invitation could only be something to do with chaplaincy work. I had heard on the grapevine that there were two vacancies for chaplains in the Birmingham Archdiocese, Keele, and Assistant to the Oxford Chaplain. Well, of course, I immediately thought, 'He's going to ask me to go to Oxford.' I didn't really, my background was such that I knew it would be Keele. This did not upset me very much but the thought of actually leaving Ystradgynlais and going there was a different matter.

I was not a stranger to Keele University. You may remember how, when I was an undergraduate at Manchester, I had been invited to officiate at my Demonstrator's wedding. She was to marry a Keele lecturer and the wedding was to be in the Keele Chapel. That was almost twenty years earlier. I well remember it was the scene of one of my all-too-infrequent triumphs. The chapel was full of Manchester and Keele academics and there was I, a humble undergraduate reading for an ordinary degree in charge of the proceedings. I remember beginning the ceremony by saying to them, 'Now it's my turn.' They had the grace to laugh. Later, Keele was to become the Mecca for those doing diploma courses in school counselling. Dr Dawes had introduced Non-Directive Counselling into this country from the USA. A school counsellor with a Keele diploma was the bees knees. When I was doing my diploma at Manchester I remember being quite envious of them. So this was my Keele background as I went, one October evening, looking very smart and academic, to dine with His Grace.

I expect it was an oversight on his part that the main course was Welsh lamb. But he made up for this with a bottle of the best wine 'From the cellar, Father', he said. Archbishop Maurice was an aristocrat in his own right so he knew about these things. After dinner we had coffee in his drawing room. I have never understood why such a room is called a drawing room in an Archbishop's house. I think originally a drawing room was for the ladies who withdrew after dinner so that the men could drink port and tell dirty jokes. That reminds me, actually, of a dinner night in the Officers' Mess during my TA days. It was a mixed Mess, being a medical unit, and the ladies withdrew in grand style following the female colonel a bit like sheep. It was traditional for the padre to lead the jokes. Being an innocent soul, of course I didn't know any. One night when our priests were at recreation and the Superior of our community had provided a bottle of whisky, I mentioned my dilemma to some of the old stagers. Well, they began to help me out and as the whisky got lower in the bottle, so the jokes rolled out. I finished up with quite a repertoire but none that was suitable even for the Officers' Mess.

Well, sitting in the drawing room with the Archbishop he began to tell me he had to find two chaplains and he wondered if I would go to Keele. He described the job and I promised I would 'go and see' not before reminding him that I was parish priest of a lovely parish and that it would be difficult to leave them and vice versa.

It was November when I went up to see Keele at the invitation of the retiring chaplain. To say, 'see' is an exaggeration for it was pitch black and all the buildings were surrounded with fog. It took me ages to find the building where I was to meet the retiring chaplain.

I had been invited to stay overnight and I was put into one of the best rooms. They certainly pulled out all the stops. The next morning the fog had cleared and I could see the campus in broad daylight. There was a shared church in the centre of the campus and I was shown around and met one or two of the Catholic staff. The idea was that they looked me over and I reciprocated. I could see one of them, at least, was not impressed. I was ancient for a campus university being fifty-eight. I had about three teeth and no dentures. I was five feet four inches and not the most impressive of profiles. The retiring chaplain was a very impressive, extrovert, tall man. The sort that slaps you on the back and nearly knocks you into the middle of next week. Moreover, he had an Oxford degree. However, on this occasion at least I was able to boast of my academic achievements especially the diploma in counselling. I didn't say anything about my second-class ordinary degree but I had a real ace up my sleeve.

You will remember my account of the interview I had to get into Aston University and how a learned member of staff mistook my TD for a Doctor of Theology. I noticed the Keele people were quite impressed with the initials and I didn't disabuse them. It would have been bad manners. You will remember that it is in fact the Territorial Decoration which an officer in the TA gets after twelve years service. It has stood me in good standing on a number of occasions.

I think they were trying to impress me when they told me that the chaplaincy was a local ecumenical project with a shared church with a very strong ecumenical flavour. They didn't know of my ecumenical experiences at Aston and that he was in fact throwing at me all the negative aspects of the job. I thought of my days back at Aston. I thought of my parish at the side of the river Tawe and I decided it would be better to stay where I was. I wrote to the Archbishop and declined his invitation. He and one or two members of staff wrote and asked me to reconsider. I said I would. I realised that while there are many good men trained for parish work it wasn't easy to find priests who could get on with young people. I could. I thought it was because I had never grown up. I am still wondering what to do when I grow up! Perhaps more realistically it was due to my constant support of the underdog, and of course everybody knows that there is nothing lower in the academic world than the undergraduate. It is the same with novices in religious life. So I embarked on a period of 'should I, shouldn't I?'

I knew that the Archbishop's invitation rested on the fact that I had spent most of my priestly life with secular students until I went to the Borough. Thinking of these things I went on holiday, I remember saying to the parishioners at Mass the week before Lent began, 'I don't know what you are doing for Lent but I'm off to China.' In fact, I was off to Hong Kong and it was there I received the answer to my prayer of 'should I, shouldn't I?'

I didn't know what to do. I had got to know the parishioners and we were getting on well together. It was quiet and peaceful and really altogether an idyllic spot to spend the rest of my days. As I said earlier I was fifty-eight at this time. I had looked forward to finishing my days in such a beautiful

234

place as Ystradgynlais with the mountains in my back garden and the sea in the front – and this was it. Moreover, it was a Salvatorian parish so it was a very acceptable apostolate in terms of the Order. The people wanted me to stay. I was not terribly inclined to go back to the student world having already spent so much time there. It is a solitary post and right at the front line of the apostolate, i.e. the stony ground. It was a very stressful job. Few priests relate to students but I had found that it was my niche, in fact, shades of standing on that street platform again.

I had been invited to Hong Kong by some students who had been at Aston University with me. Off I went to spend ten days with them. In Hong Kong there is a Catholic Centre and I used to say Mass there each day. Opposite the Centre there was a bookshop and as I was browsing around one day I came across some posters. I pulled the first one out of the holder and, do you know, it was as though God was speaking to me. The picture was of a ship out at sea on a very stormy day. The wind and the rain were battering the ship about. The caption read, 'A ship in harbour is very safe but that is not what ships are for.' It was as though I was being told to leave the safety of my parish and go to the hostile shores of the student world. I bought the poster and brought it back with me. It hangs on my wall to this day. I had to go to the other end of the world to discover God's will. A rather expensive way of finding it!

'Oh I wish I looked after 'me teeth....'

Back in Ystradgynlais I told the parishioners of my impending move and made plans for departure. I was to start at Keele at the beginning of the summer term. Remembering the look which that member of staff had been giving to my teeth, I decided I should do something about them. So with great bravery I went off to the dentist and asked him to give me a top deck so to speak. I had always associated false teeth with old age and I thought I was too young to die. So I compromised with the top set. I thought I looked quite good. I still had one tooth on the bottom shelf but I was not going to part with that. Besides nobody could see the bottom teeth so I looked quite good when I arrive at Keele. They noticed it too incidentally. Little did I know that my teeth had already been the cause of my heart valves being invaded by the dreaded potential killer, sub-acute bacteria endocarditis (SBE). This was the cause of my going into hospital just six years later, but already they were at it within my body. It seems SBE can have two sources, rheumatic fever as a child or decaying teeth. In Everton we had never had such luxuries as toothbrushes or toothpaste. We would rub salt into our teeth and gums and I very rarely did that. So I paid the price. Fortunately open-heart surgery was available by the time my little sub-acute bacteria made themselves known and I recovered. But we had one wonderful priest in whom it had been diagnosed long before me and he had been given ten years to live. It was before open-heart surgery. He died almost to the day – Fr Edward Bagnall. We used to call him Big Ed to distinguish him from Little Ed, a priest called Edmund who also died from heart problems but much later. I shall be saying quite a lot about Little Ed later.

One of the outstanding events in the hospital before my operation was a compulsory visit to the dentist before the operation. He was after my last tooth. I must confess that another reason for hanging on to that tooth was sheer fear. The fact that it hadn't fallen out like so many of my teeth indicated to me that it was deeply embedded. So I was too scared to go to the dentist thinking he would have to excavate for it. I sat in the dentist's chair without any anaesthetic. The dentist forced open my mouth, saw my last solitary tooth, put his fingernail to it and just flicked it out. I was mortified. And, of course with him flicking it out I could not keep it as a souvenir. No chance of a tooth fairy of course after that. Actually, I have had some unique experiences with my teeth. I once left one in Sandhurst of all places. The Military Academy no less. I was at a TA camp and was suffering from toothache. Being of officer class and not far from Sandhurst at the time I was whisked off to this noble college and I am sure it must have been one of the royal dentists who extracted my tooth. He asked me if I wanted it but I rather liked the idea of leaving a tooth in this venerable college. Just think, it might even now be lying alongside one of Montgomery's or even Churchill's.

But talking of fairies reminds me of a farewell party a Hall of Residence put on at Keele University some time later. The warden had been in office for some time. He was now forty and he was retiring as warden though keeping his position of lecturer. It was a good evening and there was a 'homemade' band which entertained the many guests. As the evening came to an end, the band master came to the microphone and announced a special song they were going to sing as a tribute to the out-going warden who had incidentally 'outed' sometime before. The song? 'Everybody loves a fairy over forty.' It was taken very well and proved to be a good ending to a great evening. This warden and myself used to have a drink together from time to time and we had some really lively conversations.

The time had come to leave Ystradgynlais and we had one of our regular parties at the home of Lucy and Trevor Thomas. All the stalwarts of the parish were there and as the evening came to an end they sang as only the Welsh can, 'We'll keep a welcome in the hillside'. They certainly have done and I have been back to enjoy it on a number of occasions. On 25 April 1985 I left Ystradgynlais and arrived at Keele to begin what was to prove, not the happiest time of my life, but certainly the most fruitful of my entire priesthood.

20

Keele University

At Keele I was appointed to the staff and became a member of the Senior Common Room. I felt that I had at last arrived academically, though in my wildest dreams as a child this was not one of my ambitions. It was at Keele that I was finally recognised in terms of the province when I was elected Provincial.

So all things were coming together and though this was not the happiest period of my life it was the most fruitful. I still used my psychology in giving extra-curriculum lectures in para-psychology but counselling took the form of spiritual guidance. At Keele I was seen as more of a priest than a lecturer and so my role veered very strongly towards the pastoral.

I found my own spiritual life re-awakened and though light years away from my previous attitudes, things spiritual began to assume the importance they had in my earlier years.

I was getting into my stride when my life came to an abrupt halt. I was diagnosed as having sub-acute bacteria endocarditis and rushed to hospital for life-saving operations.

To enter religious life in the 1940s at the age of twenty-six was considered to be very late. In fact anybody over eighteen was called a 'Late Vocation' and would go to a college designed for such. Over forty-years-old and you were more or less entitled to go to the English Bede College in Rome for the short course of four years. At the present time it is considered advisable to enter when older and having had some experience of the real world as they call it. The consequence of this for me was that I was always considered older if not old. So, for example, I was ordained at thirty-five when the normal age was twenty-four. I entered university for my first degree at the age of thirty-nine when the usual undergraduate was eighteen. I have always been doing things late. I have always felt that I was eight or even ten years behind everybody else and this might explain why I have always been in a hurry. This attitude of feeling old was endorsed when I was appointed chaplain to Keele University. Apart from trouble with my teeth, which I outlined previously, the local newspaper reported that the new Keele Chaplain was over fifty-eight as though that was ancient, but I expect it seemed so to an eighteen-year-old undergraduate.

It was Easter Monday 1985 when I took up office as chaplain to Keele University. I was following in the wake of some eminent men. The Jesuits (here we go again) had had responsibility for the chaplaincy. They had succeeded such men as Fr John Tolkien the son of the 'Lord of the Rings' man. The chaplains had lived in a small cottage in the village of Keele since the university began and it was to this cottage I took myself that Easter Monday. As in my move to the Borough, parishioners helped me to move my luggage and I was pleased to find that at this cottage they did accept tramps. At least, no notice seemed to be taken of my tramp-like appearance. That reminds me that during my days at Keele, if people wanted to point me out to newcomers they would single me out from the other two chaplains by saying, 'he is the one that looks like a tramp' — flippin' cheek. Actually, I was also known by a much more respectable trademark. Well, respectable to some—I smoked a pipe.

I actually learnt the dangers of smoking when a policeman chased me the length and breadth of two streets in Liverpool trying to catch me because he saw me smoking a cigarette. He never caught me probably because I was a lot younger than he was. I was eleven. That has not been my only brush with the law. In my early teens I was stopped for riding a bicycle without lights. I got a good telling-off that night and the fact that I was returning from visiting the dead body of my pal's father made no difference to him. In fact it was the first corpse I had ever seen and I had forgotten all about the lights on the bike. Those incidents and a few minor skirmishes with the dreaded knights of the road, the traffic police, constitute my criminal record. But getting back to smoking my pipe, I picked up the habit back in the days of the RAF. Apart from an occasional excursion into the cigarette world and those times in the religious order when I was not allowed to smoke I kept to the pipe until 13 August 1991.

Eventually I was smoking my pipe from dawn to dusk. I had caught the compulsive habit while I was at Manchester University back in the 1960s. I smoked sporadically until I came across this priest, who was an assistant chaplain and I admired him greatly. He was never without a pipe in his mouth and I thought it was really something. So I took it up in a similar manner. I must say I found it very useful when I counselled as I had something to do with my hands and a pipe-smoking priest looks very wise and saintly. All to do with image. It was also very useful to fill in time when a client was crying. To fill and pad down the tobacco somehow seemed comforting. But best of all, I found that if I was sitting alone in a public hall or conference I never felt alone smoking my pipe.

One day as I shall recall later, I was told to go into hospital. I stood outside that hospital puffing my pipe waiting for my twelve-noon appointment when it dawned upon me that I wouldn't be able to smoke inside. So at five minutes to twelve on 13 August 1991 I solemnly had my last puff, knocked out the ash, put the pipe in my pocket and bravely went where I had never been before – into the hospital.

I haven't put my pipe into my mouth to this day. I still have my pipes in the hope that one day I shall give in to temptation but if I am to smoke again it won't be in this life I fear. After my operation, I was very pleased to hear that my physical condition had nothing to do with my smoking habits.

So, as I was saying, I arrived at the cottage that was to be my home for almost nine years. On this occasion it was a former student of Mary Ward, Veronica Middleton, who opened the door. She was waiting for me with a lovely meal of steak casserole and the house was spotless. She had even begun to decorate the walls.

I have been very fortunate with former students. Wherever I have gone many of them have kept in touch and visited me ensuring that I lacked for nothing. Naturally some got away either deliberately or by lack of communication. I don't like to enquire which.

Keele University is different than the other colleges in which I have served in that it is a campus university. At the centre of the campus is a very big church which is shared by all the Christian denominations and surrounding that are the lecture halls and offices of administration. On the periphery of the campus are four halls of residence each with its warden and own social structure. Opposite the church is the Student's Union and some shops for the benefit of those involved in self-catering. Scattered around the campus grounds are five lakes. Imagine! As the population of the university has grown another hall of residence has been added and many students live out in digs. Unlike Aston, Keele is unashamedly Christian and all congregations for the conferment of degrees are opened with a prayer read by one of the chaplains.

I thought the ultimate academic accolade for a boy asked to leave school because I couldn't pass my exams was when I was asked to open the Degree Ceremony with prayer in the presence of HRH Princess Margaret, the Chancellor. I thought I could never better that but more was to come as I shall tell you later on.

As I said, the church was shared between the three major Christian denominations. Inside was a main chapel used by all for their Sunday services and any major ecumenical event such as the annual Carol Service and so on. Inside the church but to the side of the main chapel there is the east chapel and within that two apses which were really little chapels. The Free Church and the Roman Catholics used the two little chapels and the Anglicans ostensibly used the rest of the east chapel. Each of these chapels had an altar, etc. I said ostensibly because on Sundays the Roman Catholics used the Anglicans' part of the east chapel for an early morning Mass. On weekdays the Roman Catholic apse was plenty big enough for our needs. The Anglicans and the Free Church united for their Sunday service which was known as the 10.30 service and the Catholics would follow at noon. Often there would be congestion in the passages as Catholics jostled (friendly like!) with the other Christians as they departed and we entered, ecumenism being a bit like ships that pass in the night. That's not true, of course. Ecumenism was very strong at Keele and did give a true Christian Witness for the most part. There are three chaplains, one each from the major denominations and the chaplain is appointed by the university. He is considered a member of staff and receives a small remuneration for his work. The particular denomination is expected to subsidise the salary.

The method of appointment was quite different to that of Aston. A few days before the official interview the prospective chaplain is invited to meet with chosen representative staff and students who have an interest in the chapel. They meet purely on a social level over tea and biscuits so that they can all look at each other and decide if they are going to get on. Should there be more than one applicant they are all invited. In the case of the Catholics, again the Archbishop decides whom he will send for interview and again if necessary there will be a 'sleeping partner'. I hasten to add that this was not deliberate subterfuge but necessitated by the shortage of priests in general. The thoughts of the students and staff present at the tea are fed into the interviewing panel prior to the interview. The applicant is interviewed by the Deputy Vice Chancellor and other relevant members of staff and a representative student from the denomination of the applicant.

Whoever is appointed becomes automatically a member of staff. I shall never forget walking into the Senior Common Room for the first time. From lecturing at a College of Education, to visiting lecturer and chaplain at Aston and the Birmingham Polytechnic to full membership of the University Senior Common Room, I felt, at last, I had arrived.

Accommodation for lectures, conferences, orchestral recitals, etc. was very limited on campus and everybody wanted to use the church from the Vice Chancellor to way-out so-called religious groups with funny-sounding names. But my 'bette noire' was the music department. The music department was forever practising in the main chapel especially whenever there was a big orchestra from London or some other capital city. And they always seemed to practise at lunchtime when I was about to say Mass in the East chapel. I remember one occasion when there was a very well-known orchestra practising in the main chapel. There were notices all over the place about daily Mass at 12.15. The east and the main chapel were divided by a wooden partition and, of course, in no way soundproof. I went into the main chapel ready to do battle with the conductor who was waving his baton frenetically at the orchestra and I stopped him in full flight. I said, politely, 'I am sorry but you will have to stop now as I am saying Mass next door.' He nearly fell off his podium with apoplexy. He said, 'you can't stop an orchestra in the middle of a rehearsal' and turned around ready to raise his baton again. I said, 'You've stopped now haven't you?' He had, of course, to speak to me. Had he continued to rehearse I was all ready to say Mass there and then in the main chapel accompanied by lots of incense and holy water. However, common sense prevailed and he realised he should have read the notices and he quietly withdrew. Then there was another priceless incident. I went to say the 12.15 Mass and there, actually in the east chapel, was an orchestra practising one of Beethoven's Masses. I think it was Beethoven but it might have been one of those other classical chaps. Did women ever write Masses? It is interesting isn't it that women seem to be the best 'who done it' writers but they haven't ventured into music. No doubt it was due to the attitude towards women in those days. Just a thought! But not forgetting Beethoven, with very quick thinking I went up to the conductor and said to him, 'It is wonderful to hear you practising one of the Masses. I am about to say Mass, perhaps you would like to accompany me with your music.' Well you never saw an orchestra disappear so quickly in all your life – and not a grain of incense in sight!

Actually my music lessons have nothing to do with my attitude towards musicians. I must confess that this attitude comes to the fore whenever I feel threatened, whether that be my religious superior, in spite of my vow of obedience, or the lady who opened the door to me at the Borough and said she didn't want any tramps. I was on one of these self-awareness courses once and we were sitting in an encounter group for what seemed like hours. It turned out to actually be hours by the time it finished. But I was not terribly keen on the group leader. As with all these strange beings, they just sit there saying nothing as the tension builds up. Eventually someone explodes and so interaction begins. I have to say that I have used this technique myself, but in a much more genteel way of course!!! I think I must have exploded during one of the sessions and gave vent to my anger towards him. Very calmly, he said to me, 'You don't like your father do you?' Honestly! I nearly hit him. But equally calmly by now, I replied, 'I loved my father, I just don't like you.' He was quite taken aback at his Freudian views being challenged. Years later I went over to Vienna to visit a young lady for counselling purposes and I had occasion to visit Freud's house where he began his psychoanalytical sessions. It is now a museum and there in the centre is the original couch upon which his patients where asked to lie and reveal all – mentally of course. Do you know it is made of iron and there wasn't a cushion in sight. No wonder the patients had problems. If they didn't going in, I'll bet they certainly did coming out. It's a bit like with some counsellors or group leaders isn't it?

Actually that group leader might not have been too far from the truth regarding my father. Although I didn't particularly know him all that well I certainly loved him in his later years. But one incident stands out that could well influence my attitude to authority to this day. I don't think I mentioned that in my young days I was a boy scout. That was another uniform I wore with great pride. I don't know how I came by it but I distinctly remember wearing the hat proudly. I can't remember winning any badges but I know I would never have got one for the art of deceit. One weekend my troop was going to camp and I dearly wanted to go. But I was in the choir and I had to sing at the eleven o'clock Mass on the Sunday. There was no question of asking my mother for permission to skip the choir. But, not to miss out, I told her that it was the choir going to camp and asked if I could go with them. No problem! Permission was given without hesitation. Fool that I was I had forgotten that my father always went to the eleven o'clock Mass. He went to Mass, he heard the choir singing and then went home and told my mother. He was waiting for me at Lime Street Station and battered me all the way home to Everton. Today this would have been classed as child abuse but in those days it was considered normal practice. 'Spare the rod and spoil the child' was the great maxim. I am not sure if it was on that same occasion or another time when I hid under the table from my father and just refused to come out. One thing I do know is that it was then my stubbornness was born. This stubbornness has since proved to be a quality that has seen me weather the failures, determined to succeed.

I have always found it difficult to cope with personal threat, imagined or otherwise. And along with the experiences with my father, I am sure it goes back to that teacher telling my mother 'No good will come of him'. Do teachers realise the tremendous effect their words have on children? I bet that most, if not all, of my readers could tell a similar story. But I got to grips with this when I was a student. There were twelve of us and as I mentioned before we lived very closely together for nine years. Part of the rule was that we had to recreate after dinner and supper for half to three-quarters of an hour each day. Unless we played cards there was not an awful lot to do. Television was in its infancy and we were only allowed to watch the news. We could read the newspapers and religious magazines. But the idea was to socialise and learn social skills. It was due to these recreations that I developed the will-power not to allow anybody to disturb my inner peace. I mentioned earlier about the student who used to bait me on these occasions. Very slowly and deliberately he would throw nut after nut at me waiting for me to explode. Anybody who has been bullied will know the feelings I endured. But I was determined not to weaken. The stubbornness I had developed in my childhood stood me in good stead and I never flinched. And to this day I can hear a gun go off behind me and I don't move a muscle. This was borne out only recently here at Chew Valley. Although it wasn't exactly a gun going off. During Mass on Sundays I invite the young members of the congregation to join me and the altar staff in the Sanctuary for the Lord's Prayer which finishes with the sign of peace. The idea is that they receive the peace at the altar and then take it to their parents. On one occasion, without any warning, I was assaulted. I felt myself being thumped in the leg and when I looked down I realised it was one of the children aged three having a go at me. But thanks to my childhood I never moved a muscle. A person can present a face to the world and I reached the stage where that man never knew what I was thinking no matter what he said or did to me. As a result of those recreations and that person who later became a priest and did great work before he died, I learned the art of self control. The only people who can hurt me now or get through to me or who even see the real me are those I love and who love me. I am happy to say they still have the ability to hurt me.

If the chapel was a hive of industry the cottage where I lived was a haven of refuge and peace – most of the time. It wasn't long before I realised that, like the flat at Aston, the cottage was home to the Catholic. Society. My first introduction to the social life in the cottage came when I was told

there was a tradition that the chaplain provided Sunday lunch for students after the noon Mass. This took place in the cottage. I was told that about forty normally came and that my predecessor was quite a dab hand at making garlic pate. It was a simple lunch. I might have told you that garlic and myself don't mix and the very thought of having garlic in the cottage never mind in the food made me want to throw up. I decided that change was necessary. Back in Liverpool our local dish is scouse. All you do is get some meat, usually mutton, add some onions, carrots and spuds and you've got a meal. My brother, along with many like-minded fans, always had this on a Saturday before going to the match. I decided to begin my Sunday lunches with scouse and prepared enough for fifty in case a few extra came. In fact four came and I was eating scouse for the rest of the term. The following Sunday I prepared a beef casserole for about twenty and forty came. It was not long before word got around that the Sunday lunches at the cottage were OK and sometimes we would have as many as seventy there. By this time we were serving soup, main course and pud and we suggested £1 donation. We never really covered the cost this way but the goodwill engendered by the meal was well worth the out of pocket expense. Many a couple met at the cottage and many was the wedding I did as a result. I even went to Singapore and Malaysia to marry former students. As at Aston there were many different nationalities at Keele and this was reflected in the Catholic community. Gradually as I settled in we began to have ethnic meals on a Sunday. Students from a particular country would come up to the cottage on Saturday and prepare the meal. They would then race up after the Sunday Mass and put the final touches to it. So we had Spanish, French, German, Danish, Belgium even Hungarian meals but the favourite was always the Chinese meal. The first time we did a Chinese meal we prepared enough for forty. Sixty arrived and we ran out of food. Not to be daunted, I searched the freezer and found a lot of beefburgers. We defrosted them, rolled them into balls and doused them in soy sauce. They tasted delicious and nobody knew they were not eating Chinese food other than the cooks. I always kept the role of Master Chef to myself and supervised the cooking if I didn't actually cook. One of my younger visitors aged seven saw me cooking one Saturday and then saw me saying Mass on the Sunday. That week during the RE class a teacher asked if anybody knew what a priest was. As quick as a flash my young friend put his hand up and said, 'Yes Miss, a priest is a man who prays and cooks.' A sound theologian!

One side-effect of the Sunday lunches was that people could mix and make friends and we had a policy that everyone circulated and mixed freely. One Sunday there was a small group who had been together for some time. I asked them to circulate. About ten minutes later I saw the same group in a different part of the cottage. I told them about circulating and they responded, 'We have. We've moved here.' They probably got Firsts!

Another policy was that it didn't matter what religion you practised or even if you were an atheist or agnostic everybody was welcome at the cottage. In addition to the Sunday lunch I organised Sunday wine and cheese evenings. This was very useful for students who had been away for the weekend. I would rent a popular video and have that on in one room for those who just wanted to lounge and I advertised good conversation in the other room. This was extremely valuable because good conversation for students meant catching up with the gossip. One rather unwelcome side-effect of an open house was that sometimes the occasional undesirable would get in. We had the Groper for a while. No girl would sit near him and then we had the mature atheist student whose self-confessed aim in coming to the cottage was to meet 'nice' girls, and hopefully seduce them. I had the policy of closing down at 11p.m. and would go around thanking people for leaving – 'thank you for coming, thank you very much for going'. This man would often refuse to go and we would get the vacuum cleaner out to clean up. He would sit there and we would hoover around him. One day he disappeared off campus and nobody saw or heard from him ever again. We wondered if he had drifted into one of the five very beautiful lakes that adorned the campus. I don't think anybody attempted to find out.

Other social events at the cottage were pancake parties, Halloween parties, Christmas parties, etc. These tended to be fancy-dress affairs and one Halloween all sorts of terrifying figures could be seen in the cottage, Dracula, Frankenstein, dreadful goblins and all. The doorbell went and some children were doing the rounds, trick or treating. We had a student almost seven-feet tall and he had this terrible wolf's head mask on. We sent him to answer the doorbell and the poor children screamed and screamed. Since those days, a movement to ban Halloween parties has succeeded in preventing such 'goings on'. It was at the cottage that I learnt my second method of survival in a student world. Before I answered the door I would put my coat on and depending who was at the door I was just coming in or just going out. If any of you reading this saw me going out I apologise. But sometimes a chaplain was just too tired to give full attention to a person and this subterfuge was better than rejection.

Overseas students always enjoyed the parties and would really enter the spirit of the thing. One evening at a Christmas party a French student arrived looking very sylph-like in a beautiful diaphanous white dress. As true as I am sitting here she looked the spitting image of the Mona Lisa. And thinking I was paying her a compliment I said, 'welcome to my home, Mona Lisa'. Well, the look I got. You'd swear I had said, welcome wife of Dracula. Some years later I visited her in Paris and we went to see the original Mona Lisa. I made her stand at the side and I took a photograph. Of course she was much more beautiful. Whenever she writes to me now she signs her letters Mona Lisa. I suspect I have been forgiven.

As well as being the venue for most Cath. Soc. events the cottage was my home. I tended to get a lot of visitors, mostly former students who would stay a while. In addition to attending to them I would host a dinner party once a week to which I would invite about eight students. I would try and mix them as in Aston days and I began my spider's web approach again. For each dinner party I would receive eight invitations to different groups in return and so gradually I got to know many students whom I would never meet otherwise. I would be invited to parties such as birthday parties and the like and I always made a point of leaving at an appropriate time. My criterion was to leave when the smooching began. Using this criterion I would be invited again and to other parties. It wasn't the parties I was interested in so much as the opportunity to meet people who would never talk to a priest outside of party life.

I was a great believer that the way to a student's soul is through his/her bladder and so I founded the Chateau Ricardo. I appointed a manager who designed a label and we used this red and white wine for our cheese and wine parties as well as other functions.

As you can imagine it reached the stage where the kitchen wasn't big enough and I got permission from the Archbishop to extend it. This permission and the loan of the money needed was granted with the proviso that we would have to pay it back—£10,000. I was in my office one day giving an instruction to a potential student convert when there was a knock at the door. A member of staff stood there and asked if he could see me. I asked him to wait and told him why. He waited about fifteen minutes. When the student had gone he came in and simply said, 'Will you let me pay for the extension to the kitchen?' And I had kept him waiting! He sat and he wrote a cheque for £10,000. He insisted on anonymity but God knows, I know and he knows what a tremendous help that kitchen was to many, many students' welfare.

It wasn't all beer and skittles as they say. My role as chaplain was more to do with the spiritual welfare of the students rather than their material welfare. But I am a great believer in the spiritual life building on the material life and so it proved to be. If the students liked the chaplain they met at social events they were more likely to go to the services he organised. It was a great feeling to go into the chapel on a Sunday morning and find it packed with students from all over the world and from various religions as well as my own. This was borne out on my sixtieth birthday which happened to be on a Sunday. After Holy Communion two Malaysian girls, one Catholic, one Methodist carried to the altar a big cake on which were lit sixty candles. A Muslim student had made the cake and he stood in the passage outside the chapel as the cake was carried in. He felt he shouldn't attend Mass because of his faith. That was interesting because on this Muslim's graduation day I met his parents. The father was a member of the Malay Government and they told me that they were worried when they heard that their son was associating with a Catholic priest. But now that they had met me they were no longer worried. I think it was meant as a compliment!

We had what are called Special Ministers of the Eucharist at Mass. Since the Second Vatican Council lay members of the congregation are allowed to distribute Holy Communion and take the Blessed Sacrament to the sick. These Ministers are especially commissioned for this noble task. One day I asked an Indian student if she would be prepared to take on this ministry. She was at Mass every Sunday and she agreed. After a while I realised that I had failed to ask her boyfriend who was with her every Sunday. He declined graciously and I didn't try to persuade him. I presumed he had his reasons and I didn't want to invade his privacy. Years later after he had graduated, he wrote to me. He told me that he had felt guilty all those years because he hadn't told me why he didn't take on the Ministry. 'I'm not a Catholic', he said. I wrote back and thanked him for declining my invitation. But such was the situation that for the most part I didn't know who were Catholics and who weren't.

We had a wonderful folk group throughout my time at Keele under the direction of a member of staff, Professor Peter de Cruz. He had a wonderful way with him and with musical instruments and could transpose music at the drop of a hat. We had flautists, guitarists, organists, singers. One instrument I could never get him to use was the drum. I failed miserably on that one. But I forgive him now looking back for on my Silver Jubilee he and his wife, Lois, composed the most beautiful hymn for me, and another on my leaving. Of course his being a musician I suspected his motives in picking hymns at times. In fact on one occasion I gave him the sack. But thankfully he wouldn't take it.

I had only been at Keele twelve months when I celebrated the Silver Jubilee of my ordination to the priesthood. We decide to have a celebration worthy of the occasion as far as we could. We invited former students, particularly those who had been in the folk groups where I had served. Peter got them together and moulded them into one group and we had a wonderful Mass. It was during this Mass that Peter 'unveiled' the hymn he had written in honour of the occasion. In addition to the usual folk hymns one of the students was really professional on the organ and he brought the Mass to an end with some really rousing music. Years later when I was at the Borough in London I received a telephone call from this person from the States. He had done very well and he began the conversation, 'I want to pay the debt I owe you.' My immediate thought was, 'how much did I lend him.' But he went on to say, 'You remember that we had a bargain? If you prayed and I got a First, I would take you to the theatre.' I had forgotten completely but he asked me what I would like to see in the West End and he booked the tickets from the States. Along with two other former students we went to see 'Mojo'. We had a wonderful evening.

The culmination of Peter's contribution to my life came here at Chew Magna when I held a mega party to celebrate my forty years of priesthood, my seventy-fifth birthday and ten years of bionic life. (my artificial valve). As with my Silver Jubilee Mass we invited musicians and singers from wherever I had served. This was fifteen years later. We sent them the music individually in advance and asked them to arrive an hour earlier than the beginning of the ceremony. In that hour Peter moulded them into the finest folk group you could ever wish to hear. As I walked into the marquee that day, accompanied by a bishop and twelve priests, over 450 guests from all over the world and local villagers stood up and, led by Peter and the group, broke into 'Awake From Your Slumber'. What a wonderful occasion that was. And, believe it or not, my friend in the States flew in that morning, played the keyboard and flew out again the next day. What a man! It was on this occasion that my newly formed family here at Chew Magna proved themselves. Virtually the whole parish volunteered for some task or other and there wasn't a hitch the whole day.

I mentioned that students of all denominations and none attended Mass at Keele. A student knocked at the cottage door during a wine and cheese evening. 'Can I come in, I'm not a Catholic', she asked. Well, of course she could and she became a regular visitor. She was a German Lutheran and I quickly learnt she played the guitar, the trumpet and I don't know how many other instruments. I introduced her to Peter and she joined the folk group. Each year I would invite the archbishop along for an Academic Mass when I would invite all the staff and local 'bigwigs' along. I would try and get a few trumpeters from the music department to come along and sound a fanfare at various dramatic points during the Mass. The leader of the trumpeters was an Austrian Jew. He would lead the fanfares and, not being particularly interested in the Mass, he would look around the congregation inbetween times. On one of these occasions his eyes lit upon the German girl. Afterwards he asked her out and they became very good friends. A German Lutheran met an Austrian Jew at a Catholic Mass. I reckon that's ecumenism.

Peter would take the folk group out to local old people's homes and give secular concerts and from time to time they would go to convents where there were large communities and accompany me saying Mass.

Talking of villagers, quite a few grown-ups, as I called them, including members of staff would attend the student mass at Keele. They were a Godsend in a number of ways. They reminded the students of their own families. They made the Mass more of a realistic community rather than just a student body and they helped in various ways not least through their financial contributions. I kept in touch with the local villagers as they provided me with a non-academic refuge from time to time. In the local village of Keele there was a small group of the WI and they asked me if I would give them a talk on women priests in the Catholic Church. I thought as there were only a few of them no harm would be done so I agreed. Somehow or other word got out. It was published on the local radio and the place was packed with ministers of religion and laity from all over the Potteries. The WI had changed the venue from their Village Hall to the east chapel on campus. I began by telling them I was in fact the only female priest in the Catholic Church in that I had been made an honorary woman at Mary Ward. I continued in this vein and by the end of the talk they were no wiser as to whether I supported the motion or not. A reporter from the local radio appeared complete with mike and asked me if I would like to say a few words. Thinking of the archbishop listening in at Barnt Green, I declined her invitation. But it was a good night and there was a lot of lively discussion at the end.

I mustn't forget that the Chaplains were part of the whole university and not simply chaplain to their own denomination. We were members of staff and so had all the amenities shared by the staff such as the Senior Common Room. Among the facilities offered to the staff was the use of the Salvin Room. This was a magnificent room with crystal chandeliers, and polished tables, the slightest fingerprint on the polished tables could be seen miles away. I mentioned that former students would come to see me. On the occasion of my Silver Jubilee a coach of my Ystradgynlais parishioners came and brought with them crates of their own home-made beer. They had a great time in the Salvin Room and stayed long after others had left. They sang with such great feeling, 'We'll Keep a Welcome in the Hillside' and their very own 'Oggie, Oggie, Oggie'. The next morning I was sent a bill for £30 from the Bursar for cleaning up beer stains on the beautiful carpets. Ystradgynlais still owe me that £30. But talking of drink I must tell you about the overseas freshers dinners. At the beginning of each session new students were invited to dinner with the support services. Speeches were made in the manner of induction as I described at Aston. As the overseas students came up before the national students they had their dinner first. Chaplains were always invited and they were great opportunities to get to see the students and to be seen by them. On each table there would be a bottle of wine which provided a single glass each unless, of course, you sat at a table where there were few drinkers. It didn't take me long to suss this out and you can imagine which table I normally made for. Where else but the table where the Muslims were sitting. I had virtually the whole bottle to myself. In spite of this I got on very well with the Muslims and particularly one who used to come to Mass with his friends. He would sit at the back of the chapel wearing the most flamboyant clothes you ever saw. It was his way of showing respect. One Sunday I reminded him that the archbishop was coming for the Academic Mass the following week. I asked him to wear something special for the occasion. He did. He sat at the back of the chapel wearing a huge sombrero which he kept on all through the service. Afterwards I introduced him to the archbishop and wondered who would come off best. They both turned up trumps. The Arch said to him, 'I like your hat', I could almost see my friend grow in stature.

So many memories but I won't bore you with many more. I often think that we priests are so busy teaching others and showing them the way to God that we miss lessons hidden all around us and especially within the very people we teach. I had occasion one night to visit a lecturer who was blind. He answered the door and invited me in. It was only when he heard me stumbling around that he realised there were no lights on. He apologised and was about to put them on when I stopped him. I thought that if I have entered his world I should 'see' it as he did. It was a salutary lesson. A similar thing had occurred when I was visiting a friend in Brno which was then in Czechoslovakia. I had arranged to meet him in the square but he was late. I sat there in the sweltering heat wanting to buy an ice cream. But I didn't know how to ask for one, I didn't know the language. I could hear people all around me talking away among themselves but I couldn't understand a word they were saying. Putting both these together I thought this is what it must be like to be deaf and dumb.

Some time ago I promised I would tell you about the gift of a bike the students made to me. I had been to Rome and when I returned to the cottage the Spoggles as they called themselves presented me with a T-shirt. Spoggles were a zany offshoot of the Catholic Society (Cath Soc) and quite mad as only students can be. The T-shirt was emblazoned with slogans of my tour to the Vatican such as 'tea with JPII' etc. Anyway, I was admiring this when a couple of them brought in a fantastic bike with about ten gears. 'This is your real welcome home present', they said and solemnly handed it over to me. I admired it and mounted it to see if it was the right size. Then just as I began to thank them in walked the supply priest, Fr Michael, and asked 'Has anybody seen my bike?' Some time before this I had discovered the restrictions of driving to parties – don't drink and drive, etc. I had decided to overcome this by buying a bike. On the first evening of its purchase off I rode proudly to dinner at the house of members of staff, Rowena and Phil Gay. We had good food and good wine and I mounted my bike and proudly rode home again. Five minutes down the road I fell off it. My first reaction was, 'has anybody seen me?' Somebody must have done, hence the gift of the 'nicked' bike.

I am tempted at this point to tell you about spirits of another kind— the ghostly ones. From time to time I was called out to 'exorcise' a room or a building where ghosts had allegedly been seen. Over my student years, I was called out to many and it would take too long to tell you about them all here. So I shall limit myself to one or two examples. There were a number at Keele but this one happened at Mary Ward. You remember I told you all men had to be out of the students' rooms by 11p.m. Priests were not classed as men it seems, because we were allowed to stay later. I visited a student one evening and she had been expecting a visit from her boyfriend. He was delayed and because of the rule, it was too late for him to visit. He sent her a note on which was written, 'I shall visit you on the astral plane. You will know I am there when the light bulb falls out of the socket.' Sure enough a little while later the bulb fell out. There was a ps to the note which read, 'I will visit Fr Richard afterwards. He will know I am there when the picture by his front door falls off the wall.' I have to say he had never been in my house. I went home, shut the front door and the picture fell off the wall. Honest! I shrugged my shoulders and told him to make himself at home as I was going to bed.

Then there was the lady who came to Mass at the Borough. She would curse and swear like a trooper. She was into voodoo and believed she was possessed. Every time she would open her mouth to speak the devil would take over. It reached the stage where she was afraid to leave her house in case she swore at passers-by and got into trouble. I went to see her and found the door of her house festooned with garlic—to keep out the evil spirits. Well, I can tell you it kept me out until someone got rid of it. I went in and the lady was in bed, a bed, would you believe it, festooned with garlic. I got rid of the garlic and really went into battle against whichever spirit was playing around. I doused the lady's tongue with holy water, scattered some around the place and not a spirit disturbed that lady again. What do you think of that?

Other occult phenomena I have been involved in could well be the subject of another book. Who knows? Watch out for 'things that bumped in the night'.

I had been at Keele over six years when the illness requiring major heart surgery made itself known. I have written about this extensively in the next chapter. The original rules of tenure for chaplains were three years and then another three if everybody was happy. I was the first to be given the opportunity to serve a third term of three years. I mentioned in an earlier chapter that once I began to succeed I was always asked to stay on longer wherever I served. This held good until my next post which was that of Provincial but I have written about that in Chapter 22.

Suffice it to say that I had a most wonderful nine years at Keele. They were not the easiest of my years but they were certainly the most fruitful. Over thirty asked to be received into the church and there was a tremendous Christian spirit on the campus due to our Cath Soc. We were the largest non-sporting society. I also had tremendous support from the staff and, as I said before, the villagers.

But all good things must come to an end and on 20 April 1993 I took up the office of Provincial of the British Province of the Society of the Divine Saviour. I stayed at Keele until the end of the academic year and come 30 June I left the student world. I had spent thirty years with students and I cannot think of a more wonderful way I could have spent my life.

I was well-prepared for my travels as Provincial by invitations I had received from overseas students, and my holiday that year took me to places such as Sri Lanka, Malaysia, Singapore, Hong Kong and Sabah in Borneo. I have written specifically about this latter holiday in another chapter. A parent once asked me how I coped with the responsibility of being in *loco parentis* to students. She was surprised when I told her that I did not see it as my responsibility. My responsibility was to introduce them to God and then, like any relationship, let them get on with it. Hence my newsletter which had begun in Ystradgynlais as *The Fireside* became *The Matchmaker*. In my editorial of the first issue I wrote:

> *I don't see myself as your Leader, nor as the First Catholic*
> *on the Campus but rather I see my role here at Keele as that*
> *of Facilitator – someone who eases things and my role*
> *is to ease relationships between you and Jesus Christ;*
> *to help you to get to know him better and then to leave it*
>   *to you and Him to develop that relationship –*
> *a sort of Matchmaker!*

My next role was to be that to my priests. How successful I was at that only God and the priests know. This said it all: a poem sent in with a demand that it be published in the last *Matchmaker*.

Valediction

Going from Keele, going from Staffordshire
After hundreds of sermons and hot Sunday lunches,

One or two traumas and many more triumphs,
With cards by the shelf full and flowers in bunches.
Going to London, going to Wealdstone
To take up a high and challenging labour –
(Keele's loss is the gain of the province of Britain)
Spreading the love of God and neighbour.
Gone to the city, gone to the Capital
Down the M6 to green pastures new –
(there's nothing provincial about this Provincial)
To streets paved with promise under skies ever blue.
So shed not a tear; heave not a sigh-
Farewell, Richard: Au revoir, not goodbye!

Third Interlude

The Operation

I reckon that this is as good a place as any to talk about my operation. Prior to 1991 I had never had a day's illness in my life. As a child I used to pray to be ill so that I wouldn't have to go to school I hated it so much. There was one occasion when I actually thought of putting flour on my face so my mother would think I was ill. I did have a fall once and had to have stitches in my hand where I fell on broken glass. I still have that scar to this day though it is so small, about half an inch, that it has never appeared on my passport as a distinguishing mark. I went through the war without a scratch.

Anyway, by the time 1991 came around I had never been to see a doctor off my own bat apart from when I had that cold back in 1947. As we enrolled for war each of us was seen by seven doctors ranging from the GP to the Consultant Psychiatrist but that was compulsory and anyway I was passed A1. I remember now that I also had to see one before I entered religious life but again that was compulsory and again I was passed fit to take on whatever religious life threw at me—much more than the war years I can tell you in terms of the vows.

August 1991. It had been a strenuous academic year and I was very tired. As with my usual practice I went over to Burnham Market to do a supply in a little parish we had there near the Norfolk coast. I had looked forward to this break for some time. The parishioners, who knew me from previous years were rather surprised to see me looking so tired and expressed their concern. In fact one of them had a brother, a retired doctor, living with her and she got him to come to the daily Mass on the Friday to look at me. The first thing I knew about this was when the doctor came into the presbytery after Mass to apologise for his covert operation but he advised me to visit the local clinic for a check-up. I pooh-poohed the idea but already a parishioner had made an appointment. She virtually frog-marched me along the road to the clinic and then stood outside until the doctor could see me.

Dr Dumphy was the doctor at Mass—he has since died, Lord have mercy on him—and it was Millicent Spence who stood on guard and I have to admit with hindsight, saved my life by so doing. Sadly, it fell to my lot some years later to have to withdraw the Salvatorians from this parish and hand it over to the Diocese. The parishioners were heartbroken and you can imagine my feelings when I knew that if it hadn't been for me going there on supply regularly I would never have visited that doctor and started on the road which saved my life. What a world we live in!

The doctor examined me. I was on the surgery bed and he poked around my stomach, looked at my finger and toe nails and took my blood pressure. Then he told me that I would have to go to the hospital for blood tests immediately. Well I had come down to say the weekend Masses in this village at the weekend and this was Friday. No way could I have got another priest so I said I would go on Monday. He asked me what time the last Mass was on Sunday and when I told him 10a.m. he said to go the hospital immediately afterwards. I went back to the presbytery little realising how serious it was. I thought about it and realised that if I was to go to the local hospital which was at Kings Lynn I could well be kept in. I had no friends in the area other than a few of the parishioners so I rang the doctor and asked him if I could go back to Newcastle-under-Lyme and go to a hospital there. Probably believing that I was doomed anyway, he agreed. The point was that I had to attend my doctor there to get the necessary authorisation to go to the hospital—and I wasn't registered with any doctor. I didn't have one. So I rang some friends at Keele and asked them to get me one for Monday.

After the 10a.m. Mass on Sunday I packed my bags and went back to Keele to await whatever fate had in store for me. The doctor in Norfolk had not told me what he thought was wrong. He simply gave me an envelope to give to 'my' doctor in Newcastle. Well, an appointment had been made for 9a.m. on the Monday and the doctor there, a lovely, kind lady, did much the same as the Norfolk man. Poked around and then told me to go straight into the local hospital for tests. 'Come back on Friday and the results should be in', she said. Come back on Friday! I was halfway to heaven or the other place by then.

I gave my sample of blood and returned home to await the results. 9a.m. on Tuesday morning I received a phone call from the doctor and she said I had to go into the hospital immediately. I rang my sister, Flo, and the friend who had found the doctor and told them. I wanted to tell my good friend Helen but she was with her family touring France. I didn't want her to come home and find I was in hospital and perhaps seriously ill. Seriously ill—the understatement of the year—though I didn't know that yet.

I went straight down and, of course not having been in hospital before knew nothing about taking things in with me. I just took some books and letters that needed replies thinking I would be out in a few days.

I was 'registered', if that's the word, placed on a trolley and left there in the passage. Fortunately I'd had the good sense to take a book in with me. The officials there had an advantage over me. They had the results of the blood test about which I knew nothing and no one was going to tell me. Eventually, after about two hours, this huge giant of a man in white garments came and said he was going to take me to a ward. He could have been the senior consultant or the lowest porter for all I knew. What I did know was the business with bedpans so I asked him if he could drop me off at a toilet before we got to the ward. He actually laughed and said that I wouldn't be needing a bedpan in the ward I was going to. Then after a pause he said, 'You're going to the isolation ward and you will have your own room which is en suite.' Let me say now that from that moment on to this very day I have had nothing but admiration for our health service. I was there as an ordinary member of the public aged sixty-five on the National Health and I have had nothing but the best of treatment from that day to this. Incidentally, the medical profession got their own back on me for not going to see a doctor all my life. From that day in 1991 the longest I have gone without seeing a doctor is six weeks.

There was a time when the health service and I nearly fell out. After they had diagnosed my illness they began a four-hourly intravenous programme. Every four hours, day and night somebody would come along, crush some tablets and wait for them to dissolve. Then they would attach the hypodermic needle to a little funnel like thing that was strapped to my hand. A squeeze and the liquid would go straight into the blood stream. This was OK during the day but to be woken up in the middle of the night and half-way through the early hours was just too much. At one time I had three or four of these things embedded in me so as not to risk infection. The time came when the nurse said they could all come out. Little did I realise that something far worse would be sticking into me—the surgeon's knife. However, I had a brilliant idea and I asked her if she would leave one of these funnel like objects in my hand. She looked puzzled at this and asked me why. With a rather serious face I said to her, 'It will be great for the gin and tonic.' Alas, she had no sense of humour or didn't think I should be joking about these things. With a quick movement that only nurses have to perfection she whipped it out removing the grin off my face very swiftly.

So I was safely ensconced in my own en suite room in the isolation ward of the Newcastle Royal Infirmary. This was the Newcastle-under-Lyme in Staffordshire. It is interesting that not having been in hospital before I didn't know the duties of a patient. So to the surprise of the nurses I would be up and dressed about 7.00a.m., walk to the hospital chapel for morning prayers and then write letters while waiting for my breakfast. Of course I had not intended to be in hospital for long so didn't even have a change of clothing with me. Rowena, she who had found me a doctor, came to my rescue. She bought pyjamas, things I had never ever worn and changes of clothing. She even took my washing home and did it, bringing it back clean and fresh. Eventually the powers that be came and told me the result of their tests. Three doctors came to me. One was an obviously experienced doctor and the other two had recently qualified. I suspected things were serious when, in a very serious voice, he said 'you have SBE, sub-acute bacteria endocarditis'. Obviously that meant nothing to me so he explained that bacteria had seeded itself on the valves of the heart. When he said this, the young lady doctor interrupted him and told me in a very sympathetic voice 'it is eminently curable'. Well, I thought, that was a relief. In the old days it was a killer as I have recounted earlier. The doctor told me that I would have intravenous injections every four hours for two weeks and then I could go home and take tablets for two weeks and all should be well. Two weeks passed and I was having regular blood tests and scans. But at the end of the two weeks the doctor said I would need another week and then I could go home. On the Friday morning of the third week I was taken for a scan just to be on the safe side. That evening I was packing up ready to go home the following morning. I saw the nurses looking at something and nodding rather seriously. Then the Sister came in and asked what I was doing. I told her I was going home in the morning. She looked at me and said 'you may not be'. Nothing happened until about 7p.m. when a man came in to see me. He sat opposite me and said that he was a heart surgeon and that the scan had shown up vegetation growing on the walls of the artery. I needed surgery to remove the vegetation and also to implant an artificial aortic valve. 'You can live with the SBE', he said, with a poorer quality of life but if the vegetation came loose it could block an artery and all sorts of damage could result, such as brain damage or kidney failure. 'But', he said, 'it is your decision.' Being very brave I asked him what risk to life was involved in surgery. All my life I had dreaded having surgery and here was the big one facing me. The doctor said that I had a forty per cent chance. I thought that with my luck I would probably go. I asked him how long I had to decide and he said, 'well now'. They had to get the theatre staff back in and find twenty-four pints of blood.

I was devastated. There was no one with me with whom I could discuss it and so I rang Flo. In her usual way she simply said 'it's your decision. You must decide.' I realised that I had no option. I thought that if I didn't have the operation I might have the blocked arteries the Doctor had told me about. In that case I would be causing people to look after me for the rest of my life. Then I took refuge in the thought of my past failures. I had never passed a public exam first time in my life. So I thought I am unlikely to get to heaven first go. However, from the moment I said yes to the operation I prepared myself for death. About nine o'clock that night the surgeon came in to see me to tell me about the operation. What would happen during it, immediately after it and for the next few days. He then discussed the valve they were going to put in and he asked me, 'Which do you prefer, tissue valve or artificial?' I thought, well, I've never gone shopping for a valve before so I'm not the best person to judge. He told me if I had the tissue valve I would have to have the operation repeated every seven years and he smiled secretly to himself, though I caught a glimmer of it. I was sixty-five and he probably thought I wouldn't last that long anyway. Then he said that with the artificial valve I would be on warfarin for the rest of my life. That seemed a better proposition but there were still remnants of the old religious life left in me. We were taught that if we were ill our vow of obedience was 'sort of' transferred to the doctors. In other words, we had to do what we were told. So I said to him 'You do what you think best when you open me up.' He said that they normally implanted tissue valves if the patient was over sixty-five and he left me. I have to say that Mr Smallpiece, the surgeon, could not have done more to put me at my ease and, though I didn't know it at the time, I was to owe my life to him and his team.

Things happened fairly quickly after that. I remember my friend had returned from France and she came over from Reading to see me. Around midnight I was transferred from the medical ward to the surgical ward by ambulance. What a ride! I felt I knew what condemned men felt like when they walked to the scaffold. I was put to bed and Helen stayed in a side ward. The operation was timed for the following morning. I woke up and I thought 'This is it—my last day on earth.' I remember being given one of those gowns that fasten down the back and going into the showers. One would expect a person who had been a priest many years and had taught about the joys of eternal life that I should have been delighted. But I re-member my feelings as though it was yesterday—feelings of resentment. I had only just come (on earth) and now I was going and I hadn't done half of what I intended to do.

Helen was in attendance that morning and was a great comfort as they wheeled me down to the theatre. I remember somebody wafting a form in front of me as I was being wheeled along on the stretcher and asking me to sign it. They had forgotten to get me to sign permission for the opera-tion. As I said, I was convinced I was going to die and had been praying non-stop since I was informed about the operation. I remember waiting outside the theatre with these two giants at the side of me. I knew that they knocked you out before going into the theatre and so I said to one of these nurses, 'Will you let me know before you knock me out please.' I wanted to make a last prayer of resignation. This was now Saturday morning. The next thing I knew it was Tuesday evening.

Let Helen take up the story: 'I thought you looked dreadful before you went down to theatre. Like a condemned man, not at peace with himself. When the theatre porters arrived to take you down the image was com-plete. Dr Johnson, the anaesthetist, still dressed in tweed jacket and look-ing like a salesman told me that it was routine and to phone about 1.30p.m. He said that you would be heavily sedated until 9p.m. but would probably be conscious and able to have a brief word or two with me then. I rang at 1.30 and after being put off by various nurses who refused to give information one nurse told me, "he is still in theatre, his condition is criti-cal" and that the next of kin have been called.

'I returned to the hospital about 5.10p.m. When we, Mike and myself, got to the visitors room there was Father Noel by the door. That was a relief, in one sense. The other priest I assumed wrongly was the Provincial, but turned out to be Father Adrian. About 6–7ish they brought you out of the theatre. Still with us but only just. Mr Smallpiece, the surgeon, came in looking haggard and weary and told us that it had not been as straightforward as they had hoped. The valve was very badly damaged and as they tried to replace it some of the tissue they were attaching it to fragmented and they could not stop the bleeding. They had put in another replacement valve but the length of the operation had been a struggle for the heart and lungs and you were in a very critical state, and still bleeding. They were going to monitor you for a couple of hours and hope the bleeding would stop. When asked what were your chances, they said nothing optimistic, only that you were still alive and that was astonishing to them all. Momentarily, people felt that it was at least something that you were out of the theatre. Noel was extremely pessimistic. Adrian was resigned but slightly more hopeful than Noel.

'Adrian asked if he could give you the last rites. They let him do that. Sometime after that we got an update that you were still bleeding but that we could come in and see you in twos if we wanted. When it was my turn to go in and see you it suddenly dawned on me why they were doing this. I think they did not feel you were going to pull through.'

Me again: People talk of 'out of the body' experience. I don't know if I was out of my body but I remember an experience vividly. I felt myself being carried along in a sluice, I was floating on the water and it was all dark. In the distance behind me I could see two of our priests, Adrian and Noel. Noel was urging me to keep going. By that I presumed he meant keep fighting, rather than keep going down the sluice but knowing Noel … God bless him. I felt myself going around this bend and, suddenly, I found myself coming back. (I know what people mean now when they say they met themselves coming back.) I told the surgeon afterwards and he explained it as far as he could.

It seems that when they opened me up they found my heart was in a bad way. I am told that the surgeon asked my sister my age and when she told him he said my heart was older than that. I thought afterwards that I must have been issued with a second-hand heart when I was born. To cut (pardon the pun) a long story short, after eight hours they couldn't stop the bleeding and gave me up. The water in the sluice was my blood and my life was floating away. When Adrian heard I was at the point of death he had given me the Sacrament of the Sick and Noel at the side of him had been urging me to persevere.

They called out the next of kin and prepared them for the end. I was told afterwards that my sister, Lily, the nun, started to prepare the funeral. She was furious with me when I came around!!! The archbishop came out and said the rosary and Flo and my dear family sat in the waiting room eating fish and chips. Would you believe it and there I was dying???

I vaguely remember being on a stretcher in a little room and these people around me talking of blood. It seemed this is when they were bringing me back up to die.

Helen again: 'When I saw you, you were surrounded by surgeons, who, assuming that the last relative had been, were preparing you for the theatre. They looked weary themselves but they were kindly. You were multi-linked to tubes and gadgets and covered in a foil sheet. There was a huge bleeding wound on your chest. There were two thick tubes draining from your chest and even your hand had tubes and drips in it.

You went down around midnight. Just before you were brought back Dr Johnson came in and told us that the bleeding was not from the valve but from the chest wound and they had managed to stop that. The bad news was that you hadn't liked going on the heart and lung machine again and your blood pressure was dangerously low.'

Me again: To cut a very long story and four days short I remember opening my eyes and being given a glass of water by the Sister in the intensive care unit. To this day I have never tasted anything like it. Now I know what the elixir of life is. It tasted like I imagined liquid crystal would taste.

Helen was at the side of the bed and I was full of tubes. It seems I had been there four days and it had been touch and go during that time. What dreadful agony I put my friends and relatives through during that time only they can tell. I remember being transferred to another ward and being asked by a nurse what side I normally slept on. When I told her, I was padded in and from that day onwards until I was discharged a king or a pope couldn't have been treated better. There was a constant battle between nurses on duty and students who wanted to come and see me. The nurses won—most of the time. I had to have three months convalescent. It began in Colwyn Bay when I was signed into a posh nursing home run by the Sisters of Mercy. I arrived using a walking stick and flanked by Adrian and Noel, those of my 'out of the body experience'. The three of us stood in a line as the Matron opened the door. She looked at the three of us and asked, 'Which one is the patient?' Adrian and Noel still haven't forgiven her or me for that.

I wasn't very comfortable in Colwyn Bay as it was more a nursing home for the elderly than a convalescent home. It was very regimental and although I was given the best of food they wouldn't let me have my favourites: sausages and pork pie. I heard about self-catering flats down the road in Llandudno and so I transferred there after a week. I was very happy there and stayed until it was time to end that period of my convalescence. And what added to my joy was that the flats belonged to the Loreto Sisters whom I served at Mary Ward. The flats in fact were converted from a college, one of the colleges in which I had started my retreat work with sixth formers all those years before. It's a funny old world. Eventually when that period of the convalescence ended Monsignor Corrigan, the local Dean, who had had major surgery himself sometime before, took me in and gave me a room in his house rather than let me go back to the cottage. He was concerned I would start work too soon or that I would receive too many visitors. He joined the ranks of those who saved my life.

Three months after the operation on 8 December I returned to work. It was a Sunday and I made my appearance during the evening Mass at Keele. As I walked into the chapel I received a standing ovation. I was home.

THE OPERATION

Just before I finish this saga let me tell you about the warfarin. Fortunately for me they had implanted an artificial valve. This meant no more operations but warfarin for the rest of my life. What I didn't know was that I would have to have six-weekly blood tests for the rest of my life to ensure I was on the right dosage. But it is a small price to pay for life.

PART FIVE

The Phoenix

Although I had lived most of my apostolic life in individual apostolates I had returned to community and taken part in community exercises regularly.

I was on the short list of nominees for the office of Provincial regularly as each election came around and I served on the Provincial Council on and off for thirteen years. Eventually I was elected Provincial.

Since I had joined the Territorial Army I took the annual camps as my annual break. Now, however, I was free to roam wider at my own choice. On one of these annual breaks I went to Rome and Assisi.

21

The Mr Nearly Man

I mentioned before that I belonged to the Society of the Divine Saviour, a Religious Order. Religious Orders are a bit like Regiments in the army, each founded for a different purpose. Some were founded to teach, others to nurse. Some were founded to give retreats, i.e. courses on the spiritual life, others to preach the Gospel of Christ. The Salvatorians were founded to preach the Goodness and Kindness of the Divine Saviour 'by all ways and means'. The Salvatorians were not limited in their work. Thus whatever gifts a person had could be used to spread the Gospel of Christ. What attracted me to the Salvatorians was the global nature of their apostolate, i.e. its aims. I thought surely there must be a place for me in such an organisation.

Religious Orders tend to be international organisations and so are highly structured. Our 'Head-man' was the General living in Rome. He was assisted in his work by a council of four men (Consulters). The General is responsible for the whole order and each Consultor has a particular area of responsibility. The Order is divided into national provinces and each province is governed by a Provincial supported by four Consulters. All those in office serve for a fixed period of time but are then back in the ranks.

Around about the time of my Silver Jubilee of priesthood in 1986 I was becoming known in the Province, if not in the Society as 'the Mr Nearly man'.

I had nearly been Provincial. I had nearly been Novice Master. I had nearly been a local Superior but I had in fact been none of these. I was nearly so in that I was a Provincial Consultor on and off for thirteen years and during that time Vicar Provincial, i.e. Deputy Provincial, twice. I have to say that I was considered for the office of Novice Master, for local Superior of our biggest community in London and even considered for Prefect of Students but alas nothing came of it. But to explain this I need to take you back to 1970, when I left community life for the first time to live on my own.

In accepting the position of Lecturer at Mary Ward College I was undertaking what our Constitutions call 'an individual apostolate'. Most superiors are not keen on such but as the concept was in its infancy in 1970 I was given permission without too much trouble. After all, the Founder listed among his works of the Society, education of the youth. Until this time the Provincial had been appointed by the General having consulted certain people in the province. There was no question of voting. Fr Aloysius was the last Provincial to be appointed under this system but by the time his first term of office ended the new system had evolved. To cut a long story short I was on the short list of the first free election.

To understand why I wasn't elected I need to take you even further back than the 1970s. In fact, to the time when I was in that Jesuit parish of St Francis Xavier. My mother was a very religious person and she lived for the church. She would be at Mass every morning and on Sundays we would go to Mass in the morning, Sunday School in the afternoon and then 'Rosary, Sermon and Benediction' in the evening. The last being a devotion during which some of the finest Jesuit preachers would wax eloquently for half an hour or more. I would sit listening to them spellbound, dreaming of the day when I would mount that pulpit. Strangely enough I don't ever remember saying family prayers at home, nor do I remember my brother and sisters having to go to the church services. They must have done as they would have had to have their church cards stamped like the rest of us. In fact the Sisters of Mercy who taught my sisters had less mercy than the Jesuits. I mentioned those cards in a previous chapter. These were my formative years and you can imagine the atmosphere in which I was brought up. Anything connected with the church took priority. Thus I had no other pursuits other than going to church, attending Church 'things'. I was in the choir as a boy soprano and then I was an altar boy. These days altar servers simply serve Mass and have no other duties, whereas in those days there were all sorts of services to attend, many of which went on for hours. For example, the Good Friday service was a three-hour devotion starting at 1p.m.. In the morning we served a special Mass which was called the 'Mass of the pre-sanctified' which went on for two hours and then in the evening we would be back for the Stations of the Cross. The Holy Saturday service began at 6a.m. and went on until noon when Lent officially ended. We would go behind the high altar from time to time for refreshments. In addition to the religious duties, we would be given other work such as painting statues, polishing brass candlesticks, etc., etc.

This was my childhood and back at home strict morals were enforced. Thus I was brought up in a quasi-Jansenist's atmosphere where anything pleasurable was a sin. I remember being told that everything had three uses. Take beer. Too much was a sin, a certain amount was the right use of alcohol but the real virtue lay in giving it up altogether. I remember giving up oranges once because they gave me pleasure.

It goes without saying that sex was never mentioned except to emphasise the sinful nature of its misuse and I can vividly remember walking along College Road near our school at the age of fifteen thinking how dirty sexual intercourse was.

So it was with this background of strict religious formation that I arrived at Abbots Langley to begin my lifelong commitment to Almighty God. I presumed that everybody was brought up the same way so it was a real shock to discover my fellow candidates had been brought up in a much more liberal atmosphere which showed in their behaviour. For me the rule was meant to be kept literally, for others it was a guide for good living. I was shocked and scandalised in those first weeks and months. I seriously thought I had made a wrong decision and I think it was only the shame of failing yet again that kept me in the college. I had given up a good job, publicly proclaimed my withdrawal from the world and received money and gifts to help me on my way. This was not the best of motives for staying on but God has his own way of getting people to do his will and gradually my motive for staying became more positive.

So I arrived at the Salvatorians with a very strict religious outlook bordering on the scrupulous. Here was I trying to live what amounted to a Jesuit way of life in a Salvatorian community. I have to admit that those training us to be Salvatorians were right and I was wrong. Perhaps I should have left then and joined the Jesuits but I had put my hand to the plough and decided that this was where God wanted me. But to this day I still feel very influenced by my Jesuit upbringing. My strict conscience became stricter as I advanced from one temporary profession to the next until by the time I took final vows I must have been a real pain to all I lived with. I would keep the rule as literally as I could. As they say, for one saint in the community there are ten martyrs.

This continued into my priesthood. The day after we were ordained we were scattered to the four winds, some on the foreign missions, others to different parts of the British Isles. So my fellow students were left with the impression of me as the ultra-strict religious priest. It was many years later before we met up again. Meanwhile my name kept coming up on the short list for the office of Provincial every three years. In no way were those who had known me in the student days going to vote for me and rightly so with the memories they had. The support I had was from those with whom I had lived and worked since ordination. So what had happened?

I have written above about what happened to me after ordination. At the age of thirty-five I had gone to night school and sat with fifteen-year-olds studying 'O' and 'A' levels. Then I had spent three years with undergraduates of eighteen to twenty-one years of age studying zoology and psychology. From then on I had lived in a very secular environment, teaching secular subjects and keeping the rules of my religious life as far as I could. And without being aware of it, imperceptibly, I changed. Over those years I turned 180 degrees in terms of my spiritual and religious life.

When the Second Vatican Council took place I was ready for it and became an enthusiastic supporter of change and renewal. Those I lived with saw this. Those who had left me after ordination day still saw in their mind's eye the strict Sullivan of the old days. And ironically among those I lived with, the traditionalists wouldn't vote for me and, coupled with the others, won the day. But God gets his way eventually. It took twenty-three years but on 13 January 1993 I was finally elected Provincial.

But let's have another break.

Fourth Interlude

Part One: All Roads Lead to Rome

Among the advantages of being a chaplain in the academic world was the opportunity for holidays and travel. Students from all over the world would invite me to their homes for a break and such invitations were genuine and sincere. I wasn't able to take advantage of all the offers though hopefully there is still time. But allied with this was the advantage of belonging to an International Religious Order. We have houses in over thirty-three countries and I could visit these any time whenever I had the opportunity. It is a bit like visiting your aunt or cousin. You are part of the family as soon as you walk in and, of course, no mention of money.

I remember one Summer I was sitting in the Colosseum in Rome wondering what had possessed me to come to Rome in September when the Romans were all leaving their beautiful city because of the heat. Looking back it must have been that large gin and tonic that prompted me to pick up the phone and call our Mother House in Rome. Headquarters of Religious Orders are always called 'Mother Houses'. July and August had passed with various half-hearted attempts to take a holiday. Two days in South Wales followed by a cancelled week in North Wales. Then a two-week booking in Ireland cancelled before the dates were even confirmed. Time was drawing on and commitments at the end of September meant that it was now or never.

A voice answered the phone in Italian, then changed to very broken English to tell me there would be a spare room for me from 8–18 September. I was to find out later that there were about fifteen spare rooms, and the Italian speaking to me on the phone was in fact Indian. However, I booked the room in our Mother House which is quite literally next door to the Vatican. The next step was transport. Our provincial Bursar advised me that Alitalia was the cheapest and gave me their telephone number in London. I rang them half hoping there would be no seats on the dates I wanted. But there were and without any fuss the booking was made and if I would send the cheque for £160, they would send the tickets. Before the effects of the gin wore off I sent the cheque sealing my fate. This took place towards the end of August and the next day I went off on a week's Summer School at Strawberry Hill, confident that the ticket would have arrived before my return. It hadn't. With only four days to go the ticket still hadn't arrived and hope began to arise that perhaps the trip could be called off. I rang them, they apologised and promised express delivery. Two days before departure it arrived, only for me to realise I hadn't asked for insurance. More phone calls and insurance arrived one day before departure. It would seem my heart was not really in the trip at all. I hear people planning their holidays long in advance and having everything ready with months to spare.

I had decided to spend the night before my flight in London so as to get to Heathrow for the 11.30 booking in time and without any haste.

I had been informed by one of our priests that most of the community in our house in the Borough, South East London, would be away for a first profession of vows' ceremony in Dublin. So I knew there would be a room free for the night. I had been parish priest in the Borough some years previously so one or two of my past students who lived in the parish came up for the evening. We spent a very pleasant evening putting the world to rights and making proposals for me to put to the Pope should I bump into him. The actual bump which I described earlier was to come much later in fact. By then the proposals seemed to have lost their impact.

Monday 8 September dawned bright and clear, and without mishap I boarded the 12.50 flight to Rome clutching my duty-free Glenlivet and Balkan Sobranie tobacco.

I had rung Rome and written to tell them the time of my arrival and on the plane it occurred to me that I might have told them the wrong time. I was due in at 15.25 local time and I suspected that I had told them 5.25, getting confused with the 24-hour clock. Sure enough, nobody was there to meet me at 15.25 so I waited until 1800hrs and still nobody arrived. Fortunately I had armed myself with lire in England so I was able to pay the 5000 needed to take a bus in to Rome. This took me into Rome railway station from where I had to find a local bus going to the Vatican. The Italian bus system differs from ours. One has to buy tickets at a tobacconist's or kiosk before boarding the bus and journeys within cities are all the same price, be it a five-minute or a thirty-minute trip. Each ticket lasts a certain length of time. The seasoned traveller gets a book of these tickets and even knows how to get cheap tickets for a whole day's travel or a week's travel – a bit like our season tickets. Before I could get a ticket to the Mother House, I had to find a place to buy a ticket, then find a bus on which to use it. I had no knowledge of Italian but using the principle that if you shout loud enough foreigners understand, I eventually bought my 700 lire ticket, boarded the No. 64 at the railway station and set off for San Pietro. It is well-known in Rome that a bus is never full. There is always room for one more and you can imagine that by the time we got to St Peter's we were packed in like sardines. The London underground at its busiest peak hour is empty compared with a bus going to St Peter's at any time of the day.

We arrived. It was now about 19.20hrs. I had been to the Mother House on a previous occasion and similarly been left standing at the airport. Then I had arrived at 11p.m. It used to be the custom in our Mother House to hide the doorbell under one of the carved leaves on the huge front door. This was to deter would-be tramps from disturbing siestas, etc. I hadn't known this on my first visit and consequently had to sit on the doorstep hoping for a late-night reveller to return. I was fortunate. As you would expect, there are no late-night revellers living in the Mother House but a priest returning from visiting his family let me in at 3a.m.

So it was with confidence that I went up to the Mother House prepared to push aside the magic leaf and press the bell. But I was fooled again. The leaf had gone and with it the doorbell. Imagine a door that would make the entry into Strangeways prison look small, a door full of bits of carving, but none moveable. I searched and searched to no avail. I went round the back trudging my luggage with me. Part of our Mother House had been leased to the Poles as a pilgrim centre, and so I went in there thinking there might be access to the main part of the building. Alas, no matter how loud I shouted the Poles couldn't or wouldn't understand me. So back I went to the front door expecting to sit once again until some good soul returned from a sick call or some such.

As I placed my luggage down I happened to glance up to the side and there, in all its glory, was a brand new bell complete with light and one of those gratings that talk to you. Modernisation had come to Rome in my absence. With relief, I rang the bell. It was 19.45 and by 20.00 hours a voice answered, 'Ya?' (they speak a lot of German in the Mother House). I told the grille I was Richard, and it echoed 'Ricardo?' I replied 'Ya' this time. I was beginning to understand the language even though I was in Italy. The word 'Ya' worked like magic and just like in one of those Frankenstein films the huge door with creaking hinges opened of its own accord. Nobody was in sight but I quickly stepped in. The doors closed behind me. My holiday had begun.

Anyone who has been locked in a dark dungeon will know what it is like when the door closes upon you as you enter the Mother House. Complete blackness even in daytime. Fumbling along the wall looking for a light switch is to no avail. The switch is behind you on the door post. I found myself in a room a bit like a large rectangle turned up on its end. On the right-hand side is a small window which enables the receptionist to vet you prior to opening another door to admit you into the courtyard. Being after 7.00p.m. there was no receptionist, but fortunately my ring at the outer door had caused someone to leave the dining room in order to let me in. This person emerged through the inner door just as I had found the light switch. He was an Indian layman who turned out to be the receptionist. In broken English he welcomed me and took my bag, and we went through into the courtyard. The courtyard is a bit like the Palm Court Hotel. It is square in shape with a path going around three sides. The fourth side consists of large iron doors leading to the side street. This street is named after our first Superior General, Fr Pancratius who was instrumental in ensuring that Rome remained an 'open city' during the Second World War. The centre of the courtyard is taken up with beautiful palm trees and a fountain. We walked through and came to another door. This door was in fact an iron grille which gave access to the house proper. We used the lift and went up to the dining room on the third floor. About seven priests and brothers were just finishing off their evening meal. They made me welcome and I was invited to share the leftovers. This consisted of a clear soup with bits of scrambled eggs floating in it, fried eggs with a variety of cold meats, and figs and grapes to follow. Mineral water and a typically Italian table wine were offered to wash it down.

Seated at the table were priests from Germany, from Columbia, and from Poland. These were the General Consultors. The General and English-speaking member were both in the States on visitation. Other members of the community present were from Germany, Poland and Italy. Finally making up the community was Fr Spelluci from Germany. The latter was about eighty-five and had had the distinguished honour of being chaplain to the Blessed Sacrament Chapel in St Peter's.

Of all these, about three spoke broken English and the Acting Superior showed me to my room on the third floor. He explained where everything was and then told me that the community rose at 6.15a.m. and the community Mass in Italian was at 6.45a.m. As an afterthought he suggested that having travelled a long way perhaps I 'might like to lie in the first day'. At this point I decided his English was not clear enough for me to understand and for the whole of my stay I went down to the chapel about 8.30 and said Mass in English on my own. After the instruction about Mass, Fr Superior wished me 'a happy night' and promptly left. He had previously given me a key to unlock the two front doors and the grille and a key to my bedroom. It was the next day when one of them copiously apologised for not meeting me at the airport. It seemed that there had been a burglary and the priest deputed to meet me had had to go to the police station to make a statement.

It was about 8.30p.m. when I was abandoned to my 'happy night'. It was a pleasant enough bedroom with a bed, upright chair, desk, wardrobe and wash basin. Being Italy, there were shutters outside the windows which operated from a 'button' in the wall. Press and the shutters closed. Press again and they opened – real magic. The temperature was about 85F so I left shutters and windows open and tried to sleep. My first night's experience was the pattern for the whole week. The noise of traffic with blaring horns crashed through the open window. So I closed the windows and the heat of the room reminded me of my air-conditioned car waiting for me at Heathrow. This in turn reminded me of all the delights of England which now seemed a million miles away. Eventually, about 4.00a.m., I fell asleep to be awakened at 6.15 with the bell summoning the 'monks' to rise for prayer.

I arose at about 8.00, said Mass and went into breakfast. Bread rolls and butter, cold meats such as salami, etc. and cheese. Coffee completed the meal. Leading off from the refectory is a very beautiful veranda complete with garden chairs, tables and potted plants. This overlooks the splendid palm courtyard beneath. I sat there and drank my coffee and planned my first day in Rome. It was Tuesday 9 September. About 10.00a.m. I went over to St Peter's and renewed my acquaintance with the Vatican. Paul VI was gloriously reigning on my previous visit so I went down to the crypt and paid my respects to him in his resting place. It is marked by a simple marble slab with his name and the dates of his reign. It is slightly raised from the floor at an angle of 30°. Opposite his resting place is a large sarcophagus bearing the name of John Paul I. I spent the morning viewing St Peter's and its environs and returned 'home' at 1.30 to find all food had been cleared away. The inevitable bread and butter was there, and coffee, so lunch was rather a primitive affair.

Before I went to Rome I had written to Michael Sharkey, my successor at Aston University, to tell him my address. Imagine my surprise when on returning from St Peter's, I was handed a message from him. He had just called and had left his phone number. I was to ring him between 5.30 and 7.30p.m. that night.

After my exotic lunch taken on the veranda, I went for a walk along the Tiber, passing the castle St Angelo and visiting the mausoleum of Augustus and one or two other places less worthy of note. On my return I went down to ring Michael and found him sitting there waiting for me. He works for the Sacred Congregation of Catholic Education and his office in the Curia is almost opposite the Mother House. He took me over there and showed me the offices of the whole congregation, including the cardinal's room, waiting rooms, etc. and even the room where the various hierarchies meet the cardinal on their 'ad limina' visits to Rome. Every five years the Hierarchy of a particular country has to report to the Pope and the Roman Curia on what is happening in the church in their respective countries It is a sort of self-assessment visit and is called 'ad limina'. It was really interesting and the holiday began to perk up. Michael always played down his role in the Vatican but he was obviously well-known and well-liked. He was in the process of drafting a report for the hierarchy of the USA based on his analysis of reports from each seminary in the USA. As it was not such a favourable report he had also prepared a press release. It was interesting to see in that week's *Tablet* the journalist's view 'Rome comes down against USA'. Michael had more influence than he admitted to. I must say he was at home in Rome and I felt sure he would go far. His working day, as with all Curial members, was 8.30–1.30 Monday to Saturday and 5.30–7.30p.m. Tuesdays and Fridays. This being a Tuesday we waited until 7.30 and then went out for a meal. We walked for about fifteen minutes to his 'home', the international hotel for clergy and then found a restaurant nearby. It was a friendly restaurant and the manager had worked for a long time in England. We had a very nice pasta, and as this left us too full for a main course, we finished off with coffee and cheese. A litre of wine had been consumed with the pasta and that, or the water, or the pasta, began my stomach trouble which was to last until I returned to England and a bacon butty on the train home. I never did isolate the cause of the trouble but it came and went like waves throughout the holiday, even in Assisi. Fortunately, I had taken Enos fruit salts with me and it helped a lot.

I left Michael that night about 9.30 and took a bus home. I arranged to meet him at 10.00a.m. the next day when, he said, he would show me the Vatican behind St Peter's. It was dark now, and St. Peter's Square was almost deserted. The lamps were on by the two fountains and one or two couples were sitting around talking. I strolled around for a while and then went in. Not a soul stirred. So I went to my room. I had brought the bottle of whisky to give to the community for a drink at recreation. But as I hadn't yet encountered any community life other than at meals, the bottle was still in my room. I resisted the temptation to open it and went to bed. This time I kept the windows closed.

I woke up on the morning of Wednesday the tenth and thought I was back in England. Rain was pouring down, and as the day wore on the weather got worse. Thunder and lightning and torrential rain. God didn't want me to tour the Vatican and at about 9.45 I went downstairs intending to ring Michael and postpone the trip. Walking through the courtyard I saw two young ladies who seemed to have difficulty making the receptionist understand their needs. As I walked towards them to see if I could help (I never could resist a pretty girl) they gasped in astonishment. I thought for a moment I had left my teeth out or committed some horrendous gaffe in my appearance when one of them cried out, 'Fr Richard!' They turned out to be two Keele students backpacking around Europe on a railcard. One of them, a beautiful blonde, all blue-eyed, knew one of our priests in Wealdstone and he had recommended they call at the Mother House to get decent tickets for the Papal Audience. Her companion was a very beautiful Indian girl also from Keele.

They knew me though I didn't recognise them and I didn't want to embarrass them by asking if they came to the university chapel on Sundays. On subsequent meetings it emerged that the English girl, whom I shall call Mary had attended during the first term but dropped off. She had started again during the holidays. The other lady obviously wasn't a Catholic.

Mary later volunteered the information that she had stopped going to church because of the identification of all Christians with the Christian Union on the campus, at least in the eyes of the students. The Christian Union tended to be a very evangelical group of Christians. Anyway, Brother Cassius, the guest Master, emerged and arranged for the tickets for the following Wednesday - it being too late for the present day. We arranged to meet for dinner on the following Tuesday and off they went. There was a gap in the rain clouds so I 'dashed' across to Michael's office. He was in the throes of searching for two lost English people. I should explain that Wednesday morning around the Vatican is chaotic. The world and his wife seem to converge on the Square for the 10.00a.m. audience. Queues begin about 7.00a.m. although entry is not allowed until 8.30a.m. These two people were on a tour and had left Assisi the previous day and were due to meet Michael who was to show them how to find their seats at the Audience. In fact, they were elderly people who had been burgled in Assisi and had lost their medicines. Michael eventually found them, took them to a pharmacy and then showed them to the right entrance. But with the rains, the Audience had been moved into the Audience Hall. Sales at Harrods seem like a Sunday School outing compared to people trying to get into the Audience Hall when their tickets are for the Piazza. No queues–just thousands of people milling around the doors all wanting to be first. In the event, these two people got into the entrance hall but did-n't even see the Pope. Anyway, Michael and I had coffee and agreed to postpone our visit to the Vatican to the following day and arranged to meet that night for dinner. I went back to my room and used the time to write some cards.

In the evening the rain wore off so after studying the map of Rome I went on foot to find Michael's home. I was very pleased with myself for discov-ering it with only one wrong turning. Streets in Rome can be really scary in the dark.

The day of surprises was not over. I walked into the lift to go up to Mi-chael's office, and walking out of it were two priests. Bernard Boardman and Bernard Grouney. I hadn't seen them for over twenty years. I had been with them in the Catholic Evidence Guild and used to speak with

Bernard Boardman about our becoming priests. You may remember I mentioned Bernard when I spoke about the Catholic Evidence Guild in Chapter 9. Sadly, we only had a few minutes together but vowed to meet again back home. We didn't, of course.

After an aperitif in Michael's room we went to dinner in a nearby restaurant, being nearly knocked down on the way by the Prime Minister's car which raced by on its way, no doubt, to some important function. It was a very beautiful night after all the rain so we sat out on the terrace which was like sitting in the middle of Trafalgar Square. Traffic roaring by with the inevitable hooting of horns and passers-by jostling with each other on the pavements. Tramps were having a field day preying on the guilt of those eating superb meals in the presence of the hungry. Being priests of course we didn't succumb! I went home by bus to the quiet, peaceful house and to my restless bed.

It was always an adventure to open the shutters of a morning and to see what sort of a day it was. Expecting more rain and thunder, I opened the shutters this particular morning and found the sun blazing down. I had decided that today would be my sightseeing day as I was off to Assisi on Friday until Monday and the girls would be with me on Tuesday and Wednesday. They would already have done their own sightseeing. So at 10.00a.m. I went over to see Michael. Knowing I would be out for the day I had collected some bread and butter and the cold meats from the breakfast table, and armed myself with some sandwiches.

Michael took me into the 'tradesman's' entrance at the side of St Peter's and showed me the inside as far as he was allowed to go. We went into the Vatican Bank, the Vatican gardens, railway station, saw the Secretariat of State, Doctrine of Faith building, etc., etc. It was a wonderful experience and Michael excelled himself as a guide. Everywhere we went we were saluted by the Swiss guard resplendent in their fancy pyjamas and halberds. Salutes consisted of them springing to attention and crashing their halberds onto the ground – quite frightening the first time. After our tour on foot and by car we went to an office where they issue tickets to go under the Basilica to see the excavations and the bones of St Peter. You have to apply days in advance and as I had wondered where I would take the girls on Tuesday, Mike suggested this, so it was all arranged. I left Mike after coffee and began my tour of Rome in one day. I walked and walked and walked. Following the map, I saw most, if not all, the principal sights – at least, those I had not seen on previous visits. Castle St Angelo, fountains of three coins fame, Pantheon, various churches, Colosseum, Forum, etc., etc. I sat in the Colosseum absolutely exhausted and ate my sandwiches. It was then I discovered that in Italy they sell gin and tonic and so I had my first real drink since I had left England.

Lots of ice and tonic with a suggestion of gin, it was wonderful, and cheap at £1.50. My feet perked up and I was ready for the rest of the day. I finished up at the station where I enquired about trains for Assisi. Long queues and lots of shoving!   Fortunately, I had bought my ticket in England so that was one problem I didn't have to face. The lady at the desk gave me a brochure and I went off happy. Little did I realise what was ahead of me the following day, but that was still in the future. I was very pleased that I had travelled to Rome alone without any mishap. So I bought some fruit—grapes and pears—and headed back to the Mother House. I had started buying the Daily Mail (75p) as there was no English reading matter in the Mother House so I looked forward to an evening with the crossword.

RULE BRITANNIA

This is the time to mention the whisky again. There had still been no signs of community life at recreation in the Mother House but I still resisted the urge to open the bottle.

However, when I returned at 6.00p.m. (supper was at 7.00) it was such a beautiful evening I gave in to temptation and opened my bottle of Glenlivet. I poured a large drink and with my Daily Mail went up on to the roof and indulged in my grapes, whisky and English paper. This was what the Empire was made of!

Before I went to bed I packed my bag ready for Assisi and went to bed. The next day I began one of those periods that are forever indelibly etched on one's mind. I went to Assisi, (see Part 2 of this Interlude).

On my return to Rome from Assisi five days later I very quickly reached the Mother House. By this time I could have had shares in the 64 bus route. I had become an adept in bus travelling in Rome. The train from Assisi had been over an hour late arriving in Rome and it was 3.00p.m. before I reached St Peter's Square. I went to my room without seeing a soul, and then went off souvenir hunting. I had left Assisi early deliberately so that I would have time to do some shopping as it would be the last opportunity. Near the Vatican there is a shop called Sapranie's which sells cards and religious souvenirs very cheaply. Cards are lp whereas anywhere else they are l5p and they have an abundance of medals, rosaries, etc. all at knock-down prices. I bought a lot of these so that I would have them as gifts for baptisms, etc. and bought a few more expensive gifts for friends. On my journey back home I bought the Daily Mail and having brought back from Assisi the remainder of the gin, I went up to the roof and had a really lazy hour in the evening sun with my Daily Mail and G and T. Pure bliss. I met the community at supper. They all seemed pleased to see me and chatted away. It was interesting to see that the longer I stayed the more of them admitted to knowing English and by now four or five were engaging me in conversation.

At supper I was seated next to a Polish priest who happened to belong to the British Province. He was working in Tanzania. He spoke good English and we had mutual Salvatorian friends in England. So it was a pleasant meal. After the meal everybody disappeared as usual. I was beginning to note that people disappeared in language groups and I suspected that recreation took place in private rooms rather than the community room. This was proved to be accurate the next night when the USA Salvatorian returned. I retired to my room and wrote some final cards accompanied by a little of my Glenlivet. By now it had become a warm drink due to the oven-like temperature of my room. I went and posted my cards and retired to bed at about 10.00p.m.

Only two whole days left. I continued my practice of saying Mass alone and breakfasting on the veranda. The temperature today was 81F. At 10.00a.m. I went downstairs and found the two lovely Keele students waiting for me. We went off to collect our tickets for the excavations, passing through the Swiss guards and into the Vatican grounds. I felt sure I was impressing the students with my confidence as I addressed one of the Swiss guards with the word: 'excavationes'. It was then the other Swiss guard saw my clerical collar and decided to salute. In spite of my earlier boasting about my self control, I nearly jumped out of my skin as the halberd crashed onto the cobbled pavement. We were allowed through and as we had to wait for half an hour we wandered around the Vatican. At least, we wandered about 100 yards until some security man spotted us and re-directed us to the ticket office. We were issued with a radio guide – a sort of walkie-talkie machine which was designed to perch on the shoulder as the wearer walked around. It was tuned into English and about ten of us followed a guide down under St Peter's. I found this tour the most interesting of my whole holiday. It took us back 2000 years into the Roman Empire. It was in fact the old Roman cemetery, and sarcophagi of people who had given us headaches in our Latin studies were there before us. A deeper knowledge of Roman history and culture would have helped but I had sufficient knowledge to appreciate what I was looking at. The radio guide was very good. It was activated by photo-electric cells placed high in the corner of each chamber we entered. High technology has come to the Vatican. The tour culminated at the mausoleum of Constantine which had been built over the tomb of St Peter. The bones of St Peter were there to be seen. A most profound moment. We were told later by Michael that Pius XII had kept what was thought to be the bones of Peter in his room until further excavations revealed the genuine bones. On further examination of the bones in Pius XII's room, they were found to be those of a goat.

Our tour finished up in the crypt of St Peter's where recent popes are buried and we then made our way to Michael's office as previously arranged. He had very kindly invited us to lunch at his hotel and thither we repaired on foot. The girls must have been even more impressed than I was at the grandeur of the dining room. We were shown to our seats and treated like royalty. Waitresses attended us and Michael had chosen beforehand a sumptuous repast. Special pasta in an edible sauce, stuffed beef without the oily substance, vegetables and CHIPS. This was followed by cakes, fruit, Liquore Strega and coffee. On the next table were three Columbian bishops who were in Rome to arrange the forthcoming visit of the Pope to that country, and various bishops and curial officials were scattered around the room. When Michael had been at Aston he was a teetotaller but now he drank as well as any Roman and so a good wine accompanied the meal. We were there until about 3.30p.m. The girls still had some sightseeing to do, Michael had to return to the office at 5.00p.m., as my feet were still sore from Assisi I excused myself from the girls' company and took myself back home, walking slowly and enjoying the postprandial glow of satisfaction.

It was about 5.00p.m. when I eventually reached the roof of the Mother House clutching my Daily Mail and G and T. I was just about to sit in my usual chair when I heard English-speaking voices. Sitting a few yards away was the American General Consulter, with two other Americans. They were, of course, drinking bourbon and martini. It was the sacred cocktail hour. It was then that my views about language grouping in the community were confirmed. I joined them. There was not a lot of bourbon so with great generosity I fetched what was left of my Glenlivet and offered to share it. Alas, it was too strong for them. The two other Yanks turned out to be USA army chaplains celebrating their promotion to colonel. One was a Salvatorian, the other a diocesan priest.

So it was a very satisfactory meal although I have forgotten what we had to eat. The two Americans had gone out to dinner and I was about to return to my room when one of the Italians who was a member of the Mother-House community, Fr Gabrielle, took me by the arm and said 'Community'. At last there was communal recreation to welcome back the Consultor from America. He had been in the States for a month. It was what I used to know as a real Salvatorian evening. A lot of laughs, some serious conversation and a real genuine family atmosphere – and they spoke in English. That may have been due to the presence of liqueurs. There were drinks to suit every national taste. Imagine my shame and guilt when, especially for the 'Britisher', they produced a bottle of Glenlivet.

We retired about 10.00p.m. The holiday was coming to an end and tomorrow I was to see the Pope.

The day began at 80F and I was up early. I had got our tickets for the Audience the previous evening, rejoicing to find that they were for 'A' seats and immediately behind the dignitaries. I had arranged to meet the students as soon as they could get to the Mother House and at about 7.30a.m. I wandered out and over to the Vatican to check which entrance we were to use. The Audience was to be held in the square. Already nuns were queuing up.

Although the tickets were lettered according to a particular 'pen', each pen held around 500 people and it was a matter of first there got the best seats. Entrance wasn't allowed until 8.30a.m. anyway so I went home and said Mass. The usual invasion of the Vatican was beginning. Coaches, cars, invalids and hikers converged on the Vatican for the next two hours. About 9.00a.m. my fellow travellers arrived and we joined the queue to get to our seats. Our bags were searched thoroughly. I had taken water because it was such a dry day but this was confiscated as an offensive weapon—it was in a glass bottle. We received good seats after a lot of elbowing and shoving and sat waiting for the arrival of JPII. The square was crammed with about 70,000 people from all races, countries and creeds. It was a wonderful experience to sit there and feel that we belonged to all this. Eventually the Pope-mobile appeared to the tumultuous applause of the crowds. We could only see him in the distance but it was obvious he was getting out of the car to greet people and shake hands. Eventually he climbed the dais and began his speech in Italian. We were at right angles to the dais and about fifty yards away. After the Italian speech came synopses in five languages including English and a welcome to special groups who were present from each country. He welcomed among others the International Congress of Diabetics who were in Rome, and I immediately thought of friends I knew at Aston University who were specialists in diabetes. They always attend the Congress so I felt sure they must be somewhere amongst the crowd. I found out later, they were in Rome but had not been able to get tickets for the Audience. Only a limited number had been given to the Congress. After all the speeches, blessings, etc., the Pope began his walkabout, beginning with a group of singers on the steps of St Peter's and very near us. There was a mass movement towards the barricades; people leaping over each other in a mad rush to shake his hand. Mary literally took off and seemed to fly through the air. She got within a few feet of the Pope and took some very good pictures with my camera. After it was all over, we went and had a good long, cold, drink and waited for Michael to join us as arranged. He had offered to take us to the hills and lakes above Rome where I would entertain the group to lunch. We collected his car which was in the Vatican car park and he gave us another little tour of the Vatican grounds emerging into Rome at the side of the Congregation for the Doctrine of the Faith—successor to the Holy Office—the KGB of the Vatican. God still hadn't dispensed all his gifts to us this holiday. As we passed the door out came, as though by a miracle—the great Cardinal Ratzinger and actually bowed to us—well, to Michael. He recognised Michael, who had worked with him. We basked in reflected glory and on seeing such a lovely, gentle, silvery-haired person with the kindest of eyes I immediately changed my views of him. Views I had acquired mainly through reading Hebblethwaite.

We gatecrashed our way through the Roman traffic and passing Castel Gandolfo arrived at a lovely little village overlooking a lake which was breathtaking in its beauty: deep blue, absolutely still and peaceful. Michael knew a very good restaurant overlooking the lake and there we had our lunch at the side of a large window which gave a commanding view of the panorama. The girls were to move on to Florence the next day and I was to return to England. It was about 5.00p.m. when we left the little village. We dropped the students off at the station near where they lived and said farewell to them. Michael and myself went back to his room where we had a final drink together. I walked back to the Mother House along the Tiber and crossed the Castel Sant Angelo bridge where there was a book exhibition. I sauntered up the Via della Conciliazione and took a last look at St Peter's by lamplight. It was about 10.30p.m. when I found my room and my bed. My last day in Rome and with it my holiday had come to an end.

Time to go home. I got up early and said Mass in the Founder's Chapel alone and in English. Then went in to breakfast. I made my farewells to the community. Then it was time to pop over and say farewell to Michael. Without him the holiday would have been a real flop – at least the Roman chapter. What could I give him to show my appreciation? I had brought him a little icon from Assisi which I now intended to give him. But was this enough? I pondered and pondered and then decided he was worth the ultimate sacrifice. I parcelled up what was left of the gin and the Glenlivet and took it over to his office where I solemnly presented it to him. Of course, he was delighted. We then went out and had coffee and I bade him farewell, leaving him in the bosom of St Peter's and feeling he would one day go far in the Curia. God provided a final gift. We shared the lift with Cardinal Homer, Secretary of the Congregation of Clergy and I met Sr Mary Lynscott SND. She achieved worldwide fame in being the only female to have reached great heights in the Curia. As Michael said, had she been a man she would have been a cardinal. She didn't seem very impressed when I mentioned she had been on a retreat I once gave back in England.

One last sight concluded my stay with Michael. Walking or doddering down the street was a very old cardinal, scarlet skull-cap on his head, scarlet buttons on his cassock, rings on his fingers—and on his toes? a pair of trainers. I had seen it all. It was time to go. I collected my gear from the Mother House, boarded the number 64 bus for the last time and took myself to the airport. I arrived in plenty of time, had coffee and a ham and cheese bun, visited the duty free and bought some more tobacco and Liquore Strega and waited to be called for embarkation. There was no delay. We set off at 3.50p.m. and soon after take-off were served a light meal. After coffee I sat back and had a think. On the whole it had been a wonderful holiday, the best, I think, for many years. Assisi had been an uplifting experience looking at it in retrospect.

'Fasten your seat belts, we are approaching Heathrow.' What wonderful words which broke into my reverie. We landed safely and I seriously thought of kissing the ground. But these days you don't know who has been kissing it before you so I restrained myself and went through the immigration and customs procedures and on to collect my baggage. The train from Euston was at 7.30p.m. and it was now 5.45p.m. I felt comfortable until a note came up on the computer to tell Rome passengers to wait. Thirty minutes later our baggage arrived. I had one and a quarter hours to get to Euston, including time spent changing stations. I got to Euston with five minutes to spare. The joy of being able to ask the guards for directions was indescribable. I was assured that this was the train. Just change at Stafford. In spite of a chirpy voice that kept coming over the microphone assuring us that BR was getting there, we were delayed for about fifteen minutes just outside London. Only a short delay but long enough to ensure that I missed the connection at Stafford, but that was still unknown to me as I settled back and had the most delicious bacon butty I have ever tasted. My stomach felt better already. At Stafford we were told our connection had gone. Had all gone well we would have been at

(..... rings on his fingers,
and bells on his toes ....

Stoke by 10p.m. We had to wait for nearly an hour at Stafford and then caught the last train for the night, which stopped at every station, arriving in Stoke at 11.30p.m. As luck would have it, of my two train companions on that last trip, one was a student just back from backpacking around Europe and the other was one who wished he had and who went on and on about his psychiatrist. Still, it didn't seem so bad. After all, they were British. At Stoke there were no taxis and no phone number for taxis, so the student who lived near Keele and myself set off hopefully in the right direction in search of some means of transport. Eventually we spotted a taxi. We shared it, and after dropping off the student nearby I was deposited on my doorstep at 12.05a.m. I had arrived home.

Fourth Interlude

Part Two: Some Roads Lead to Assisi As Well

Although I set forth to Assisi from Rome my journey really originated back in Manchester in 1967. As an undergraduate living in the university chaplaincy I had to find money to pay for my digs. I am sure the Salvatorians would have paid but I have always been independent as far as I could be when it comes to money. I decided to do what we call among the clergy, 'supply work'. It's a bit like being a locum in the world of pharmacy. A priest stands in for another if he is ill or needs a break. Obviously remuneration is given for this, albeit not a lot. A priest in charge of a parish on the outskirts of Manchester fell ill and needed to take a long time off. I was given permission to look after the parish at the weekends thereby earning my keep at the chaplaincy. Each Saturday evening I would take a bus out to this parish and one of the parishioners would meet me at the bus stop and take me to the church. He and his wife, Bob and Mollie Johnson, were stalwarts and virtually looked after the parish during the week. We became great friends and from time to time they would invite me to have a meal with them and their three children. One of the happiest Christmas dinners of my life was spent with them. The whole family were devotees of Assisi and would invite student friars over for holidays. They were well-known in Assisi and it was they who first put the idea of visiting Assisi into my head. I was involved in another way in that if the students on holiday showed any signs of stress or in need of counselling, I would be brought in as the 'expert'. So I already knew some of the friars before I put my foot in Assisi.

The days seemed to be getting warmer in Rome and the temperature had risen to 85F when I took off on my pilgrimage. But as Rome is notorious for its heat and I wasn't so sure of Assisi I packed a jumper, made sandwiches from the breakfast tray in the Mother House and set off for the station. The train was due out at 11.25a.m. and as I reached the station at l0.00a.m., I had plenty of time to check up on platforms, etc. So far so good but my problems were about to begin. The departure notice board listed every train due to leave during the next few hours and against each one the platform number—except mine. The train was listed but no platform. I consulted wall timetables and tried to translate the Italian. Instinct is not the best means of translation, but when I saw little letters like E and R I began to feel a little uneasy. I suspected the 'R' next to my train meant rapid but my brochure had said to change at Fumiglia. With no one to ask and seeing the train come in I took a bold step and decided God would guide me. Back in England I had been advised to get a first-class ticket, so when I saw '1' written on a coach I boarded it. The compartment I entered looked strange—one seat, like a long table. I was about to try the next one when the guard came in. With great faith and childlike confidence I showed him my ticket. I might have been showing him secret plans to assassinate the president. He started waving his arms about and pointing towards the platform. He must have known the principle of shouting when speaking to foreigners for he nearly burst his lungs. The less I understood, the more and the louder he shouted. Eventually I realised that the 'R' did mean rapid and that one had to pay a supplementary fee and even worse one had to actually book a seat. He told me to get off and do all these things, but with the train about to leave, I looked very simple and English-like and he gave in. He told me to try and find a seat. So I promptly sat down on the one in the compartment, thinking he meant that one. Alas, it was his. I was in the guard's van. He nearly blew another gasket and waved his arms towards the front coaches. I went and decided I would travel third class if it meant finding a seat. I found one, sat down for three minutes only to be ousted by someone with a numbered ticket. I went further forward and decided to stand. By accident I stumbled into what looked like the cockpit of Concorde. Seats lined the nose of the train—very plush seats. I realised this was first class and as there were vacant seats I sat down and waited for someone to come and move me.

I spent the next two hours clutching my bag, secretly eating my sandwiches and waiting for the guard to come and put me off the train. I also prayed that the wretched train would stop at Fumiglia or I would probably spend the night in Istanbul. I needn't have worried. It stopped, I managed to find the right platform and I boarded the train to Assisi accompanied by two terribly English people in the first-class coach. Twenty minutes later, I was in Assisi where Fr Imedio, a Franciscan priest, was waiting patiently to greet me in his Franciscan habit and bare feet. I had never met him, simply been told about him. The Johnsons, God bless them, had asked him to meet me and take me to Santa Maria de Angelo. He clasped me to his bosom and gave me a resounding kiss on both cheeks, saying, 'Welcome to Assisi Ricardo'.

As you come into Assisi on the train it is as though you are coming into fairyland. You look out of the window and you see layer upon layer of houses, vineyards, trees and all sorts of vegetation. There is no other way to describe it other than a many layered elongated wedding cake.

It was about 3.00p.m. and Imedio took me to the Franciscan convent, as they call it, where I was to stay. It was about three-quarters of a mile away, all downhill and we talked as we went. Imedio had been to England and knew quite a bit of English. When we reached Santa Maria de Angelo he gave me a conducted tour of the church and grounds before showing me to my room. The church is a basilica and unique in that when you enter there is another church inside it. It is called the 'Portiuncula' and is the church St Francis repaired when he heard God telling him, 'repair my Church'. It has become the focal point for all Franciscans throughout the world. It became the first Franciscan Church and around it were built mud huts for each friar to dwell in. Those huts are now represented by side chapels inside the basilica.

In the Portiuncula St Francis gave St Clare the habit and shaved her head, thus founding the very strict female religious order called Poor Clares. Nearby is the place on which Francis' hut was built and the place of his death. Imedio showed me all this, then the museum of the most beautiful vestments and finally the old friary which had been built after St Francis died. There was so much history, so much atmosphere here that it was quite breathtaking. I knew I was going to enjoy Assisi by the time I reached my room.

Franciscan monasteries are called convents and Franciscan convents are called monasteries. So I was living in the convent which was the head-quarters of all Franciscans throughout the world. It was huge. I went up to the first floor and into a large corridor, all marble, with very high walls. Each side of the corridor were doors leading into cells – ten on each side. At the end of the corridor another corridor at right angles contained another twenty cells and so it went on to complete a square. Eighty cells altogether, all looked out onto a beautiful courtyard or to breathtaking views of the city or of fields full of vines heavily laden with grapes. My cell, which was typical, was about the size of the whole ground floor of my cottage. Marble or stone floor, sink, wardrobe, desk, an upright chair and bed were the only contents.

I unpacked and as it was some time before the evening meal, I took a walk and explored the geography of the locale. I discovered a little restaurant across the road from the convent and so with an hour to spare had a very refreshing gin and tonic. Feeling very happy with myself and with the world at large I went back to the convent and waited for the dinner bell which was to ring at 6.30p.m. Imedio had arranged for one of the friars to come for me and introduce me to the dining room. A brother who spoke no English came for me and led me down. Going through the doors of the refectory was like stepping back into pre-Vatican II religious life. It was a typical refectory with long tables running the length of the room. These tables could accommodate forty people comfortably and seating took the form of what looked like choir stalls. In the old days seating was arranged according to seniority based on the time a person took first vows but these days a friar would take whatever 'stall' was free when he entered the room – with two exceptions. At the end of the room there was another table at right angles to the others and in the centre the Guardian (Superior) sat beneath a large crucifix. Senior friars who held an office of some sort in the friary would have their own places alongside him.

In the centre of the room some tables had been placed together to make a more conventional dining room table and it was to this I was shown. As I entered I saw the friars all standing motionless with their hands tucked into the large sleeves of their habits waiting for grace. I was shown to a place and stood there also waiting for grace to begin. A few other monks came in and stood alongside me and opposite me and eventually grace was said in Italian. I learnt that the centre table was for the junior monks and visitors. Then occurred the first of a series of coincidences which punctuated every day of my visit. The monk next to me was American, the one opposite me was an English-speaking Pole, and the one on my other side was an English-speaking Italian from Venice. I felt more at home than I had in Rome and these men were most hospitable and caring. They went out of their way to see I had all I wanted and engaged me in conversation. Another priest at the table came from San Salvador but did not speak English. I then had a really sumptuous meal.

I had been given a key to the cell but not to the house. The house closed at 9.30p.m. and everybody was expected to be in by then. A card on the desk in the room which gave times of meals, etc. also stated that visitors were expected to wear their habits and were not expected to stay too long at local bars or restaurants. Time of community Mass in Italian was again at 6.45a.m. and one of the brothers kindly lent me an alarm clock in case I didn't hear the bell calling the monks to prayer. He needn't have bothered. The church bell boomed out every quarter hour throughout the night, but as I had just about managed to fall asleep about 5.00a.m. I missed the boom, the bell and the alarm clock.

I now understand why sleeping on the floor was part of monastic asceticism. It's impossible to sleep on the bed. The bed was designed so narrow that you slept to attention if you wanted to stay on it. No question of turning over without falling off. And as it was a high bed you could do serious damage to yourself by turning over. But not only that. The bed was a virtual trampoline. To jump on it unsuspectingly was to be bounced up to the roof again and again. The sheet was narrower than the bed and more like a loin cloth than a sheet. However, I had been shown blankets in the cupboard and at about 2.00a.m. I put the mattress on the floor and covered myself with the blanket and listened patiently to the bells of St Mary's. It had been quite a day.

Travel is a great educator. At 8.00a.m. I went looking for the sacristy to arrange Mass. Imedio had seen the nun the previous evening and asked her to let me have English missals, etc. I had timidly asked if there was any chance of saying Mass in the Portiuncula. They looked (a) horrified and then (b) amused at the simplicity of the Englishman. It seems you

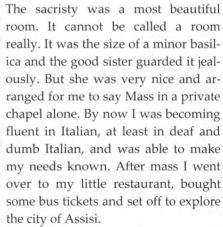

have to write months and months in advance to book a time.

The sacristy was a most beautiful room. It cannot be called a room really. It was the size of a minor basilica and the good sister guarded it jealously. But she was very nice and arranged for me to say Mass in a private chapel alone. By now I was becoming fluent in Italian, at least in deaf and dumb Italian, and was able to make my needs known. After mass I went over to my little restaurant, bought some bus tickets and set off to explore the city of Assisi.

Over the years Bob and Mollie Johnson had been urging me to go to Assisi. For some reason I had not felt any urge to go but when I told them I had at last decided to go they kindly arranged everything with the friars in terms of my being met and being housed. They also gave me a little pamphlet describing a pilgrimage to Assisi and I followed this now as I boarded the bus. Assisi is a unique and very friendly city no longer than about three miles and no broader than one mile. Full of tiers of streets, shops and churches, I 'did the sights': Church of St Clare which houses her body and which is attached to the Poor Clare monastery; the birthplace of St Francis; and various places made famous through St Francis culminating in a visit to the basilica of St Francis where his body lies. As always in Italy, churches were built upon churches and St Francis' basilica is a church built over a church built over the tomb of St Francis. There were thousands there. Masses were going on in various chapels. Thousands milled around and down at the tomb another Mass at the altar prevented us going close enough to see it. After Mass we were able to walk around the tomb and see the resting places of St Francis' early companions. I would imagine that on a quiet day it would be very peaceful and prayerful. After my visit to St Francis' basilica, I made my way back to the city centre intending to go on to visit San Domiano—the original monastery of the Poor Clares. Passing through the city, I noticed a fast-food shop actually selling hamburgers and chips. This I couldn't resist so I joined the small queue, my mouth already watering at the thought of real food. Alas, it must have been an illusion. Twenty minutes later the queue hadn't moved and the assistant was still fiddling with the cash register. I moved on, wondering about static fast-food restaurants. I walked down the hill looking for signs to San Domiano. It was in this monastery that the crucifix spoke to St Francis and told him to repair his church. Here St Clare had lived for over forty years and her place in the refectory is still covered with flowers. I found no sign but called in at a tourist agency and got directions. It was very hot and I had been walking all morning so when I came across a little restaurant I sat down and had some of the delicious Italian gelati (ice cream). Refreshed, I took to the road and following the directions I had been given, I reached San Domiano about one mile away. It was closed. No sign of life at all and no notice of opening times. It was very peaceful and hidden away in the undergrowth so I stretched out and

302

had my siesta. It was about 1.15p.m. At 1.45p.m. with no signs of opening, I went and found the bus stop and returned home. I had spotted a shop selling drink so I bought a bottle of gin for about £3 (poor quality, I might add), some tonic and smuggled them into the friary. There on the roof I sat and drank. Then a visit to 'my' restaurant and a toasted sandwich gave me the energy I needed to continue my pilgrimage. I took the bus back to nearby San Domiano and this time it was open. It was the most peaceful of all the shrines and quite a reflective place. We saw the place where the crucifix had spoken to St Francis (the crucifix is now in St Clare's Church), the spot where Clare died and her choir stall and refectory seat. It was a little off the tourist track so was more peaceful than the other places. As I wandered around I bumped into the two 'terribly English people' I had met on the train. They were not Catholics but came to Assisi regularly. Their son was an Oxford don who had just joined them for a holiday. They were very nice people. I went home by bus and waited for supper sitting on the roof again—this time reflecting on the day's events and the places I had visited.

I thought of the basilica which is looked after by the Conventual Franciscans. I should mention that there are three Franciscan orders. There are the Conventuals who are distinguished by their black habits, the Franciscans Minor who are the traditional friars people are accustomed to see in their brown habits and bare feet and then there are the Capuchins who are distinguished by wearing beards. There is controversy as to which was founded by St Francis. Each would claim to be the one founded by St Francis and that the other two were founded from the original one.

I also thought of the two Franciscans I had seen walking down the road arm in arm. In England there could have only one explanation but here in Assisi it seemed quite natural and even comforting. The supper bell broke into my thoughts and I went down to the refectory. All were in their places but Brother Pater was there with a walkie-talkie. A Japanese visitor had been so impressed with Assisi that he installed the system into the friary and Brother Pater accompanied his meal with constant overs and outs to somebody at the front door. It had been a really good and interesting day and I went to my mattress on the floor with a peaceful, happy tiredness.

303

Sunday seemed to bring even more tourists to Assisi and they all seemed to want Mass at the same time. I went into the sacristy expecting my private chapel only to find the sacristy inundated by priests leading pilgrimages and all wanting to say Mass. By 'accident' I bumped into an English priest whose group were present in the crypt waiting for Mass so I joined him and we concelebrated in the crypt. It was very beautiful and the group of elderly people very devout. The courier was from Liverpool – of course. It was a pilgrimage 'doing' the shrines of Europe and heading for Rome. Again 'by accident' the priest's sister belonged to our parish in Wotton-under-Edge, Gloucestershire, a Salvatorian parish.

The temperature in Assisi was little different than Rome though it was not as stuffy. I spent the morning resting—my feet were beginning to complain—and so I had coffee over the road and then sat on the roof writing cards and drinking my aperitif.

Sundays are feast days in every religious house and Assisi certainly knew how to celebrate. For lunch we began with a very thin, cold, smoked ham with olives. This was followed by a ribbon pasta with tomatoes. Then half a chicken, beans, salad, CHIPS and boiled potatoes. This was followed by grapes, apples, etc. and then cakes of various sorts. The whole accompanied by wine. It was a feast. Sadly, the chicken had been treated with some wretched garlicky substance and I had to leave it. But it was a lovely meal and everybody was really friendly and chatty.

Death by le garlic

After dinner I took the bus to Assisi again. I wanted to visit the caves up on Mount Subiaco where St Francis and his companions had prayed. There was no transport other than private car or taxi so I decided to walk or, rather, climb. It was four kilometres upwards under the scorching sun. On the bus to Assisi I met two English ladies who appeared lost and were looking for a particular convent in Assisi—there are dozens of them. One of them was shouting at the driver in order to make him understand, but of course, he didn't. To my surprise, I was able to direct them, even being able to tell them where to get off the bus and which road to take. I felt a native of Assisi.

I climbed from the bus terminus and climbed and climbed. Cars passed by with only one destination—the caves—but they didn't stop. I thought St Francis would have climbed so I was in good company. Eventually, after about an hour, I reached the caves and went in. The caves are interconnected by archways and are like little open cells carved in the rock. They are the same as when St Francis first used them except in each one there is now an altar. I felt it spoilt the atmosphere but again this proved to be a very peaceful place and probably a place to pray when the tourists had gone.

I walked back and rested a while at the bus terminus. Then I came home and wrote down a few reflections on how Francis would react if he visited Assisi today and saw how his city had changed. Not only his city but his Order.

I cannot remember what supper was like that night but I remember the friendliness of the friars and their help in organising my return journey to Rome the following day. I didn't know the platform changes I might have to make. They helped me as far as they could but there were still a number of unanswered questions I would have to face alone at the station the next day. Nobody at the station spoke English. I did a farewell tour of Santa Maria de Angelo and went to bed.

My train to Rome was at 10.07a.m. and I wondered if I should say Mass before I went or back in Rome. I was up about 7.30a.m., put the mattress back on the bed and folded the loin cloth. So as there was plenty of time to spare I went again to the sacristy. I prepared for my little private chapel when the nun in charge stopped me. She was muttering something about the Portiuncula. Even with my fluent sign language I couldn't understand her but she signalled me to wait. About ten minutes later a Texan-type American blew in as though he owned the place. He was one of those who months and months ago had written and booked the Portiuncula for 8.30a.m. Monday 15 September. His little band of fourteen wealthy Americans who were 'doing' Europe in ten days had gathered in the little church and I was invited to concelebrate. So St Francis got his way in spite of his monks and I got the Portiuncula. It was less than the spiritual experience I expected, principally due to the Yanks popping up every minute to 'snap' Father preaching, snap Father raising the Host, etc., etc. and when the Our Father came they all held hands. There had been an unsuspecting friar kneeling on the floor in the middle of the church. It's a very small church with about five or six chairs lining the sides and enough room for perhaps four men to stand between them shoulder to shoulder. Suddenly this poor man's hand was 'yanked' out of his sleeve and this good holy American clutched him as they said the Our Father. The friar showed his sanctity by leaving his hand with the woman and not showing the slightest distraction. Our American Father must have got my signals for he kept his hands to himself. It was amusing to hear him bellowing out in this tiny church and I'm afraid no matter how much I tried, I couldn't really say I was spiritually uplifted by the experience.

After Mass I collected my bag and, armed with sandwiches, boarded the bus to Assisi station. I had made my farewells to the friars the night before, especially the American Fr Benedict (not the Texan), Fr Donald from San Salvador and the Pole, also Fr Benedict. Imagine my surprise when I arrived at the station to find Fr Benedict (USA) there with Donald. They had been waiting one hour for a nun from Rome who must have missed her train. They were waiting for the next one and so they were able to find out for me and a few other stranded passengers how to get to Rome. We had to change twice—Orte and Fumiglio. We made our farewells again and when the train arrived I climbed aboard, sat in the nearest seat regardless of class and waited for my first change. This happened without mishap and when I got on the next train I didn't bother about first class again. This is very significant in view of what happened later. From Fumiglio to Ortone is about a two hour journey in the particular train I was on. It stopped at Spoletto and a young, very beautiful but sad-looking lady boarded the train. She sat on the opposite side and a few seats further forward. Soon after Spoletto the train stopped at a place called Santa Guillaume. An announcement was made, in Italian of course, and a lot of people seemed to be getting off. The young lady moved and as I was looking out of the window rather puzzled she signalled me to get off (not come on!). Then in perfect English she told me there was a fault on the line and we had to go to the next station, Terne, by bus. She took charge of me for the rest of the journey, guided me from bus to station, platform to platform until we finally arrived in Rome. She was an interior design student and had just said farewell in Spoletto to her boyfriend with whom she had been spending the weekend. She was a Roman and lived in the Piazza Venetia and her name was Francesca Tranconi. We spent the train journey exchanging views on England and Italy and when in Rome I thanked her for looking after me she said, 'It was a pleasure to be in the company of such a nice person'. The pain in my stomach disappeared, the blisters on my feet from my walk to the caves healed and I walked head held high to the bus terminus. There was life in the old boy yet!

22

The Provincial Years

I had skirmished with the Salvatorian international scene by attending conferences from time to time but now I had the opportunity to mix with Provincials from all over the Salvatorian world and to be able to influence decisions on an international level. I was hampered a little with my lack of languages but most of the conferences I attended were facilitated by members trained in instant translation.

It was a great privilege to lead the Province for six years but by the end of my second term I was beginning to feel the strain. Members wanted me to stand for a third term and I agreed reluctantly.

I was elected Provincial for the statutory three years by one vote. Three years later when the Provincial elections came around again I was re-elected unanimously. I had been on the Provincial Council for thirteen years off and on and I had observed a number of Provincials close at hand, so the office was no stranger to me.

I believed very strongly in the 'hands on' approach and I made it my first task to visit the houses and meet each member of the Province personally. In the old days members would include priests and brothers. But these days we only have priests. Morale was not very high in the province as vocations (recruits) were not terribly numerous and the members were overworked. Some members had personal problems which reduced their level of activity causing the rest of the membership extra work and responsibility.

I felt we were at a crossroads in the life of the Province. The form of religious life we undertook to follow had disappeared as a result of the Second Vatican Council but we were privileged to have the opportunity to build the religious life of the future. Consequently I took the phoenix as my symbol of office.

It is alleged that the phoenix is a bird about the size of an eagle, brilliantly coloured in plumage. It is the only one of its kind and lives in Arabia; at the end of an epoch, as it feels death is drawing near, it builds a pyre of the sweetest spices, on which it then sits singing a song of rare beauty. The rays of the sun ignite the nest, and both this and the bird are consumed by the flames and burnt to ashes. From the ashes there arises a worm, which eventually grows into a new phoenix more beautiful than its parent.

The symbolism was obvious. Many priests and thousands of Salvatorian parishioners had gone before. Based on the traditions they established and the sacrifices they made in order to establish our Society in these islands, I wanted the membership to place their hope on the emergence of a renewed Province rising from the flames of the Holy Spirit.

One of my friends drew a picture of the phoenix rising up from praying hands and that became my inspiration. History will record how successful the scheme was but I pursued it to the end of my second term of office when I returned to the ranks. As I left office there were two members waiting to be ordained and no one had given up membership during the six years. Subsequently those two members were ordained Salvatorian priests. When I left office each of our parishes had a Lay Vocation Group whose task it was to pray and work for vocations identifying any possible or likely male in a particular parish.

One of the first tasks I had to face after my election was to go to Krakov in Poland for a General Chapter of the Society. A General Chapter is a gathering of Salvatorian representatives from all over the world. I found Krakov to be a most beautiful city with a square and market place unequalled anywhere except possibly by Prague. In the enclosed market there are stalls offering the most exquisite handmade jewellery, leather goods, paintings by local artists and popular, locally carved images representing Polish culture. The market was particularly noted for its amber, which was at the height of its popularity in 1993.

We had a very heavy schedule over a period of four weeks but there was always time for some sightseeing. Once a week, a trip was arranged by the Host province and we visited among other places, Czestochowa, and Auschwitz.

Czestochowa is the Polish national shrine of Our Lady. Installed in a very special chapel is a painting of the Virgin Mother and child and it is known as the Protector of Poland. An interesting feature of the painting are the sword marks on the Virgin's cheek. It is alleged that when Sweden invaded Poland in 1655, the Swedes tried to remove the painting in a horse-drawn wagon, but could not budge it an inch. Exasperated, two Swedish soldiers drew their swords and slashed at the Virgin's cheek. As soon as the swords touched the canvas, the soldiers fell dead. And nobody has since been able to cover up the scars.

Our Lady of Czestochowa was first said to have been painted by St Luke but it is now believed to have been painted by an unknown Italian artist in 1383. The painting took on a very special significance after the heroic defence of the monastery in 1655 when the invading Swedes were defeated after a seventy-day siege. Following this miraculous victory, King Casimar of Poland proclaimed: 'To touch Our Lady of Czestochowa is to touch the very soul of Poland.' Whether by Swedish swords or not, the Virgin's cheek remains scarred, and every year thousands of pilgrims go to see it.

The painting is locked in behind a golden screen on the altar of the chapel and twice a day a priest, to the accompaniment of a trumpet blast, slowly unveils the Icon. The unveiling begins at the waist and gradually, very slowly, almost imperceptibly, moves up to the neck and gradually reveals the face and the whole painting. To see the Polish people kneeling in prayer before it was a deep lessen in faith. 'Important people' who have travelled from afar are allowed in the sanctuary within touching distance of the Icon. But the Polish people, no matter how far they may have travelled, were not allowed inside the sanctuary. Two Polish officials had a very long pole held horizontally which they used to hold back the crowds from getting too close. The Polish people simply knelt outside the sanctuary on their knees. I must say that what left a lasting impression of Czestochowa on me was the faith of those Polish people on their knees rather than the Icon of Our Lady.

I don't need to tell you about Auschwitz. Suffice it to say it was like standing on holy ground and one could only stand, stare at the relics of Holocaust and pray that one day man will turn away from evil and embrace good.

I spent some time in one particular building which housed the cell where St Maximilian Khobe was executed. The cell is empty now except for a large Easter candle which burns twenty-four hours a day in the centre of the cell. This was first lit by Pope John Paul II. Fr Maximilian was imprisoned in Auschwitz in 1941. One day a prisoner escaped and as a reprisal all the prisoners were lined up and every tenth man was sent to their deaths by starvation. One of the tenth men was a man who was married with a number of children. He begged the wardens to let him go for the sake of his wife and children. When they refused Fr Maximilian who stood next to him stepped forward and volunteered to go in his place. He had no wife, no children. The guards didn't care who went as long as it was one in ten. And so Maximilian went to the starvation chamber and kept the morale of the condemned alive with prayer and song until the last man but one died. Maximilian was the last and so to hasten his death gas pellets were thrown into the cell and Maximilian breathed his last with a prayer on his lips. He was canonised by Pope John Paul just recently.

The food in the Polish Provincial Mother House was very good but very Polish. I longed for a bag of chips. One evening while I was out walking on a beautiful summer evening I could hardly believe my eyes when I saw before me a kiosk actually selling chips. Talk about an answer to my prayers. From that day on, a walk was scheduled into my programme and I would buy an English paper from a nearby hotel and a bag of chips from the kiosk. I would then sit on a park bench and have the most enjoyable half hour of the day.

A meal made in heaven

A Provincial is responsible for all the members of his Province wherever they are situated. Ideally the Provincial visits each member wherever he is working to ensure his personal health and wellbeing. Members of the British Province were living and working in a number of countries including the UK, USA, Australia, Tanzania, India, Sri Lanka and Rome. I was able to visit all these countries with the exception of Tanzania and India. The most interesting of all the places I visited had to be the USA. For it was there I met the Apache Native Americans. One of our priests ran a mission on the Cibecue reservation near Phoenix, Arizona. I spent ten very happy days with the Apaches. I think what surprised me most was the fact that they were little different than us in terms of personal problems and difficulties. I met one who looked like a real Indian warrior as one would imagine him. Talking to him one day after Mass he told me that he had volunteered for the Vietnam War. He suffered from a mental illness and his life had been so difficult he had hoped that he might stop a bullet and so end his life. But this was not to be and now he was back home living in a caravan and drawing sketches as a form of therapy. Most of his work combined the violence of war with the peaceful culture of his own Tribe. He was a lovely man and we spent a lot of time together. While I was there on the reservation I came across a very old man who could have stood in for Geronimo without any difficulty. I was so impressed with him that I asked him if I could take a photograph of him. He was delighted and posed for me quite readily. I thanked him and was about to say goodbye when he held out his hand and said, 'That will be ten dollars please.'

But I think the most lasting memory of my trip to Phoenix was the plane flight out of Chicago. We were late leaving and as we climbed into the skies the pilot came on the intercom welcoming us on board and reassuring us: 'I'm sorry we are late leaving Chicago but don't worry if you have onward connections. We shall arrive in Phoenix dead on time'.

' The fastest mass .... in the West '

I thought this was a bit much and when I reached home I wrote to American Airlines and told them that I didn't want to arrive dead on time. I told them that I would prefer to arrive late but alive. I received a letter of apology and gratitude for drawing my attention to this and I was given a $100 voucher for when I travelled on American Airlines next time. As it seemed highly unlikely that I would fly American Airlines again I sent it to my Salvatorian host on the mission. I am sure he put it to good use. But I did benefit from a £4 food voucher they had also sent me to spend at Luton airport. I had complained about the food too and this was their way of saying sorry. I have never complained to airlines before but what compelled me to do so this time was seeing a child being refused permission to go to the toilet because she would disrupt the food trolley's progress down the passageway. Later I read in a newspaper of a man who made his living by complaining. His was full of 'apologetic gifts' and he travelled free fairly regularly in compensation for his complaints.

If visiting the Apaches was my most interesting trip abroad as Provincial my most moving visit was to Sri Lanka. I received a most warm welcome from our Salvatorian Sisters when I visited them in the Sri Lankan novici-ate. There were novices from India, the Philippines and Sri Lanka. As I pulled up to the door of the convent the novices with the professed sisters were all there lined up to greet me. They presented me with a sort of wreath of leaves which was obviously a welcome ceremony of some sort. I equally obviously hadn't a clue how to respond so I gave them my best smile and said thank you. I also asked the person who seemed to be the leader what her name was. She answered 'Piumella'. Without a thought I said, 'What a lovely name.' We went into dinner which was conducted in virtual total silence. I wondered if my lack of Sri Lankan etiquette was the cause. And yes, it was! The next day I learnt that because of my being the Provincial they were waiting for me to start the conversation! I also learnt that Piumella couldn't sleep all night thinking that I had told her she had a lovely name. The magic is still there – or was! But isn't it interesting that it never occurred to me that in their eyes I was somebody special. Old Mr Hignet had done his work well.

And so my six years moved on and although I found it very stressful at times I enjoyed it and am grateful for the opportunity given me to serve my brethren and also for the great support I received from 'most' of them.

Back at home, there was the day-to-day work of the Province to attend to. I couldn't have achieved half of what I did if it had not been for the help of 'Little Ed' as we called him. He was only called little to distinguish him in size to 'Big Ed' about whom I wrote earlier. What Little Ed lacked in physique he more than made up in stature. He had served as Provincial Secretary for many years and at his funeral oration four former Provincials paid tribute to the great debt they owed to him. It was on the occasion of his funeral that I realised just how much Ed had done as well as administering the Province. Chaplain to nursing homes, visiting hospitals, accompanying the sick to Lourdes, preaching missionary appeals were only some of the tasks he had set himself quietly and without fuss. If any member told him he had a problem, invariably his reply was 'Leave it to me', and the problem would be solved. I was unfortunate to lose him during my first term of office when he died suddenly from a massive heart attack. The mould was broken when God made 'Little Ed'. I used to think that there he was lying all at peace up in the cemetery and leaving me to do all this work. But I couldn't begrudge him his rest and I am sure he kept at my side, guiding me from heaven as the next few years unfolded.

One of the things I noticed going around our parishes was that parishioners did not seem to be aware that their parish was run by the Salvatorians. I encouraged our parish priests to ensure that their parishioners knew they were Salvatorians. To this end I had banners made and erected in all our parish churches announcing to all those who entered that they were entering a Salvatorian parish church. I knew that the Notre Dame Sisters in Liverpool had made some splendid banners for the Liverpool Cathedral to welcome the Pope's visit in 1982. I contacted the Sister in charge and she was delighted to make the banners for me. They still hang in our parish churches.

Before I became a Provincial I had worked with students for almost thirty years and during that time I would tell finalists to get involved in their local parish when they went home. Sadly, reports came back that some parish priests didn't want them. Consequently a number of students lapsed after university. I had hoped to start some sort of society which would act as a half-way house between the cosy Catholic atmosphere of the university chaplaincy and the harsh almost anonymous world of the parish. A number of past students joined me in this venture but alas it ceased to function when I came out of office.

There were a lot of privileges attached to the office as well as travel. In the Mother House in Rome a Provincial was always shown the greatest respect and given one of the better rooms to lay his weary head. And if there was anything happening across the road at the Pope's place the Provincials would always get the best seats. I was fortunate to be in Rome on the occasion that Archbishop Polycarp Pengo received the Red Hat. He had lived on our mission in Tanzania and he used our Mother House as his base. 'Receiving the Red Hat' is the expression used when the Pope personally hands to a bishop the scarlet biretta, a symbol of his being elevated to the Sacred College. Thirty bishops were being 'made up' that day and there was I in the best seats beside National Leaders and other 'big nobs' from around the world. I thought I might receive a hat myself but I was told there were none small enough for my head!! It was a fantastic occasion and the nearest I could ever get to a Papal Consecration.

I thought that after this, I could never ever again experience or be conscious of failure or rejection but God always has something up his sleeve doesn't he?

I mentioned that having served three years plus three a Provincial returns to the ranks. Occasionally a Provincial is asked to serve a third term. When nominations were called for my successor, a number of members asked if I would stand for a third term. For a third term to be granted by the General Council the candidate has to receive two thirds of the votes at the election and have the approval from Rome to stand for election. As the number of those asking me to stand easily exceeded two thirds of the Province membership I accepted nomination. Approval was given by Rome and it looked as though I would be elected. I had found the last year of my office very stressful and had no great desire to do a third term. Moreover, those asking me to stand normally added, 'there is no one else' and so it seemed to be. Those who would obviously make good Provincials were serving in important positions and it would be very difficult to replace them.

When the Chapter gathered for the election I addressed the assembly and told them this. I added that to say there was no one else was to deny the action of the Holy Spirit and said that everybody present was a possible Provincial. They must have listened, for the election that ensued went to three or four ballots even though I had had the majority of nominations. Had I been allowed to be elected by a simple majority, as the other candidates on the short list were, I would have been home and dry. However I needed two-thirds of the vote. Finally another member got the required number of votes and was declared elected. I was out. I could hardly believe it and a number of others, including the General Council, were 'gobsmacked'. But my prayers had been listened to and God had spoken. Although I was eventually pleased not to have to serve a third time I must say my first reaction was one of total rejection. It reminded me of the story Bruce Marshall told in his book, Every Man a Penny. A French cardinal was flying back to Paris after the papal election. He was in a really bad temper. First, the coffee was cold. Second, he was still a cardinal.

And one final story before I move on. A Provincial is given the respect due to a bishop when he travels to other houses and a General receives the respect given to a cardinal. Thus when the General came on visitation from Rome I arranged for him to meet with Cardinal Hume to express his good wishes – a sort of courtesy visit. The cardinal had just written his book, Basil in Blunderland and the General wanted a signed copy. He asked the cardinal for this and the latter said, 'of course' and he held out his hand for the book. There was an embarrassed silence. The General had expected the cardinal to give him the book. After what you might call a pregnant pause the cardinal let out a guffaw and said, 'I don't have one' and the incident passed off happily. But I made sure afterwards that I got a copy and I got a friend to get the cardinal to sign it for the General. So everybody was happy.

And so the king was dead. Long live the king! I returned to the ranks and it was a case of what next? Where would my personal phoenix lead me?

23

On The Market

In spite of being reluctant to stand for a third term and encouraging the members to elect another I felt very rejected
when I was not elected. I knew my reaction was unreason-
able but I think my deep-rooted memories of failure and rejection in childhood reared their ugly heads again.

By now I knew that if I failed at anything it was just a blip. I
had proved myself a success in the public arena. I had experienced slight rejection when I left the Borough but this
time it really hurt.

I know that my term of office as Provincial was considered
successful and there was no reason to hide my head in
shame which is what I felt like doing.

I could have taken a sabbatical at this point but as I was seventy-three years of age. I felt I had no time for such a luxury.
There was no obvious Salvatorian Community apostolate
immediately available and the new Provincial gave me permission to look for one that suited my gifts. Thus I placed
myself on the market, once again an unemployed priest.

The time came for me to hand over office to the newly elected Provincial. Fortunately for me he didn't wish to take up the Provincial's accommodation so I was allowed to remain there until it suited me to move. I had been making tentative enquiries about my next apostolate. Normally after coming out of such an onerous office a person is allowed to take a sabbatical. However, I felt at my age it wouldn't be long before I took a permanent sabbatical so I was anxious to find a position as soon as possible. Of course, I expected every bishop in the country to be head-hunting me once it became known that I was on the market, so to speak. Well, I let it get around that I was available and waited for the letters to pour in. Alas not one. Was I about to return to my failure status I asked myself.

I had recovered, more or less, from the rejection I had felt at not being allowed a third term of office. So I thought while the bishops were fighting each other for my services I would take a holiday. Give them time sort of thing. So I took up a long-standing invitation from some friends in Germany. I had known Julia back at Keele when she was a student. After many years

"AT LAST A WINDOW THAT OPENS!"

without any correspondence between us I got a letter out of the blue from her. God bless her, she had remembered me all that time and thought it would be a good idea to meet up again. After an exchange of letters we met eventually in London and we became good friends. This was during the time when I was living in Wealdstone and we would meet up whenever she was in London.

She would stay with the sisters of Our Lady of the Missions opposite my house. I received a number of invitations from her parents to spend a holiday with them. They lived in Fribourg in Germany, an idyllic spot as I was to discover, but much later. I promised to visit but never got around to it until 1996. I arranged to go. I had my ticket and even got as far as the airport. But then something came over me. I don't know what it was but I felt too ill to travel. I turned round and went back home. I was not email literate in those days and we would exchange faxes. So on my return I faxed Julia's mother to tell her what had happened. If I hadn't felt guilty before then I certainly did about an hour later when Julia's mother replied. 'We are so sorry you are not coming. Here we are sitting around an open log fire wondering what advantages we can have from you not visiting us. We have spring cleaned the house. There are roses and a box of chocolates in your room and we have even groomed the dog.' Isn't that lovely, especially the bit about the dog? I thought then that if I ever did get there I would have to steer well clear of the dog, especially if he had been groomed a second time.

Thank God there was another time. In 1999, as I said, while the bishops were arguing the toss as to who should have me, I went to Heathrow and eventually found myself in Neurenberg being greeted by Julia, her mother and her younger sister Natalie. What a wonderful week that was, living with such a close-knit family who waited on my every need. They couldn't do enough for me and gave me a week to remember. Even the dog chipped in and offered me his bone.

The highlight of the week happened quite by accident. At dinner one day Natalie remarked that she had spent the previous four years at the university in Passau which was not too far away. My ears pricked up at this. Every Salvatorian has heard of Passau. It is there that the South German Province has a very big House of Studies for Salvatorian students. I mentioned this to my hosts and they decided to spend a day taking me there and showing me this beautiful city where there is the meeting of the waters of the Danube, the Inn and the Liz. We rang the Seminary and we were invited to lunch. What a wonderful surprise awaited me. The South German Province was just about to start their Provincial Chapter at Passau and German Salvatorians were gathering from all over the Province. And, of course, the most notable visitor of all was Father General from Rome. He was just about to relinquish office as I had some months previously and, like myself, was going through the trauma of letting go and

It was all Charlie's fault really. He was living in a beautiful little flat in Redfield, Bristol and was going away for a short break. I was talking to him on the phone and he said, quite out of the blue, 'Why not come and spend a few days down here while I am away.' Well it seemed a good idea at the time.

Apart from two very short spells as parish priest I had spent all my priestly life before assuming the office of Provincial back in 1993 in the academic world. And so, on coming out of office and thinking of what to do next my first thoughts naturally turned towards student work. However I was now getting rather long in the tooth and I knew that I wouldn't be able to hold down a full-time job as a student chaplain.

But with the shortage of priests and the increase in universities I knew that many chaplaincies were staffed by lay people. So I thought that if I got myself a nice little parish near a university with a lay chaplain I could supply the Eucharistic needs of the chaplaincy and also be able to fulfil a useful function as parish priest of a small parish.

So with the usual humility which has endeared me to so many people I let it be known I was in the market.

My first call was to a bishop who shall be nameless and from whom I received short shrift. 'We don't encourage religious to be parish priests in this diocese, Father.' I should explain that as I belong to a religious order I would essentially be on loan to the bishop. This means that my superior, the Provincial, could move me at short notice. However, I saw this as the

321

bishop's loss and 're-advertised'.

This time I was invited to tea in a bishop's house and he told me on the phone that he might have something for me. I put my best suit on, as one does—come to think of it, my only suit—polished my shoes, my only shoes, and put the few hairs I have in place and set off full of optimism. Well, this bishop was obvious highly intelligent and very perceptive because even before I had put the cup to my lips he had offered me a job. Full time chaplain to one of the new universities. It had been previously a college of further education and had never had the luxury of a chaplain. I was delighted and was already getting my act together and planning strategies when through my fantasies I could hear the bishop droning on, 'Of course, you could live in the local presbytery and say Mass occasionally for the parish priest.' There was to be no chaplaincy as such. I was to live in the presbytery and operate from there, visiting the university and students, etc.

You will remember that I had been offered a similar situation back in 1983 when I had offered myself to the Archbishop of Southwark as a student chaplain. Another very perceptive man, he appointed me Chaplain to the medical and nursing students of Guys and St Thomas's hospitals. But again, when I approached him for accommodation, he kindly offered me a room at Cathedral House. Such accommodation would be fine if there was a chaplaincy building of some sort at the college or university. But students would be very reluctant to knock on the door of a cathedral house or even a presbytery. So reluctantly I explained all this to the bishop, thanked him for the tea and biscuits and left.

Another bishop rang me, this time an archbishop no less, and this one had three universities on offer. By this time I had become increasingly impressed that bishops considered me able to take on a full-time chaplaincy in spite of my venerable age of seventy-three. But I didn't share their confidence and when this archbishop offered me a redbrick university chaplaincy I declined gracefully on the grounds of those long teeth. However, he knew a good thing when he saw one and, in fact, offered me two other chaplaincies. Ironically I had been chaplain to one of these some years before and in fact had served five years there. So it was a case of 'been there, done that, got the chalice'.

But the third chaplaincy this good archbishop offered me had distinct possibilities. The chaplain was a nun who was also a lecturer. She was looking for a priest who would say the Masses and do some general chaplaincy work such as counselling, etc. I met with the student's support team and we all agreed I was the best man for the job. No one mentioned I was the only man—or woman for that matter. And then came that question again—accommodation?

'Well, the last priest lived in the presbytery close by', began the good lady chaplain. 'Not a chance' I interrupted her, going over, yet again, my method of working with students. 'There is a vacant room in the student house next door,' came the next suggestion, 'or there is a room in a house nearby that belongs to the diocese. The diocesan people only use it in the evenings and so you would have it most of the time to yourself.'

Thank God, the student support services including the chaplain were very patient and listened to my needs. They appreciated my thirty years experience with students and eventually took me up on my suggestion that they look for suitable accommodation. This was in May and I was to start in the September. So we left it at that and off I went back to London to await news.

It was then, as I said, that I had what proved to be a fatalistic telephone call from Charley. 'Why not come and spend a few days in my flat while I am away', he said. Fr Charles, a fellow Salvatorian was chaplain to a nursing home and lived in a flat which was part of a complex of flats owned by the parish priest and our sisters. It was small but very comfortable and as I was at a loose end at this time, waiting for news about the accommodation, I took him up on his offer and went off for some rest and recuperation. I was not expected to do any work, simply enjoy the peace and comfort of the flat. The parish priest made me very welcome and was very solicitous for my welfare. He would constantly ring up to see if there was anything I needed and if he could do anything to make my stay more enjoyable.

On one of these occasions, without really thinking, perhaps I had been drinking, I jovially said to him, 'Well, there is one thing you can do for me. You could find me a job.' He took me seriously and so I outlined what I was looking for. Almost within the hour he had rung back and said, 'I think I've got the very thing for you. There is a small parish in the Chew Valley about to become vacant and also there is a vacancy for a chaplain at the nearby University of Western England (UWE). I have rung the bishop's secretary and he thinks you will get a positive response if you write to the Bishop.'

I never mentioned that after I came out of office as Provincial I had made a retreat to try and discern the next step God had in mind for me. I wrote down what I thought God wanted of me and, believe me, it was almost identical to the words spoken to me by that parish priest.

It seemed God had spoken to me through Charley and so I sat down and wrote to the bishop enclosing my C.V. Our sisters who were stationed in Bristol knew of the parish and the university and spoke of them in glowing terms.

Soon I received a phone call from Bishop's House inviting me to visit the bishop. I had had opportunity to meet this bishop in my role of Provincial and so it was not as strangers that we met. He was very kind and understanding and very soon told me that I was welcome to the office of parish priest of the Sacred Heart Parish at Chew Magna but that he had a diocesan priest in mind for the university. 'However, no doubt, Bristol and UWE will avail themselves of your services when they know your background.' I was on the pig's back as we say in Liverpool.

At the time I went to see the bishop I was still living in London and so enroute home from the bishop I went and had a casual look at the village of Chew Magna and the Sacred Heart Church. Everything seemed perfect. It was just a matter now of getting permission from the new Provincial, meeting the parish priest and arranging a changeover date and moving in. The Provincial had already given me permission to look for suitable work and had, more or less, given me carte blanche in this matter. There was of course the question of a contract. When a religious priest is given permission from his superior to work for a bishop a contract is drawn up concerning length of stay, financial, living and working conditions and so on. The contract is usually for a period of five years in the first instance. I mentioned this during my interview with the bishop and he smiled very nicely and said, 'According to Canon Law parish priests are expected to offer their resignation at the age of seventy-five.' I was seventy three! I changed the subject.

24

So Where Does That Leave Me?

I was back in parish work. I had hoped for a small parish with some student work on the side. However, the latter was not forthcoming and I found myself again in a rural parish very isolated and lonely.

As with the other two parishes I found the people are wonderful and warm-hearted and caring. But also, as with the other parishes I felt parish work was not really my scene.

With the shortage of priests and considering my age I decided to stay and strive to build up a real post-Vatican II parish. With the whole-hearted cooperation of the parishioners this is being achieved and when the time comes for me to leave the parish it is hoped that the parish will be able to continue without a resident priest should there not be one available.

A positive outcome of the loneliness and isolation of the parish is that there is time to write, an occupation I have wished to engage in for some time. So who knows? Perhaps there is a 'what next?'

And so it came to pass that I was appointed parish priest at the Sacred Heart parish, Chew Magna and I took up the appointment on 21 September 1999. As when I moved to the Borough from Aston University, I was helped to move by friends I had made at the Borough. This time I had hired a removal firm to take most of the luggage such as bookcase, books and all the paraphernalia of thirty-eight years in the priesthood. Most of the luggage consisted of nick-nacks given to me over the years. Of no earthly use to anybody other than myself they were constant reminders to me of having been invited into the lives of so many people at a very intimate level. I remember, when I saw how much luggage I had, thinking of one of our priests when he was moving many years before. He had been our assistant novice master and he was moving to another post. He had given us lectures on the meaning of the vows and in particular of the vow of poverty. Well, we students at that time looked out of the window as he was leaving and saw him with a simple suitcase in his hand. We were really impressed at this example of practising what he preached. Now in those days, when anybody died or was moved, the students would make a beeline to his room to see if he had left anything worth having. Imagine our surprise not to mention disappointment when we saw outside his room six tea chests full of luggage to be forwarded.

'Have collar ...... will travel.'

These thoughts came back to haunt me when it came to my turn to leave Keele. Far from one suitcase, I needed to hire a removal firm to transfer my belongings to Chew Magna. I went ahead of the luggage with the essential and fragile things and my friends helped me with this. As we were unloading the car, a man from across the road came in true village style to introduce himself and ask us if we needed any help. He was a Catholic and like in most parishes was the sort of person no parish priest should be without. Do you want a shelf putting up? Ring Chris. Do you want to know where this is or that is, ring Chris. He was a Godsend. An added attraction to Chris was that he had been part of the team that had built Concorde and was very technical as well as religious in a wholesome way. He had spare keys to the church and the presbytery and I came to learn that he would look after both if I had to go away or during my holidays. We have become good friends.

In fact I came to realise that all the parishioners were made in the same mould. If I coughed during Mass there would be a jar of honey outside the door soon after Mass ended. I have never been cared for so well by so many in my entire life. I am trying to lose weight but they won't let me!

So we unloaded the essential things we had brought by car such as the microwave and the television. In passing I am told that one of the major subjects taught in the seminaries these days is how to cook by microwave. Alas, no housekeepers these days. We were just about to settle down for a congratulatory drink when someone mentioned, 'What about the church? Shouldn't we have taken a look at that?' Well, this we did and then settled down thinking what a lovely parish this was and how lucky I was to have been appointed to such a quiet small parish with eight nuns at the bottom of the garden to keep an eye on me. 'Eight nuns?' I hear you say incredulously. Perhaps I had better explain.

The history of the parish of the Sacred Heart, Chew Magna began in East Harptree and the mother church of the parish goes back about 250 years to a wealthy pastoral farmer, William James, who owned an extensive farm. It is recorded that having hired an Irish drover at Salisbury market, William James noticed that his servant did not attend the services in the local

Anglican parish church. Rather, he retired to one of the outbuildings where he would engage in his devotions using the rosary as he had done in Ireland. William James was so intrigued by the good example of his faithful Catholic servant that he asked for an explanation and very soon was received into the Catholic Church.

To cut a long story short, as a result of this man's conversion, St Michael's Mission began in East Harptree in 1806. Eventually St Michael's Church was built and the parish took off. The Second World War opened a new chapter in its history when, in 1940, the sisters of Our Lady of the Missions bought the Manor House in Chew Magna as a reception centre for their evacuee boarders from London and the Southeast. The first Mass since the Reformation was celebrated in the manor's library by Bishop Lee of Clifton on the feast of the Sacred Heart, 14 June 1940. The vestments he wore were those worn at the marriage of Henry VIII and Catherine of Aragon.

Gradually the evacuees went home but the nuns stayed. The school grew and in time opened a preparatory school as well. The convent chapel was too small for parish services and eventually the sisters donated some of their land on which the parishioners built the present Sacred Heart Church. The parish priest moved from East Harptree and became parish priest and chaplain. In return the sisters built the present presbytery and successive parish priests have lived there to this day. By 1990 the parish was thriving and the two churches were not big enough to hold the growing congregation. In 1996 St Mary's Anglican Church in West Harptree became a shared church and so a third church was added to the parish.

However, in the course of time the nuns got older and the number of recruits diminished. Consequently the secondary school closed and the preparatory school was handed over to the care of a body of trustees and is flourishing to this day still under the title of the Sacred Heart Preparatory School. So by the time of my arrival, there were only eight nuns in the convent some of whom were working in the village among the old and the sick, others were retired. I discovered that the parish used the convent property for their meetings. But then calamity! One day six months after I arrived the Provincial of the Order in England came and told me that they were selling the manor and the nuns would be leaving Chew Magna.

Not only were we to lose our parish meeting place but also the remaining sisters who were such a great support to us. I was on my own. Fortunately the sisters left us in possession of the presbytery so at least I had a roof over my head.

But back to my arrival. Can you imagine the change in my circumstances? I had been Provincial for the last six years and in that role I had travelled the world. I had mixed with the top people such as the Pope and the General. Prior to that 'job' I had mixed with Vice Chancellors, opened degree ceremonies with a prayer and in general, I was 'something'. I remember a few weeks after my arrival I was showing a parishioner around my photographs which I had blue-tacked to walls of my kitchenette. They were mostly of graduates in their caps and gowns. With not a little nostalgia I remarked to her, 'Of course, this was when I was something.' With not a little annoyance she retorted, 'Being parish priest of Chew Magna is something, Father.' I was put in my place and rightly so. But it was all very well being reminded of the importance of Chew Magna. I had discovered by now that I was the proud possessor of three churches situated at Chew Magna, West Harptree and East Harptree. So I sat back comfortably thinking I could manage these OK. I waited in vain for the university chaplains to come rushing to my door for help, alas in vain. Eventually, however, the chaplain at UWE asked for some guidance as he had never been to a university let alone been chaplain to one. But apart from one or two visits to UWE my student work had come to an end. I was receiving regular visits from past students and had become more or less a guru to past students and staff.

But all this was just as well for no sooner had I settled down with my three villages when I heard about Chew Stoke, then Compton Martin, then Stanton Drew, Nempnett Thrubwell, Hinton Blewett then twenty-odd other villages that I discovered were on my patch.

Wistfully I recalled a letter I had received the day after my arrival in Chew

Magna. Surrounded by boxes and boxes of books, crockery, bookcases, etc., etc., I saw this letter which was from the bishop's house. I presumed that it was to welcome me to the diocese so I left it to be opened at a time when I was more relaxed. But you know what it is like. It glared at me every time I moved and so I opened it. I nearly fell off my chair. It began, 'I know this is no way to run a diocese but will you go to Bath as Chaplain to the University and take on the local parish?' 'My goodness', I thought, 'if only I had received the letter before I had started to unpack.' But then I thought, 'if only I was not so long in the tooth – (if I had any).'

It had been very kind of the Bishop to offer me this post but realistically I couldn't have done justice to the job at my age. It was at that point I think, that I realised that my student days were over. There is time in the affairs of men as somebody once said, etc. And it was time for me to let go. Thank God I was able to and I have been fortunate in that many past students have kept in touch with me and we have been able to be a help to each other as the years have rolled by.

In fact this book is a tribute to them as well as to all those others who shared their lives with me. Around this time I became aware that I was getting older. As I said earlier, I was approaching seventy-five. Working with students one forgets the passage of time. Students remain the same age and one is apt to forget that the chaplain is getting older in spite of that. I have written previously how I was caused to face death in 1993 when I had an aorticvalve replacement operation. That was a wonderful experience 'looking back on it' and I had been forced to work through my attitude to death and all that pertains to that. I remember thinking then, if I was to die now, I would have a wonderful funeral.

In accordance with our Statutes I had worked out my funeral arrangements and even devised the liturgy I wanted at the mass. Obviously it was geared to students. So now as I approached my seventy-fifth birthday my thoughts turned once again to the 'final farewell'. I was still in touch with many students and in all humility I knew that a lot of them would like to be invited to my funeral. I still had the programme I had worked out for a student funeral. It was a good one, if I may say so, and I thought that I would like to be present myself. My knowledge of theology does not extend to whether a deceased person's spirit is allowed to attend its own funeral so I thought it better to be sure than sorry.

I thought why not stage it now when we can all get together and have a great Mass and a mega-party. And that's what we did. On 8 September 2002 a call went out for everybody to attend a celebration of my seventy-fifth birthday, my fortieth anniversary of my priesthood and ten years of bionic life. And what an occasion it turned out to be. It was attended by 450 people. Guests came from all over the world, including the Far East, USA and Europe. Guests came from all the professions and included a bishop, many priests, professors, and so on. As I began Mass that day in a huge marquee I thought as I have thought on so many occasions, 'if only old Mr Hignet could see me now.' He was the one who caused my mother so much pain when he said, 'No good will ever come of him.' I was convinced that my mother was present with me and thought, 'Good on you, son. We showed him, didn't we?'

And so here I am in Chew Magna, in Chew Stoke, in the Harptrees, and all twenty-five village points west to Blagdon and beyond. It wasn't long after my arrival that I discovered I wasn't the sort of person the parishioners had expected. They had been told that their new parish priest was to be a retired old monk. I am not sure of their expectations but I did overhear a remark in the congregation as I walked down the aisle after my first Mass here, 'Well, at least, you can hear him.' They were to hear quite a lot over the next few weeks as I made my presence felt and gradually I came to believe that I was being accepted and they were happy with what they'd got. One of the worst things a priest hears when he moves in to a new position is, 'You've a hard act to follow.' I remember it being said to my successor at Keele even before I had left. As I introduced my successor to the students I told them I hadn't been acting and that I hoped the new priest wouldn't follow me. A priest has to do his own thing. So while paying tribute to the works of my predecessor here at Chew Magna I swiftly began to do my thing. From the first day I decided that our parish would be a model parish in line with the tenets of the Second Vatican Council. And what better way to start than to throw a party. When I had arrived at the Borough in 1981 I did the same thing and threw a cheese and wine party but nobody came. I was mortified until a parishioner told me that my parishioners were not cheese and wine people but beer and pie types. Well, I quickly remedied that and learnt from the experience. After some research here in the valley I was assured that the people here were definitely cheese and wine types and even the odd bit of smoked salmon wouldn't be sniffed at.

Once we got to know each other socially it was easy to recognise people at Mass and gradually as I stood at the back of the church after Mass I was able to address individuals by their names, the surest way to a person's soul not to mention heart. I have always believed that if a priest got the liturgy right then everything else would fall into place and soon there would be a genuine caring community. Being in a rural area people here were very much aware of the needs of their neighbours and so it wasn't difficult to build up a community of the People of God. Although there are three churches in the parish there is no meeting place other than the presbytery which isn't very big. So we hire the school hall or one of the village halls for our parties and set ourselves a good social programme. There were already certain annual events in place such as the parish lunch, the parish barbecue and so on. There were regular theatre trips as well. Building on this I introduced the monthly wine and cheese evenings, the medieval banquet for the grown-ups and occasional outings for the young people. The Post-Confirmation Group got together and organised fund-raising activities to help house the 'Untouchables' in India. Within six months they had raised over £2000. The scene was set for the next stage, the establishment of the Collaborative Ministry.

The foundations of Collaborative Ministry had already been laid down by my predecessor and in one sense I was just the ideal person to continue his work. I am no spring chicken and it was obvious from the outset that I would need help to run the parish. Thus the laity came into their own. Being the sort of people they are they came to my help and almost, by default, Collaborative Ministry fell into place and is working extremely well at the present time. It is a typical example of the direction the church is going in terms of the age of the clergy and the lack of recruitment of

new students. I was a visual aid if you like. The parishioners soon realised they would have to undertake more work in the parish and that, one
day, they might even have to run the parish in the absence of a residential
priest. And most importantly, they saw this not as helping the priest but
rather as exercising their ministry in the church.

So I identified thirty-five separate ministries and asked for volunteers to
undertake them. Believe me when I say practically all the parishioners
volunteered for one ministry or another and within two weeks every ministry was filled. The next step was to prepare a parish manual outlining
these ministries and giving detailed job descriptions of them.

Just one thing remains to be done before I can rest on my laurels and ask
what's next – the formation of a parish council. This is under way at the
moment and should be in evidence before long.

And then what ?

Soon after my arrival a villager asked me what I thought of the village.
Without thinking, I responded, 'Well, it's a bit like St Mary Mead, isn't it,
you know the village where Miss Marple lives.' She was very pleased with
this. Alas, I was to blot my copybook some time later. I was in one of the
villager's houses for a committee meeting of some sort. We were in this
huge kitchen gathered around a beautiful pine table. Above us hung
dried herbs and it could have been taken, lock, stock and barrel, from the
kitchen featured in the TV programme, 'Upstairs, Downstairs'. Again I
was asked, 'What do you think of the village now, Father?' And again
without thinking, and looking around at the committee, I said 'Well. It's a
bit like the Vicar of Dibley, isn't it?' There was a stunned silence. They
were not used to my Liverpool humour just yet. But then the lady of the
house came to my rescue and said to the amusement of all, 'Where does
that leave you then, Father?' With the emphasis on Father.

So, yes, where does that leave me? Where does that leave me after a long
and wonderful life? I began this book with the story of my visit to the
Pope and the great privilege of saying Mass with him. I had never

dreamed it possible and so it didn't figure among my life ambitions.

But there have been other ambitions along the road and there was just one more to fulfil when I arrived at Chew Magna. I had made one or two abortive attempts but it was in November 2002 that the opportunity came to make that 'Long Jump'.

25

The Long Jump

Back in my childhood days listening to the Jesuits talking about the life of St Francis Xavier I resolved that one day I would visit the island where he died.

The opportunity to do this came in 2002 which happened to be the four hundred and fiftieth anniversary of his death.

It was on the path leading up to the church which houses the sarcophagus in which St Francis Xavier's body lay that I experienced a moment similar to that which had come to me fifty years previously in St Mary's Church, Highfield Street. I felt the presence of God very strongly and thought, 'I have come the full circle'. Thinking on this, as I descended the mount in pitch darkness after our Mass, I thought all the failure, all the rejection, imagined or otherwise, had been worth it all.

'Jump', he said as the boat bobbed up and down in the swirling waters of the South China Sea. 'Jump and we'll catch you.' I think that was what he said but he was speaking in Cantonese. I owed my knowledge of Cantonese to the Chinese laundries back in Everton in my childhood days. We used to take our laundry to them and received it back beautifully clean and ironed all for the princely sum of twopence, (old pence of course).

There was I with my suitcase in one hand and my other bag over my shoulder looking across a three-foot gap and down on to what looked like a recycled ferry boat from the days I crossed the Mersey to Birkenhead back in the 1930s.

It was on one of these ferry trips that I conceived the idea of going to the island of San Scian in the first place. The night before on the Feast of St Francis Xavier (SFX) I had listened to a Jesuit priest giving the most inspiring sermon about the voyages of SFX and how he had travelled from Spain to Goa, then to Malacca and on to Japan establishing the church wherever he went. Eventually he had tried to get into China but, alas, that was denied him. He landed on the island of San Scian opposite the mainland and overlooking Canton and planned strategies for getting into what would have been a most lucrative mission field. But it was not to be. He caught pneumonia and three months later at the age of forty-six he died. As he was dying he asked to be taken to the beach of this island so that he could die overlooking the mainland and praying that one day China would be converted. His body lay in a large stone sarcophagus until it was taken to Malacca and then on to Goa where it rests to this day in the Basilica of Bon Jesus.

I must have been about ten when I heard that sermon and I remember thinking to myself, one day I shall go to that island. And here I was within jumping distance of fulfilling my ambition. I looked down into the choppy waves thinking, is this where it is going to end. Have I come all this way to die without having even set foot on the island.

I had left London the previous Sunday for Hong Kong where I was met in the new Hong Kong International airport by a Chinese lady who I knew from my Birmingham Polytechnic days in the 1980s. Maria escorted me from the airport to Hong Kong Island via the Tsing Ma Bridge, the world's longest combined road and rail suspension bridge. It carries six lanes of traffic on the upper deck and two more lanes below for use in bad weather. The total length of the 160,000 km suspension cable is enough to circle the world four times. The train runs across this bridge in a form of tube which makes it appear to be underground.

Fr Kane, a Jesuit priest, was waiting for us in Hong Kong. He had been my contact with those organising the pilgrimage during the past year and he had travelled from the island of Cheung Chau to meet me. This island is about an hour's ferry journey from Hong Kong. He lives there conducting a retreat house situated on the top of a very steep hill. Retreatants really do have to be serious about their spiritual lives to climb the hill to pray. And yet the centre is fully booked throughout the year.

Maria went back to work and Fr Kane took me to the place where I was to be based during the fortnight of my stay in the Far East. I don't know whether God was giving me a message but I was taken to Ricci Hall, a Hong Kong Jesuit hall of residence. From the day I was baptised in the Jesuit Church of St Francis Xavier in Liverpool to this day the Jesuits seem to have been around when I needed them. The warden of this Hall, Fr Sean Coghlin, welcomed me and showed me to my room in the Community House, a large airy room with a bed, a table and two upright chairs. In a cubicle in the corner was a shower and washbasin. A door in another corner led to a veranda overlooking the Hong Kong Harbour. I say overlook but to see the harbour waters I had to peer between huge skyscrapers so typical of the Hong Kong skyline. But I was to spend some happy hours on this veranda after my pilgrimage reading and basking in the sun with the occasional cigar and, of course, the odd G and T.

At dinner that first evening there were about seven Jesuits, two of whom were visitors. They were Irish apart from one who hailed from Macau across the harbour. He was Chinese but in the course of the table conversation I mentioned I was from Everton and his eyes lit up. He was a fanatical Everton Supporter.

The pilgrimage was to start from Macau on Saturday so I spent the next few days meeting past Chinese students who had kept in touch with me over the years. We had some lovely meals together and caught up with all the news and gossip. Gradually the week passed and as the pilgrimage was to start at 6a.m. we had to get to Macau on the Friday. I say 'we' because, fortunately, a priest staying in the house was going on the pilgrimage as well. He was also an Irish Jesuit and was returning to Ireland after a sabbatical year travelling the world. I had been concerned about finding my way to Macau on my own but God solved my problem. Fr Sean took us to the ferry and Fr Hugh, my travelling companion, knew exactly where to get the tickets and which pier to sail from. He had done a recce the day before. God bless the Jesuits.

Macau is to the Portuguese what Hong Kong was to the British. Macau had been leased over 400 years ago and was handed back to the Chinese two years after the British handed back Hong Kong. We were to spend two nights in Macau, one going and one coming. As there was no room in the local Jesuit house I was accommodated in the bishop's house nearby. And how bishops live! I had a beautiful room completely en suite with access to coffee, etc. any time of the day or night. BUT read on:

As I have travelled quite extensively over the years experience has taught me always to take a bathroom plug. Wherever you go abroad the plug in the sink or in the bath is missing. I carried mine everywhere but I was pleasantly surprised. Wherever I went on this trip, even the hotel on the remote island of San Scian, plugs were supplied except in the bishop's house. Wasn't I the proud boy to unpack my plug and with great aplomb put it into the sink outlet. My aplomb was punctured. It wouldn't fit. It was too small. I thought of having a quick shave in running water and a shower instead of a bath. I unpacked my shaving gear only to discover

one of my wildest nightmares realised. I had forgotten my razor. It was still sitting there in Hong Kong when I needed it here in Macau. What to do? Being typically British and not minding what 'foreigners' thought about me I decided I would go unshaven for the pilgrimage and let people think I was growing a beard.

So at last the day of the pilgrimage dawned and we were to meet other pilgrims at a particular rendezvous at the unearthly hour of 6.15a.m. I normally wake early but I thought, with my luck, this was probably the one morning when I would sleep in. But I needn't have worried. Up with the lark or the Chinese equivalent I packed enough for the weekend with great enthusiasm (without my razor of course), had some coffee and set off for the rendezvous. I got as far as the door of bishop's house. To my horror I found myself locked in. I couldn't get out and I had about five minutes to get to the meeting point which was the Cathedral door around the corner. My heart sunk and I thought have I come all this way only to be foiled at the last minute. I knew there was a back gate out of bishop's house but that was locked as well. These were iron grills and I thought of putting my arms through and screaming for help. But God must have been testing me. Along came another pilgrim who had been staying there and he knew another way out. Believe it or not that was locked as well. We thought of knocking on the bishop's bedroom door but we didn't know where it was. We were about to give up when a third pilgrim came along and guess what? He had a key to the gate. We got out and with one minute to spare ran like headless chickens to the Cathedral door. Our third pilgrim wondered at this and asked us had we not been told that the meeting place had been changed and it was about 500 yards away down a steep hill around the corner. Up with our luggage and again we raced and fortunately the bus had been held up in traffic and we were standing patiently composed when it drew up. It picked up a few more pilgrims at various spots and took us to the main meeting place where we boarded the buses that were to take us into China.

Four buses awaited us. Two were filled with a Portugese contingent resident in Macau. One with Chinese Macauan residents and one with an international group who had been attending a symposium in Macau prior to the pilgrimage. This group consisted of men and women from all over the world, priests and lay people, who were top academics in their own subjects. Hugh and myself had organised our pilgrimage through this symposium so we tagged along with some of the top brains in the world. Needless to say we sat together and pretended to belong. Hugh probably did but...

The pilgrimage had begun. We passed through the Macau emmigration without any bother but a different ball game greeted us at the Chinese immigration post at Gongbei. We had to disembark and go through the usual process of passport control and customs. This didn't seem to create a problem and we were back on board our buses quite quickly, all of us but one. One of the priests among the group had been detained. It seems he had been in China a few weeks previously and had spoken out publicly against the Chinese Government so was now classed as an undesirable entrant. It took about an hour for the pilgrimage Director and our Chinese courier to persuade the authorities to let him accompany us because of the nature of the journey. Eventually he was allowed through and we were on our way. But it brought home to us the tension under which the missionary priests live and the dangers there are for them in teaching the Faith.

We travelled for two hours across the south of China passing paddy fields already harvested and came to the Shanchui ferry terminal of Taishan city. It was there that the man said, 'Jump'. I virtually threw my luggage across and with the help of two sailors jumped the gap landing safely in the boat. Had I any doubts about making that leap of faith they were quickly dispelled when I saw a lady get out of a wheelchair and prepare to make the same jump. It reminded me of that time in the Territorial Army when I was required to be a 'pretend casualty' with the medical corps and allow myself to be strapped to the outside of a helicopter. You remember I was about to refuse when I saw female TA officers volunteering for the same role.

After about thirty-five minutes we came to the island of San Scian, known locally as Shangchuan Island. No jump required here. We simply crossed a rickety plank and there we were at last on the island where St Francis Xavier had returned his soul to God. It was lunchtime by now and as we were to remain on the island overnight we were taken to the hotel where we were to stay. There were no roads as such, just wide dirt tracks. It was not unlike Sri Lanka in this. The first time I arrived in Sri Lanka one of our Sri Lankan students met me and had a car ready to take me to Kandi where I was to stay. As he got into the car he took his shoes off and drove barefoot. It was pitch dark and he was driving like there was no tomorrow. Suddenly there was an almighty screech as he did an emergency stop, and I mean an emergency. We had come to the river and the bridge had gone. During the day they had moved it further up the river. Can you imagine it?

Along the dirt-track roads in San Scian the mini buses to which we had been transferred careered along scattering anybody who happened to be

APPEARANCES CAN DECEIVE ... ..
MEET THE DRIVER.

in the way. The island had been closed to visitors until recently as it was a naval base but now tourists were being encouraged and a very good hotel (3 star by our standards) had been built. As luck would have it the 'academics' were housed on the fourth floor and of course there were no lifts or escalators. I climbed the eighty stairs puffing and panting with my luggage to find I had a lovely room overlooking the South China Sea. A beautiful beach stretched out before me and it was everything one would expect to find on a tropical island. It was 30 November and the sea was warm.

We all dined together on tables of ten and sitting next to me was a young Portugese man who belonged to a Secular Institute called 'Heralds of the Gospel'. He was very enthusiastic and was convinced that some 'dodgy' looking men on the next table were probably Government agents planted among us. We became convinced of this until we got up to board the buses that were to take us to the shrine when we discovered they were the drivers.

At long last I was to fulfil that promise I made to myself over sixty years before. We drove along the dirt tracks until the buses would take no more. There were six mini buses now and they unloaded their cargo at the bottom of a steep hill from where we were to walk. The Director gathered us together in a clearing. Above us was a stone arc announcing 'The Graveyard of St Francis Xavier'. We were reminded that we were on pilgrimage and from now on we should observe a reflective silence. A priest from Goa gave us a short talk on the life of St Francis Xavier and in silence we began the ascent to the church. Half way up we stopped for another talk. This was given by an Irish Jesuit who belonged to the Indonesian Province and was working on inter-religious dialogue in Rome. He spoke about the spiritual life of St Francis and how his views on God had changed in his later years. St Francis' favourite prayer was Psalm 121 which he continually repeated as he lay dying, 'I will raise my eyes to the hills', Francis saw God as the nightwatchman guarding his people as they slept.

Then we climbed the last part of the path up steps and into the church. The first thing that strikes the visitor is the presence of a very large sarcophagus in the centre of the church. In this had lain the body of St Francis prior to his being transferred to Malacca the year after his death. I stood at the side of it and thought, at last I had fulfilled my promise and with it a lifelong ambition.

When I first went into the church I saw a priest, a Jesuit of course, on his knees at the side of the sarcophagus. I thought he was overcome with the occasion and then I realised he was scraping money off the sarcophagus, money left by a previous well-wisher. Though how he thought St Francis

Xavier would get it I don't know. St Francis has been dead 450 years and his body is now in Goa—or part of it is. A few years ago his arm had gone on tour around the world and somehow or other the wrist got separated and is now in Malacca. But I must tell you about his other arm. I am not sure about these days but in the old days when a person was canonised part of his body was used for relics. Tiny pieces (almost like small splinters) of the saint's bone were housed in beautiful small caskets for veneration by the faithful. My mother, Lord have mercy on her, had a tremendous devotion to St Francis Xavier and, after I was ordained, she asked me if I could get her such a relic of SFX. I wrote to our man in Rome and sure enough he got me one. I gave it to my mother and it became her most treasured possession. She would venerate it privately and show it off to neighbours who called. As you can imagine a neighbour fell in love with it and asked me if I would get her one. Nothing ventured nothing lost so I wrote to our man again. Again he turned up trumps and a second fragment of the body of St Francis Xavier winged its way to Liverpool. Would you believe it a third person asked for one. I thought I was really chancing my arm (pardon the pun) when I wrote and asked for another. Do you know, a third relic was sent to me but this time with a note, 'Are you trying to reconstruct the body?' I stopped at that but was very pleased to find that the Vatican had a sense of humour. (I think he was joking!)

But back to San Scian. The priest on his knees, Fr Sequira SJ, was in fact clearing the lid of the sarcophagus so that we could use it as an altar for the Mass we were about to say. Meantime the pilgrims were encouraged to look around the site, and behind the church we discovered that Stations of the Cross had been erected on the hill above the church. The stations were at equal distances but reaching up into the heavens, it looked like a tall ladder erected against a wall. I thought, dare I risk climbing this having climbed so far to the church. But, I also thought, I had come this far. How would I feel back in Everton if I reneged on this. So onwards and upwards I climbed pausing for breath from time to time. The value of making these stations was that there was no reward. It was dusk by this time so that the beautiful view that could be seen in daytime was completely obscured now. Or so I believed about the reward. By the time I got back and went into the church again it was crowded. I looked for a seat at the back and then God rewarded me for my efforts on the mountain. Fr Sequiara called me forward. A place had been reserved for me among the concelebrants at the head of the coffin. I moved through the crowds and sat down thinking, 'If my mother could see me now'.

The Mass began in Cantonese. Can you imagine it? Priests and people from all over the world gathered around this stone coffin saying Mass by the light of little red nightlights scattered around the church. I was transported back to 1984 when I had first visited China as a tourist. I remembered being in a hotel in Canton and thinking I just have to say Mass and raise the Host over China. But, of course I was not allowed to, however, in the secrecy of the hotel room, that is exactly what I did. I had bread from my sandwiches and I got wine from the hotel bar. I said Mass from memory in a very low voice, and to this day, I think that was the most devotional Mass I have ever said.

As the Mass in San Scian proceeded various languages were used, Latin, Portuguese, English, Goan and, of course, Cantonese. I think the highlight of the Mass came when Fr Sequira, the principal concelebrant invited us to share a sign of peace. From all over the world we moved around and shook the hands of people we had never met before and probably would never meet again. And do you know what we sang as we did this? 'Shalom'.

'Shalom, my friends' we sang in English as we mingled one with another.

Truly there were tears in our eyes. But more was to come. The Mass was over and it was pitch black outside. As we left the church we were each handed one of the little red nightlights to take with us and we carefully made our way down that steep hill. From the Mass the light had been given us to show us our way for the future.

We left the island early the next morning and after a day of sightseeing returned to Macau where, once again I stayed overnight in the Bishop's house – sans bath plug. Then it was back to Hong Kong to await the official celebration in honour of St Francis Xavier's anniversary.

I had been invited to concelebrate Mass in Hong Kong Cathedral on 3 December, the actual date of St Francis Xavier's death. I had spent the day with some past Chinese students and they took me to the Cathedral in plenty of time to find a parking place. I had worried a bit about this but I reminded St Josepha about the necessity of being in time. She has never ever let me down. Did you know she is the patron saint of car parking spaces? Sure enough there was just one left when we got there right in front of the cathedral. It might have had our name written on it. I don't normally tell people about this saint for obvious reasons but since the pilgrimage I have learnt to be a little less selfish in these matters. Give it a go sometime.

I had also worried about vestments as I had none with me. But again, like most worries, it was needless. Being a cathedral they were used to many priests attending celebrations and there before me were about fifty albs and red stoles waiting for the concelebrants. There must have been about forty priests there intermingling as they waited to be called for the procession. They were from different parts of the world but most of them were Chinese and Irish missionaries who have laboured in the mission fields for forty years or more and at a time when the prospect of martyrdom was very real.

I felt so proud to be among those men as we entered the Cathedral to the sound of hundreds and hundreds of people of all ages singing their hearts out. The Bishop of Hong Kong was the principal concelebrant, and, flanked by the Jesuit Deputy Provincial and a Permanent Deacon he began the Mass. It had all begun with a vision. St Francis Xavier 450 years before on that little island of San Scian had envisaged that one day the Catholic Church would have its rightful place in China.

Conclusion: My Final Vision

Throughout this book St Francis Xavier has appeared quite a lot. This is because, since my childhood, I was captivated by his vision. He spent his life determined to fulfil that ambition and in my last chapter I have described how he achieved it. It doesn't matter what a person's vision is as long as he is determined to fulfil it come what may.

From the age of seven I had a vision and no sooner was one vision fulfilled than another took its place. I have described in these pages how I saw my visions come true in spite of constant failings and being rejected. I say failings because to fail doesn't make one a failure and at no time have I seen myself as a failure. To be rejected doesn't mean a person is a reject. I have been rejected more times than I care to admit and have suffered deeply because of it. But I have never seen myself as a reject. I am what I am in spite of what others think of me or would like me to be and one thing I can safely say is that I am happy being in my own company. I am happy being me.

So what's next?

You won't believe it!

I received a letter from the Vice Chancellor of the Open University recently and I quote:

> Dear Rev Sullivan,
> The Senate of the Open University recently voted to offer you the honorary degree of Doctor of the University in recognition of your public services. It is my pleasure to inform you of this and ask, on

behalf of the Senate, whether you are
willing to accept the offer of this award.

I don't know if I get to write D.Univ. after my name but I could not
ask for greater recognition of all I have tried to say in this book. I have one
final vision, one final ambition and that is to gain an St. And you write
that in front of your name.

You've gorra laugh!

Goodbye and thank you for spending some time with me.

Richard.

OJIBWA PRAYER

Oh Great Spirit, whose voice I hear in the winds,
And whose breath gives life to everyone,
Hear me.
I come to you as one of your many children;
I am weak ... I am small ... I need your wisdom
and your strength

Let me walk in beauty, and make my eyes ever
  behold the red and purple sunsets.

Make my hands respect the things you have made,
  and make my ears sharp so I may hear your
voice.

Make me wise so that I may understand what
  you have taught my people and
The lessons you have hidden in each leaf
  and each rock.

I ask for wisdom and strength
Not to be superior to my brothers, but to be able
  to fight my greatest enemy, myself.

Make me ever ready to come before you with
  clean hands and a straight eye,

So as life fades away as a fading sunset,
My spirit may come to you without shame.

(Author unknown)

Coming soon ...

Bless and Tell Some More

If you have enjoyed and been touched by Father Richard Sullivan's extraordinary life, you will enjoy his second book in which he looks more closely at the people and events which have shaped his life and which have helped him serve others. *Bless and Tell Some More* is written in the same easy style of this autobiographical work and takes individual, real-life stories of those who have sought his friendship and his guidance, and those who have moved on and achieved so much for having been touched by his wisdom and kindness.

For more about *Bless and Tell Some More* or if you would like to contact Fr Richard, please visit www.museumware.com and click on the Bless and Tell link. We look forward to hearing from you soon.